ACKNOWLEDGEMENTS

I shall be eternally grateful to the readers of *Crystal Angel* manuscripts who offered valuable comments and suggestions for improving the story: Lynne Berry, Bill Bostick, Penny Bostick, Don Brown, Betty Dowda, Luann Hodges, Bob Morgan, Opal Norris, Marsha Preston and Patti Stanford.

Words are inadequate to express my sincere appreciation for the precise and insightful editing that Janet W. Seaman and my wife Janelle contributed to the finished work.

The painting for the cover of *Crystal Angel*
by
Mari W. Newton
Artist/Art Teacher, Shelby County Schools, Alabama

Photography
by
Rebecca Hutchinson Crum
and
Design
by
Janelle Henley Whetstone

DEDICATION

Any work of fiction begins on a note of truth and continues to develop through the characters created by the author. The portrayal of courageous Paul Peterson in *Crystal Angel,* though fictional, was inspired by some dear friends and colleagues. The late Reverends Monroe Lewis, Claude Whitehead and Calvin Gibson cast their ministries in the durable mold of compassion for the under-served. They endured the flames of social rejection for following the rightful passions of their calling. Surely there are other unheralded clergy that resist the undertows of violence and indifference among laity and clergy alike, but these three men and Reverend Warren Hamby loom large as revered colleagues with whom I was privileged to tend the Lord's vineyards during the critical historical period of Birmingham's struggle for civil rights. It is with great admiration and humility that I dedicate *Crystal Angel* to these four models of true discipleship.

> The chief office of the minister...is not to represent the view of the congregation, but to proclaim the truth as he sees it. In the pursuit of the duties of his office, the minister may from time to time, be under the necessity of giving views at variance with the views of some, or even many, members of the congregation.
> Rabbi Stephen S. Wise (1906)

CRYSTAL ANGEL

The Church and the Civil Rights Struggle in the South

By

Bob Whetstone

lulu.com

Six year old Angeline's career as a gospel singer begins in a 1950's coal mining town in Alabama, and is destroyed by an out-of-wedlock pregnancy. The college freshman drops out of school, changes her name from Lily Angeline to Crystal Angel and seeks anonymity in New Orleans as a cabaret singer where she gives up her baby for adoption. After two years of the fragile bistro circuit, Angel returns to racially-torn Birmingham to face the ghosts that haunt her. She falls in love and her engagement to Chad, a church choir director, lands her in the midst of the church's struggle with racial integration. But Angel must face her own struggle—to garner enough courage to confront the man who drove her away two years ago.

This book is a work of fiction. All characters, incidents and dialogues are created by the author and are not to be construed as real. However, references to events that occurred during the Civil Rights Movement in Birmingham, Alabama are historically accurate.

ISBN 978-0-615-25877-5

© Copyright by Bob Whetstone, 2008
www.bobwhetstone.com

1

> May 30, 1951
>
> Dear Mr. Choir Director,
>   I hear you are looking for people to sing solos in church this summer. My little girl sings good. She knows some church songs. She just won the Little Miss Walker County Talent Contest. It was in the paper. Thank you for reading this.
> God bless you.
>
> Marie Shook
>
> p.s. Her name is Lily Angeline and she is six year old.

Tucker Shook doesn't go to church but he tosses God's name around more than a hell-fire and brimstone preacher at a tent revival. "Goddammit, Marie, why don't y'all jist git dressed an' g'wan to church and leave me be." It's the usual Sunday litany he began reciting when Marie enrolled Lily Angeline in Sunday school. Ordinarily, Marie would have just slipped his breakfast back in the oven and walked downtown to First Methodist, but this Sunday is special.

"Lil Angel's gonna sing in the biggest church in town. I know you wanna be there, honey," Marie begs in a high-pitched whine, more irritating than charming.

Tucker sits up on the edge of his bed and shoots a villainous look right between her eyes. "Reckon it ain't enough for me to wallow 'round in a goddamn hellhole all week to put vittles on the table jist so…"

"Now Tuck, you know I 'preciate what you do for us, really I do," Marie strains to sound sincere. "But, today's real special for Lil Angel an' I know she wants ya' to…"

"I ain't gonna dress up jist to rub elbows with them goddamn city folk so they can look down on me." Tucker's agitation heaves up an uncontrollable coughing spell.

Marie folds her hands. "I hope the Lord don't hear ya', Tuck, takin' his name in vain an' on Sunday to boot." She sighs and opens the closet door to check her makeup in the dangling narrow mirror. "We're gonna walk on to the church. You still got time to clean up an' meet us there in the truck." Viewing her body in the mirror, Marie admires how she's recovered her figure after Angeline's birth six years ago. Living in a coal miner's shack at the end of a dirt road challenges but does not diminish her pride. Marie is determined not to walk to town looking like a coal miner's wife.

"Hurry up an' finish ya' breakfast, Lil Angel, it's time to go," Marie calls, still looking in the mirror.

"All right, Momma, I'm ready," her lilting voice reverberates against the walls of unfinished pine. Although Tucker is proud of his partially built house, Marie does not share his pride. Not only does she covet a complete house, but also the status that goes with it. She desires a *position*, something long denied to wives of pick-and-shovel seam busters in the tiny coal-mining town. Marie still struggles for release from the trap that snares so many young girls in mining towns, always has—pregnancy, quitting school to marry an older coal miner with a good income—at least, when he's not on strike. Etched across her brow are traces of a mundane and unfulfilling marriage. Bearing a child at the age of fifteen brought Marie to a brief pinnacle of pride, but she has become gradually cast aside like mine tailings. Her only hope is to polish the precious gem that has emerged from the rubble—her talented Lily Angeline, whom she believes can be molded into a stage personality—Lil Angel.

"Come in here, Angeline," Tucker yells towards the kitchen. He refuses to call her Lil Angel. Around the door peers a tiny face framed by long blonde curls, a face that has already developed an enticing pout.

"Come over here an' hug ya' daddy before ya' go, sweetheart."

"Be careful not to wrinkle her dress," Marie warns, provoking a stern look from her drowsy husband.

"Hell, Marie, I ain't gonna mess her up! Oh, excuse me, sweetheart. I meant to say 'heck'." Tucker pushes back his tangled hair and rubs his eyes. "What's that on ya' lips?"

Angeline glances up at her mother, who quickly defends her protégé. "Tell Daddy its jist a little color for…"

"Lipstick on a six-year old? On my little girl?" He wraps the bottom of his dingy undershirt around his finger and reaches toward his daughter's face. Angeline backs away before he can touch her lips.

"Don't, Tuck. It ain't lipstick, jist a little bit o' rouge. Anyway, she'll probably lick it off before we git to church." Marie leads her child out of the bedroom. "If ya'd act like any kinda daddy, ya'd put on some decent clothes an' go hear her sing."

"Damn you, woman. You'll have her all growed up…stuck up…shacked up…an'…an'… knocked up before she gits to high school." Tucker reaches for a cigarette and follows them to the kitchen looking for a match.

"Sounds right familiar, don't it?" Marie mutters as she wedges a tiny blue hat on the back of her head and pins it in place. She thinks the hat will help make her look older than twenty-one, but precocious motherhood has anticipated her wish. Marie runs her hands over her firm buttocks, proud of her well-kept figure, and adjusts the front of the oversized dress to cover her cleavage. She glances in the mirror at Tucker's face, illuminated as he touches the lighted match to his cigarette, his once ruddy cheeks now shallow and pale.

"Why don't ya' sing ya' song for ya' daddy, Lil Angel, maybe he'll change his mind about goin' to church." Angeline gazes at her mother, waiting for a signal to begin. Marie nods, so Angeline flashes a broad smile, showing two spaces where her bottom incisors are missing, and sings:
>*This little light of mine,*
>*I'm gonna let it shine.*
>*This little light of mine,*
>*I'm gonna let it shine.*

Tucker draws a long deep breath through his Camel and recovers the escaping smoke with his nostrils for a second charge of nicotine. He shifts his weight as she sings the second verse, and then another. He suddenly becomes self-conscious, standing before his daughter in wrinkled boxers and dirty undershirt, hardly a proper audience. She concludes the song with hands raised and head up, staring at the ceiling. Never once did she look at her daddy while singing, as if she was trying to block out the contrast between her parents—one dressed up neat and tidy, ready for church and the other clad in slept-in underwear.

"Ain't that the cutest thing you ever saw," squeals Marie patting her hands together. "She learned that song in Bible school jist last week."

"That was good, sweetheart," Tucker offers. "Now y'all g'wan downtown an' I'll try to git there in time." Marie sniffs at the empty promise, pointedly aware that Tucker has not crossed the threshold of any church sanctuary since the afternoon of their wedding at Burnt Creek Holiness Church six years ago. Tucker had slipped five dollars to a part-time preacher/miner after performing the ceremony in secret one Saturday before Angeline was born.

The preacher had warned Tucker, "Take my advice an' marry that girl 'fore you git arrested for fornicatin' with 'jailbait'."

Tucker has nothing against religion; he just finds no use for it. He understands the realities of life. All that's required to earn the mark of a good man is to work hard, be loyal to the union and support his wife and children. Fate and the union will take care of everything else. On the other hand, Marie views church as a blessed springboard for Angeline's rise to stardom.

Marie pauses to dab the perspiration from her face before crossing the street to the church. "Look at me Lil Angel," she checks her daughter's appearance ensuring that she is prepared for her debut. "Now remember to smile. And don't be afraid of standin' in front of all those people by y'self. Momma's gonna be right there watchin' ya'." With those final encouraging words, Marie takes Angeline's hand and leads her across the street, up the steps, and through the double doors of the large brick building.

Angeline's performance in church does not turn out quite the way Marie expects. Instead of singing a solo, she is joined by thirty-odd children of all ages. Somehow she must have misunderstood Angeline's exciting announcement Friday after Bible school, "Mommy, I'm gonna sing in big church Sunday."

Sitting on the back pew during the service, Marie vows under her breath, "This will never happen again, never, never again." Following the service, she waits until the crowd disperses before she confronts the music director.

"Mr. Ray, I'm Angeline's mother an' I…"

"Oh, Mrs. Shook, I want to tell you what a wonderful voice your daughter has. You should be very proud of her. Do you realize she's the youngest child in the group that sang today? What a voice! And when she threw her arms in the air at the end, that just put icing on the cake."

"Thank you," is the only response Marie can manage. The effervescent young choir director has unknowingly defused her complaint with a compliment. Claude Ray eases into a crouch to talk to little Angeline.

"How would you like to sing in big church again next Sunday?" Angeline looks at her mother, her big brown eyes brimming with anticipation. "This time, a solo," Claude explains. Marie's approving glance turns Angeline's anticipation into an excited grin as she nods at the director. "Good!" Claude exclaims.

"If your mother will bring you by the church Wednesday afternoon around two, I'll teach you the song."

Marie and Angeline bounce down Main Street swinging their arms like two children leaving a candy store. This time there is no misunderstanding; Lil Angel will be the star of the service. However, Claude Ray neglected to tell Marie that the following Sunday is the Fourth of July, the day that most Mimosa Methodists escape to the river. In addition, he has given the choir and regular soloists the day off. Nevertheless, the following Sunday Angeline's rendition of *God Bless America* captivates the faithful few who turn up for the service, including the Vice-President of the Mimosa Kiwanis Club. Afterwards, he approaches Claude Ray.

"Mr. Ray, do you think you could bring this cute little songbird to sing for our club meeting this Thursday?" Overhearing the offer, Marie steps forward to accept, but Claude Ray answers instead.

"I'm sure that can be arranged, Mr. Polk." Turning to Marie, Claude adds, "If her mother will allow me to escort Angeline to the meeting." He pauses with raised eyebrows.

Marie nods tentatively, realizing the invitation does not include her. The Kiwanian beams, "Good, good, good. We'll see you at noon at the Majestic Hotel."

Claude offers Marie and Angeline a ride home so he'll know where to pick her up on Thursday. Marie is quick to refuse, not wanting Claude to see that she lives in an unfinished shack on the edge of town. Neither does she want this classy gentleman to catch Tucker sitting on the front porch in his underwear with a beer in one hand and a cigarette in the other.

"We don't live far from here, we'll jist walk. I, uh…got another stop on the way home." Marie's eyes shift rapidly as she thinks of a way to keep Claude Ray away from her house. "And don't worry about pickin' up Angeline Thursday. She'll meet you here at the church about…what time?"

"Won't that be too much trouble?"

"What time?" Marie insists.

"How about eleven-thirty? We can walk down to the hotel from here." Marie responds with a nod and smiles, knowing Angeline will perform for some of the most important men in town.

During the remaining days of summer, Angeline sings her patriotic anthem for the Civitan Club, the Pony League Baseball Banquet, the Harper Family Reunion and the American Legion Labor Day Barbeque. In the blistering August sun Marie walks Angeline to the church before each performance and waits for Claude Ray to bring her back an hour or two later. Although she longs to accompany Claude to hear Angeline sing, she dares not risk rejection by asking. She rationalizes that tailgating on her daughter's journey to stardom is almost as satisfying as sharing the limelight. To avoid embarrassment, Marie gives Angeline strict instructions before each performance, "Honey, you sing pretty an' if anybody asks about ya' daddy, tell 'em they gotta talk to me about that."

In the fall, Angeline's catapult to fame follows her to the elementary school where Claude Ray teaches music. He features her frequently in school and church programs, her crystal clear voice captivating the townspeople. Then the precocious songbird's career hits a speed bump. An anonymous letter arrives at the church at the end of the school year:

Dear Mr. Ray,

As my Christian duty, I suggest there are many talented children in our church from good families whose mothers <u>and fathers</u> would come to hear them sing solos. Their names are on the back of this letter. I'd be the last one to criticize, but a word to the wise is sufficient. These children are good examples of the kind of people we appreciate in our church, and we know how to show our appreciation!

A concerned church member

Claude charges into the pastor's study and thrusts the letter at him, "What do you think, Brother John?"

The preacher doesn't bother to put on his reading glasses before replying, "Well, Claude, somebody's taking advantage of your being new in this community. Ordinarily, I'd pay little attention to a letter written by a person with too little gumption to sign her name, but…"

"*Her* name?" the astonished director interrupts. "Then you know who wrote this."

With a grimace, he pushes the letter away from his face. "Let's just say I have a strong suspicion. As I was about to say, if my hunch is correct, this lady swings a heavy club in the church. She is influential and she may have a point. If I were you I'd begin to spotlight some of the other children, let them sing a line or two here and there."

"You mean give in to her none-too-subtle elitist demand?" His astonishment escalates to anger.

"That may be too harsh a description, Claude. Being fresh out of college places you at a disadvantage in dealing with church folks. Eventually you'll learn to maneuver the narrow path between pride and jealousy. People in this church have a lot of pride. They're proud of their children as well as their ancestors who built this great church. You should have realized by now that the parents of this wonder-child you so avidly promote have staked no claim in the traditions of Mimosa First."

"What does that mean?"

"Our parishioners are only too aware that her parents are not members. As a matter of fact, no one seems to know the child's father, do you?"

Claude stiffens in his chair. "That's ridiculous, Brother John, and you know it!" Claude sputters. "Jesus didn't ask the children for their parents' I. D.'s when he said, 'Suffer little children to come unto me, forbid them not,' did he?"

"I hate it when scripture is quoted out of context, Claude. Now don't obscure the issue."

"O. K. and what if I just ignore the letter? What can she do, this mysterious praetorian guard of the status quo?"

"Let me put it this way, young man. I have only one more year to retirement. I'd like to leave Mimosa First in good graces with no conflicts, especially over something as innocuous as the music program."

Claude gazes at the letter for a moment to avoid exploding over the pastor's denigration of his profession. "So, you're saying if I ignore the demands of this letter, you'll come down on the side of the trouble maker who wrote it?"

"It's their church, son, not ours. They'll be here long after you and I are gone, so it's best that we don't leave any cankers for our successors to nurse."

Claude slaps the back of his hand against the letter. "That's bullshit and you know it. This is the Lord's church, not theirs. And we are charged with the responsibility to guide them down the path of righteousness, not the path of least resistance."

The color of John's bald head deepens like the red line of a thermometer reaching the boiling point. His words burst forth, "That's enough! This conversation has exceeded the bounds of decency. I have nothing further to say." He ushers Claude out the door and slams it forcefully behind him.

Whether by default or design, Claude Ray mysteriously detaches himself from Marie Shook and Lily Angeline over the summer. He forms a junior high ensemble to keep the church young people busy and he prepares a program for youth week. His efforts to involve more children and youth in church music meet with high praise, yet disappointing results. "At least I made the effort," Claude tells his wife, "but vacations, weekends at the lake and cheerleading camp have eroded my program. I wish the parents had just half the enthusiasm for their kids as Mrs. Shook has for Angeline," he sighs. "Maybe John has a point about music being only window dressing for his prayers and sermons."

~~~

Marie notices the change in Claude Ray's attitude toward Angeline. She confronts him after the children's first choir practice in September. She dismisses Angeline, "Lil Angel, go on out an' wait for me in front of the church." Then she boldly approaches Claude, "I'm jist wonderin' when ya' want Lil Angel to sing a solo in church again?"

His mouth drops open, suspended in disbelief at this backstage mother's lack of subtly, as the heated glare of her coal black eyes fuses his tongue to his jaw. A few painful moments later he manages to lick his dry lips as he gropes for a reply to this unexpected inquisition.

"Well?" she persists.

After poaching a few more seconds to gather his thoughts, Claude points to the front row of chairs, "Come and sit down for a minute, Mrs. Shook." Marie prances across the choir room to the nearest chair. Claude's eyes covertly follow her sensuous hips undulating beneath the thin housedress. She sits on the edge of the chair expecting a brief response from Claude, totally unaware of the uncomfortable response she had unwittingly aroused. "First, allow me to compliment you on the outstanding support you give to your talented daughter, Mrs. Shook. I recently mentioned to Brother John how much I admire your devotion to Angeline as she continues to develop the marvelous talent God has bestowed on her."

Marie, disarmed by his praise, blushes, politely crosses her legs, and settles back in the metal chair. "She does sing kinda nice, don't she?"

How can such a beautiful woman massacre her native tongue with such brutality? Claude thinks. After a year in Mimosa, he had tuned his ear to ignore local pronunciations such as "i's" that are as flat as hoecakes, but not to bad grammar. Sitting down in the chair next to Marie, Claude continues, "And I appreciate your allowing me to share her lovely voice with folks around town."

Marie presses her hand against Claude's arm, "That's all right, Mr. Ray. Ya' know what's best for my girl." Her eyes soften, sending shivers down his spine. Claude struggles to maintain control of the conversation despite his increasing sense of attachment to the alluring woman fluttering her eyelashes. Claude tells himself, *Remember your training, she isn't coming on to you. It's just a naïve trust in an authority figure.*

"Mrs. Shook, my plans here at the church this fall will not include any solos for children," he says. Marie's expression sours as if he had dismissed Angeline from the children's choir altogether. "However, I think it's time for Angeline to share her talent with other churches beyond Mimosa. With your permission, I'd like to contact some of my colleagues and arrange for her to be a guest soloist at their churches. Would that meet with your approval?" The light returns to Marie's eyes. She lifts her head and leans forward, within inches of Claude's face.

"Well," she says, eyelashes fluttering, arched eyebrows inviting further explanation, "I reckon."

"The only problem would be transportation," Claude says, patting her hand that's still on his arm. A warm flush rises to his face, so he backs away from her to finish his sentence, "So do you think you could drive her as far as Birmingham to sing at the eleven o'clock services?"

"Her daddy don't work on Sundays. I'll see to it she gits to wherever ya' say."

"Fine," Claude says, walking toward the door. Marie follows him and then hesitates near him at the threshold.

"Mr. Ray, I want ya' to know I really appreciate what ya' do for Lil Angel. If there's anythin' I can ever do for ya'…well, ya' know…all ya' gotta do is ask." Marie purses her lips, as the color returns to Claude's cheeks. He extends his hand toward the door, but Marie misreads the gesture as an invitation to hug and clamps her arms around him. "Bye," she murmurs—pushing away slowly, chagrined that Claude had kept his arms at his sides.

He stands motionless, tracking her mincing walk all the way down the hallway. She turns with a coquettish smile, wiggling her fingers toward him before disappearing around the corner. *No way, there's no way that woman knows what she's doing to my sense of morality, no way.* Claude walks over to the piano and runs his fingers wildly over the keyboard to clear his mind of the impending dilemma he senses.

On Wednesday afternoon, Marie accompanies Angeline to choir practice so she can check on Claude's promise to schedule solos in other churches. "Nothing yet," he tells Marie as he follows the children out the door, thus avoiding another uneasy session alone with her in the choir room. Having forgotten his promise, Claude pleads for more time, "I'll call you when I hear something." Taking Angeline's hand, Marie saunters down the sidewalk.

The next week, she shows up again and Claude turns her away with the same response. The following week Angeline does not appear at the usual practice after school. Claude is disappointed for two reasons—she's by far the best singer in the Angel Choir, and at last he has good news for her mother. After practice, he shoos the children out of the building, locks the outside door, snaps the hall lights out and returns to the choir room to rearrange the chairs for adult choir practice later that night.

"Hi Mr. Ray," a voice startles him as he opens the door to the choir room. Peeping around the music rack is Marie Shook, sitting on the piano bench looking like a teenager—her black hair pulled back in a ponytail.

"How...how did you get in?" he blurts, looking to see if Angeline is in the room.

"I was listening from the sanctuary, didn't wanna interrupt ya' practice."

"Oh, I see...I missed Angeline today."

"She's home in bed, sick to her stomach. Didn't go to school either."

"I hope she's all right," Claude sounds concerned, "who's taking care of...?"

"Her daddy got off work at four, so I thought I'd drop by...had to come to the drug store anyhow." Marie emerges from behind the piano, standing between Claude and the large west wall window. The sun streaming in behind Marie clearly outlines her Coke bottle figure through the delicate film of dress she always wears—except on Sundays. Praying she'll hold that pose, Claude gently eases the door shut behind him and steps toward her.

"I have good news, Mrs. Shook."

"Oh?" she exclaims edging towards Claude, her face radiating an expectant glow. But his eyes are not on her face. She stops suddenly, looks down and asks, "Is something wrong with my dress?"

Claude coughs, embarrassed at being caught ogling the profile of her figure through the dress, "Uh no, no I was just thinking."

"About what, the good news?" Marie smiles coyly, as if reading his mind.

"Yes, as a matter of fact, I've arranged for Angeline to sing at the community Thanksgiving service at Hampton this November. There will be four churches..."

Before he can finish, Marie rushes forward and throws her arms around him, pressing her face against his chest. "Thank you, thank you, I'm so happy!" Claude places his hands on her shoulders intending to push her away, but instead they glide down her back, pulling her closer. "Mmm, know what I think, Mr. Ray; I think ya' deserve a Yankee dime for helpin' Lil Angel." Marie tilts her face and pecks him on the chin with her lips.

Claude gazes into those endless dark eyes for an instant and then steps back. "That's more thanks than necessary. I'll get you the details about the service as soon as possible. I think I know just the song for her," Claude rushes to the piano and thumbs absently through the hymnal. He has to quickly distance himself from this sensual woman. "Oh well," he says tossing the book on the piano, "there's plenty of time to select just the right piece for Angeline."

Marie giggles, "I reckon you know best." She pats him on the arm, "Bye, now."

"Goodbye, Mrs. Shook. I know Angeline will be as happy as you are with the news."

"Most people my age call me Marie. I reckon we're about the same age, so…"

"All right, Marie it shall be," Claude walks her to the door, "only if you call me Claude."

As they continue down the hall, Marie tells him, "Oh, I might be gittin' some good news, too."

"And what's that?"

"I wrote a letter to my Uncle J. B. He's somebody big in the Coal City Methodist Church, so I asked if he'd let Angeline visit one weekend an' sing in his church."

"Coal City? I have a good friend, Paul Peterson, who's the new preacher there. What did your uncle say?"

"I ain't heard from him yet."

"Let me know as soon as you hear and I'll call Paul and tell him about Angeline." Claude unlocks the exterior door to let her out, but can't keep his eyes off her rhythmic gait as she crosses the lawn. *Damn, what a body! But, I must focus on tonight's practice, it certainly won't plan itself.*

2

> September 5, 1952
>
> Dear Uncle J. B.,
>   How are you and Aunt Nora Belle getting along? Fine, I hope. Are you still going to Coal City Methodist Church? Lily Angeline sings solos at Mimosa First Methodist sometimes. Would you like for her to sing at your church? Tucker said he would drive us over one weekend to visit and while we are there maybe Lily Angeline can sing for your church. You just won't believe how much she has growed since y'all saw her at Mama's funeral.
>
> Love ya,
>
> Marie

Lorna Peterson hears an automobile park on the street in front of the church next door. She parts the living room curtain and peeks through the limbs of the crepe myrtle rendered bare by an early October cool spell. "J. B. is here," she calls back to the parsonage study where Paul sits reading Bonhoeffer's *Letters and Papers from Prison*.

Her husband slips a blue ribbon inside the book and closes it. "I suppose brother Dietrich will have to wait," he sighs. "But, you won't see me breaking my neck to go waste time listening to J. B. tell me how to run the church."

"He probably figures it's his turn now since he spent some time last Sunday listening to you tell him how to run his life," Lorna laughs as she passes his study on her way to the kitchen. "I'll bring you two pillars of the church some hot chocolate and cookies in a while, so go on and feed your sheep like a good shepherd."

"Sheep I can handle, but that bull-headed goat distracts me from the rest of my flock," Paul snorts. "I'd give a month's pay to know which of my predecessors pushed ol' J. B. over the edge."

"Over the edge?"

"The edge of religiosity; centering his faith on his position in the church."

"Sounds like you're floating on a cloud of theology, Reverend Peterson. Now get your feet on the ground and go before J. B. decides to come after you."

Paul walks to the kitchen where Katy sits with her homework spread on the table and brushes his daughter's forehead with a kiss. "Tough assignment tonight?"

"No, Daddy, just boring," she thumps her pencil on the fourth grade math book.

"Then I'll say good night. You should be asleep before I get home."

With a shiver Paul closes the front door of the parsonage behind him as a crisp autumn breeze whistles through the screened porch. His thoughts focus on the task before him. *How many tedious weekly encounters with the gatekeeper of my new parish have I endured, a dozen in just three months? It seems so much longer. Bonhoeffer had his prison; I have mine.*

As Paul trudges up the church steps treble voices trail from the sanctuary piercing the nippy night air. He tugs at the heavy oak door as the anomalous blend of rich pine and burnt candlewick assails his nostrils. The visible sliver of light under the anteroom door prompts Paul to pause for a peek at his choir—an avoidance tactic before dealing with his dreaded adversary. As he swings open the double doors to the sanctuary, the singing ceases and Miss Bessie stops playing. The choir cheerfully greets the new preacher sporting his yet untarnished gloss.

"Hi folks, y'all don't let me stop you; just wanted to say I wish all goes well with your practice." With a gentle pastoral wave of his hand, Paul starts to leave.

"If you've come to bless our meager attempts at harmony, we'll gratefully accept, Brother Paul," a man quips from the back row of the choir loft.

"That's more'n our other preachers ever did," another man comments, eliciting twitters of laughter from the others.

Paul dismisses himself and backs through the doors that swing shut separating him from the choir. Reluctantly ambling across the narthex, he opens the door to the room that could double as a closet. J. B. hunches over the table, his back to the door, as his internal radar monitors Paul's every move. He anxiously begins before Paul has time to close the door.

"Been going over these figures, doesn't look too good." Paul wonders how many times J. B. has launched that loaded phrase to former pastors. He prays for the patience of Job.

Paul takes a deep breath and slides into the chair opposite the church treasurer. J. B. bends over the table with lips pursed, reminding Paul of a cartoon that hangs in the barbershop down the street—a bulldog playing poker with aces stuck in his hat. "It's so good to see you, Brother J. B., a real pleasure on this fine evening." He greets him warmly determined to disarm this keeper of the purse. J. B. extends a limp hand to his pastor, accompanied by a quick glance over his bifocals and a tiny lip movement that might be interpreted as a weak smile. That done, he turns back to the business at hand.

"Offerings haven't picked up any since you've been here, preacher," he launches a warning, aiming the shot directly across the table at Paul. *He always starts with a put down, banging me over the head with the collection plate. I should have brought my Bible or a silver cross to ward off this vampire's attempt to suck the blood out of my ministry. But I will not allow this demon of religiosity to put me on the defensive.*

"Elbert Tate came home from the hospital today, and I went by to see Margie Johnson and her new baby boy at Methodist Hospital."

J. B. skewers Paul with his rapier look. "You're spending a lot of time with folks who don't give a penny to the church."

Paul bites his lower lip. *What would Jesus say? Would he instruct this Satan to get behind him or simply admonish him with "the first shall be last and the last shall be...?" I must be positive and pleasant. This man signs my paycheck.* "Whoever ministers to the needs of the least among us shall..."

"Save your sermon for Sunday morning, let's take care of the business at hand or you might not have a pulpit to preach from," interrupts J. B. with a benign chuckle that communicates more contempt than humor.

Paul's thoughts turn to Bonhoeffer. *Here's the perfect example of a man wrapping his religion around the church's treasury making it the center of his faith, a neurotic grasp to secure his soul in paradise.* Paul chooses not to waste energy wrestling with this descendent of Judas, so he relents and follows J. B.'s finger sliding across the ledger before him. *How long has this old church been without strong spiritual leadership?*

Before Lorna can arrive with hot chocolate and cookies to temper the conflict, J. B.'s wife sticks her head in the door and coos, "I'm ready to go, honey, whenever you're done."

Paul rises quickly from his chair and seizes the opportunity to break up their session. "What happened to choir practice?"

"Brother Hugh got sick as soon as we started so we had to cancel practice," she says, "I think he's coming down with something." She drops her eyes and turns away as if to break off the discussion about Hugh Underwood, the charming relic who directs the choir. Being an excellent bass soloist, brother of the pianist, and fulfilling his duties without compensation—everyone at Coal City First Methodist overlooks Hugh's legendary courtship with the gin bottle.

Releasing a heavy sigh, J. B. closes the ledger. "I'll turn down the thermostat and switch off the lights," he says, then faces Paul for one last volley, "I hope things pick up, Brother Paul, for your sake...and ours."

Paul shakes hands with the departing choir members and then speaks to Miss Bessie as she juggles her music books, shawl and bifocals. "I'm sorry to hear your brother isn't feeling well this evening. I hope it's nothing serious."

Miss Bessie drops her eyes as J. B.'s wife had done and shakes her head. "Don't worry, Brother Paul, nothing serious. He just has these spells sometimes."

J. B. flicks off the sanctuary lights and joins their conversation. "Mighty fine playing, Miss Bessie, as usual, mighty fine, mighty fine."

Miss Bessie tucks in her double chin and giggles, "You sure know how to make a person feel proud, J. B."

He clears his throat and pulls a letter from his coat pocket. "My niece is coming to visit us soon. I understand her daughter has a fine voice. Would you play for her to sing at the church service?"

The pianist lays her books on a table, adjusts her bifocals and angles the letter to catch the dim light from the single bulb overhead. "Lily Angeline, what a precious name. Yes, fine, just be sure she picks a song I can play."

"Oh come on, Miss Bessie, everybody knows you can play any song in the book. Anyhow, Marie's girl is a little tyke, not even old enough to read." J.B. returns the letter to his pocket. "I'll write my niece and let her know you'll play for little Angeline."

Paul ignores J. B.'s incursion on the pastor's domain of planning worship services and returns to the parsonage to continue his review of the fundamental virtues of the Christian faith. The phone rings as he closes the front door. "I'll get it." Lorna emits a muffled squeal. "My goodness, it's good to hear from you. Sure, he just came in the door." Lorna hands the receiver to Paul. "It's Claude Ray."

"Hello, Claude, what a nice surprise." Paul glances at his watch. "Aren't you having choir practice tonight?...Oh, I see. Well those things happen." Paul listens for a few minutes as his wife sits on the arm of the sofa, anxious to hear news from their young friend. "Yes, I'll do that, Claude and give my regards to your lovely bride. Good bye."

"Well?"

Paul extends the suspense. "Well, what?"

"Are they expecting?"

Paul laughs. "Oh no, nothing like that, he just called to warn me about something I already know. A lady from his church in Mimosa wants her little girl to sing here for one of our services."

"Oh, I thought it was...well, you know, something important."

~~~

Tucker Shook cracks the window an inch from the top to let the smoke escape from the cab. "We're freezin', Tuck. Do ya' hafta open that window?" Marie pulls Angeline closer and adjusts the scarf around her daughter's ears.

"It's cold air or smoke, which do ya' want." Tucker's eyes are fixed on the white stripes of Highway 78 zipping beneath the truck. "This ain't no way to spend Christmas Eve—drivin' forty miles jist for Angeline to sing a song."

"Two songs! That wind's blowin' Lil Angel's hair to pieces. Now throw out that cigarette an' roll up the window."

Tucker grumbles and flips the half-spent cigarette out the narrow slit in the window. In the side mirror he watches sparks scatter on the dark asphalt. "Hope we don't git busted for startin' a woods fire."

"There's the sign," Marie exclaims, "Gallant Heights is six miles down that way." Tucker wheels the truck onto a mining road, a narrow strip of crumbling asphalt.

"Don't reckon we'll come up on any coal trucks, tonight bein' Christmas Eve. Besides, they closed Gallant mine more'n five year ago." Tucker rambles on about the uncertainty of working in coalmines, but Marie is too busy adjusting Angeline's curls to pay attention. "Here's the church," Tucker says, guiding the truck into a dirt parking area. "Looks like the crowd ain't come yet." He parks beside the only other car in the lot. "Y'all g'wan in. I'll listen to the radio, be in later."

Marie shrugs her shoulders and helps Angeline out of the truck. Tucker lights a cigarette. She knows he'll still be there when they return after the service.

"Welcome to our little church," a voice greets Marie and Angeline from the pulpit. "You must be our guest soloist," I'm Reverend Oliver Barron, the pastor." He lifts his long white robe and hops off the dais, betraying his ineptitude for wearing ecclesiastical garb. "I've heard so much about you Mrs. Shook. Our pianist will be here shortly so you can rehearse your song. What will you sing tonight?"

Marie blushes in amazement at his youth, perhaps younger than herself, as he grasps her cold hand. "Oh, I'm not...I mean...I'm not singin'."

"Oh?"

"I brought my little girl to sing for ya'. This here's Lil Angel."

"I see...I guess I misunderstood Brother John's letter. I'm afraid there won't be any children here tonight. All of our members' children are grown and..."

"Oh, that's all right, preacher. Lil Angel sings by herself a lot in big church at Mimosa. She'll do fine."

Behind Marie, a gust of cold wind ushers an elderly couple through the door. "Come on in folks and let me help you with that door," Reverend Barron says. "That wind can turn this place into a deep freeze in no time." Marie leads Angeline to the front pew near the pot-bellied stove that glows orange at the bottom. The preacher chats with the elderly couple and waits expectantly to greet others. Each time the door opens, Marie glances around hoping the pianist will arrive in time to practice with Lil Angel.

A few minutes past nine Reverend Barron marches to the pulpit and announces to a dozen people seated in the small sanctuary that the first annual Christmas Eve service will commence. Instead of joy and hope, the service honoring the nativity is cloaked in disappointment. The pianist doesn't show up, so Angeline sings two secular Christmas songs *a capella, Jingle Bells* and *Santa Claus is Coming to Town.* Reverend Barron expecting a larger crowd expresses regret that the cold has kept his "fair weather" parishioners indoors. His wavy orange locks and eyebrows give the appearance of a flaming candle as he thrashes about in his white robe delivering the sermon. Concluding his verbose homily, Barron touches a small candle to the Christ candle in the Advent wreath and passes the light to the only usher. Humming *Silent Night,* each worshipper touches a candle to the flame. As the service concludes, people extinguish their candles and drift into the bitter cold in silence.

"I can't believe this church is run by a kid just outta high school," Marie complains as she helps Angeline into the stifling truck cab. "That redheaded peckerwood thinks he's God's gift to preaching. He didn't say one word 'bout Lil Angel's songs."

"He didn't give you no money?" Tucker asks.

"He didn't give me shit."

"Angeline, you jist make like your mama ain't said 'shit'," Tucker chuckles. Marie slaps him across the shoulder causing him to laugh even louder. "Eighty miles round trip an' not a dime for gas money, what a bitch!" He revs up the idling engine and puts it in gear.

Marie bundles Angeline. "It'll pay off one day, Tuck. Jist you wait an' see. Lil Angel's gonna sing her heart out on the stage of the Alabama Theatre. They'll crown her 'Miss Alabama' an' she'll have me to thank for it."

"Yeah, I reckon. The only use I got for songbirds is down in the mine."

"Hush up, Tuck," Marie scowls, covering her sleepy daughter's ears in protest. "You're tryin' to pretend I don't know what y'all use canaries for in the mine."

"Looks like we're wastin' the whole Christmas Eve. I reckon ol' Santy Claus done come to Mimosa an' left 'cause we ain't home," Tucker says clucking his tongue, rubbing salt in Marie's chaffed ego.

"Shut up, Tuck," Marie screeches, hugging Angeline close while the truck bumps toward Mimosa.

~~~

Chad Willis follows the rusting trolley track past storefronts where decades of coal dust has melded bricks and mortar into one dark shade of gray. He stops the car where the rails veer off the road and appear to slice a diagonal alley between two stores. After checking the directions written on the back of an envelope, Chad shakes his head, proceeds along the trolley line to Main Street, and turns left. Occasional street lights shine through low hanging oaks casting eerie shadows along the road. Two blocks ahead, a soft blue hue illuminates his destination for the big interview. He eases his old Chevy to the curb beneath the source of the light—a neon sign attached to the corner tower of a brick building proclaims "COAL CITY" in vertical lettering. His directions verify this as the church, but the black Gothic lettering, "Methodist Church" painted at the base of the sign becomes visible only after he gets out of the car. It's as though the name of the denomination is expendable and can be changed with a few swipes of a paintbrush.

"Hello there, are you Chad?"

Chad turns around to greet a man of slender frame pulling a topcoat around his shoulders descending the steps from the house next door. "Yes sir."

"Paul Peterson," the man's lips emit puffs of vapor highlighted by the glow of the neon blue. Chad is relieved that the pastor's grip is gentle on his cold fingers. "How was your Christmas? Richly blessed, I trust."

"I had a nice break from school." Chad stuffs his hands in his pockets realizing his light jacket is inadequate for the late December cold spell.

"Let's go inside where it's warm. You must be freezing." Paul leads Chad to the parsonage and introduces him to Lorna and Katy. "Chad's a student at Methodist College, majoring in music.

I've asked him to consider taking Hugh Underwood's place and to help with the youth."

"Could I interest you in a cup of hot chocolate, Chad?" Lorna offers. Chad nods. Paul explains the protocol of the interview as Katy moves stealthily around the room trying to inspect this handsome guest.

"Before we go any further, Brother Paul, I'm just a freshman and haven't had a course in choral conducting yet. I'm not sure..."

"Not to worry, son. I know all about you. The fact of the matter is, this church's previous director was an amateur who donated his services and we've never had a youth director. Your roommate recommends you very highly."

"Ollie Barron?" Chad raises his eyebrows and shakes his head. "How did..."

"Didn't he tell you, he's the one who gave me your name?"

Paul stops talking and cocks his head as if receiving a message from the Holy Spirit. He sets his cup on a side table and Lorna quickly moves it to a coaster. "Excuse me," he says, slipping over to the parlor window. "J. B.'s here. I'll go and have a word with him before our meeting." Paul fumbles with the doorknob and finally jerks the door open. Lorna hands him his coat and closes the door behind him.

As soon as the screen door slams, Lorna says, "You'll have to excuse my husband. He's not always this nervous, just when a certain church member comes around." She giggles to cover her indiscretion. "That was an awful thing to say, but I only meant to warn you that getting this job depends on getting the O. K. from just one man, and it's not my husband.

With her eyes glued to Chad, Katy adds, "Yeah, he thinks he runs the whole church."

"That's quite enough from you young lady," Lorna scolds. "Don't you have homework to finish?"

"It's still holidays, Mama. I've got five more days off."

Paul ushers J. B. Colley into the parsonage living room and introduces him to Chad. "Evening son, I understand you're looking for a job." Chad grips J. B.'s extended hand. Paul gestures toward his study and follows his visitors inside.

"J. B. is a longtime member of Coal City Methodist, Chad. As a matter of fact, his father helped establish this church back in 1895..."

"...the year I was born," J. B. concludes as he seats himself in Paul's chair behind the desk. He folds his hands and leans forward pursing his lips. "Go ahead and have a seat, son. Let me say this; Coal City Methodist got along fine for over fifty years with just a preacher, and barely paying for that. Everything else was done by members—directing the choir, playing piano, cutting the grass, stoking the furnace. But Brother Paul has convinced the board to hire a combination youth and choir director." J. B. goes on voicing his reluctance to add staff as Chad squirms in his seat, glancing at Paul occasionally for signs of support.

When J. B. concludes his disclaimer of support for the position, he leans back and asks Chad, "What'll it take for you to accept the job?"

"Sir?"

"How much money are you asking for?"

Chad's mouth falls open. No one has mentioned his qualifications or the duties of the position. He looks at Paul and shrugs. Paul says, "I understand you'll have to give up your position as soloist at First Church downtown, so we'll need to compensate you for that amount. Also, we need to cover your expenses for driving over on Wednesday nights and Sundays. Perhaps we could..."

J. B. clears his throat to cut Paul off. Chad takes the cue and speaks up. "First Church pays for my voice lessons and gives me ten dollars a Sunday."

"Do you think seventy-five a month will cover everything?" Before Chad can respond, J. B. continues, "And can you start work next week?"

Chad pauses and then nods in agreement. With a grin, Paul pats him on the shoulder. J. B. adds, "Oh, I forgot to mention that the board approved the position for six months. Then, we'll take another look at it."

After J. B. leaves, Katy rushes into the study anxious to hear the news. "Is he going to do it?"

"Settle down young lady," Paul chides. "You may go tell your mother she can join the choir now that we have a new director." Katy squeals and darts off to the kitchen.

Paul is about to explain Chad's duties when J. B. barges back into the living room. "Uh oh," Paul mutters.

"Seems I left before taking care of one other piece of business." J. B. pulls an envelope from his overcoat. "I've made arrangements for my grandniece to provide special music for a couple of services in January. You may want to write down these dates and fit them into your plans."

"I really appreciate any help to get started, Mr. Colley. Does she play organ or piano?" Chad asks.

"She sings," J. B. mutters, "Miss Bessie's already agreed to play piano for her, we don't have an organ."

"Miss Bessie is our regular accompanist," Paul explains.

"Oh, I see. Maybe I know your grandniece. Does she go to Methodist College? What's her name?"

J. B. grunts. "I doubt you two have met. Lily Angeline's seven-years old…well, good night folks." With that curt farewell, J. B. disappears into the chilly night.

3

> May 5, 1953
>
> Dear Brother John,
>
> I am sorry I was unable to attend your reception Sunday. Enclosed please find a small token of our appreciation for your good works here in Mimosa. Elsa and I are especially pleased with the way you helped a certain young choir director avoid an unfortunate scandal in the church. Best wishes on your well-deserved opportunity to rest your feet in the green pastures of retirement.
>
> Sincerely,
> David Elliot, Chairman of the Board

Popularity and recognition power Angeline through the second grade. Her reputation spreads in churches from Coal City to Gallant Heights to other small churches around Birmingham. She makes brief appearances on Sunday sunrise radio programs and becomes known as Lil Angel from Mimosa with a voice "as clear as fine crystal."

"Time to rise, Lil Angel, the world's waitin' to hear ya' sing," Marie accompanies her singsong voice clanging on a bread pan in the kitchen.

"For God's sake, Marie, it ain't even daylight yet," Tucker yells from his bed. Marie ignores his complaint and dishes up three plates of scrambled eggs and grits. Then she pulls her sleepy daughter out of bed and rubs a damp cloth over her scowling face.

"I know it's early, sweetie, but that radio station ain't gonna wait for us." By five a.m. all three are heading for Birmingham with Angeline asleep between Tucker and starry-eyed Marie. They arrive at a cracker-box studio on the Bessemer Highway around six-thirty. Marie combs Angeline's hair, reddens her lips with rouge and pulls her into the studio ten minutes before airtime. Tucker slumps down in his truck, locates the station on the radio and promptly falls asleep before his daughter comes on the air.

"Tucker, Tucker, wake up, let's go home," Marie hollers, banging on the truck door. "You didn't even listen to Lil Angel sing," she fusses.

"Yeah, yeah, I did, but I dozed off soon as she was done, I swear."

"One day the devil's gonna grab a hold of ya' family jewels for lyin', Tucker, an' he ain't gonna let go 'til ya' swear to quit." But Marie is so pleased with Angeline's exposure to "radio land" that she does not stay angry with Tucker very long. She hums one of her daughter's songs all the way to Mimosa.

Radio preachers take advantage of Marie's offer to show up anytime anywhere with her little angel from Mimosa. As a result, the Shooks repeat their pre-dawn routine nearly every Sunday during the fall of '52, returning to Mimosa and sleeping the remainder of the day. Because the low wattage radio signals from outlying areas bounce off the town's surrounding hills, few people in Mimosa are aware of Angeline's newfound success.

A surprise opportunity comes along just before Thanksgiving, one that stretches far beyond Marie's hopes for Angeline—an invitation from the best-known radio station in Birmingham. Tucker drives his ecstatic wife and sleepy daughter up Red Mountain and eases his truck through the early morning mist glowing red from the WOKE-TV neon sign across the roof of the ante-bellum building.

"This ain't no radio station, Marie," Tucker says, peering at the sign.

"But this is where the man said to show up," Marie responds, "must be a radio station in there somewhere." She twists the radio dial. "I think it's 1050...here it is." She waits, listening for clues to the studio location. After a couple of gospel quartet numbers, she looks at her watch. "We'd better go on in an' see if this is the right place." Marie checks Angeline's face, pink from the neon glow, before leading her up the steps to the studio door.

Tucker keeps the radio tuned to the station until the announcer says, "You've been listening to the Harper Brothers Happy Hitters on WOKE, 1050 on your dial from our studios atop Red Mountain in good ol' Birmingham, Alabama." Assured they've come to the right place, Tucker turns down the volume, pulls his heavy coat tighter, hunkers down and drifts off to sleep.

Suddenly awakened by a tapping on the truck window, Tucker opens his eyes and sees Marie standing in the cold beside a well-groomed man wearing a heavy overcoat. Tucker quickly rolls down the window. "Mr. Shook, I'm York Little, Station Manger here at WOKE," the man beams.

Tucker extends his right hand and brushes his hair back with the other. "Yes sir, how-do."

"I was just discussing our annual March of Dimes Telethon with your wife. I'd be honored to have little Miss Shook perform on the show." Angeline steps up on the running board grinning at her daddy.

Marie pulls Tucker's arm exclaiming, "He wants our Lil Angel to sing on television, Tucker. Imagine that!"

"The telethon starts next weekend and I have a spot for another singer on Saturday morning. Mrs. Shook says I should consult you before booking your daughter," Mr. Little continues.

Tucker glances at Marie and then gazes into Angeline's hopeful eyes. "Well, I reckon so," he drawls.

"Good! She'll need to be here by eight o'clock for make-up, rehearsal and camera check." York Little whips around and heads back up the steps emitting puffs of vapor from his mouth.

"Oh, shit," Tucker bangs his hands against the steering wheel.

"Tuckerrr!" Marie scolds.

"I mean, shoot, I have to work half a day next Saturday gittin' ready for the inspectors. You'd better run in an' tell that Little fella we can't make it."

"Oh no, Tucker. I won't let her miss this chance of a lifetime." Marie lifts Angeline up to crawl over her daddy. Then she runs around the truck and climbs aboard. "Let's go," she says, "I'll think of somethin', we'll git her here someway."

Tucker rolls up the window and grumbles as he eases the truck down Red Mountain's twisted road, "Don't need nobody's charity, Marie."

She ignores her husband's declaration of independence. *It wouldn't be charity if I offered somethin' in trade.* With that thought, a tiny smile creeps across her lips as she ponders the possibilities.

By the time the Shook family arrives home, Marie has a plan. Angeline and Tucker nestle back in bed—but Marie dresses for church. She goes to the front porch to touch up her makeup in the sunlight. *Lil Angel has finished performin' today, now it's my turn,* Marie tells herself on her way to Mimosa First Methodist.

Marie continually eyes Claude Ray during the worship service, adding a coy smile when he glances her way, but he does not respond.

As choir members file out after the service, Claude's wife whispers, "Did you see Angeline's mother in the congregation? She doesn't have little Shirley Temple with her today."

"Oh, I didn't notice," Claude lies.

"Uh huh…well, she'll make sure you notice her now. She's making a beeline straight for you as we speak. I'll stay close by in case you need a lifeline, maestro," Claude's wife mutters and moves towards the choir loft stairs.

"Why Marie Shook, you're here without Angeline," Claude calls over the wall that separates the choir loft from the pulpit dais. Ignoring his attempt to talk over the barrier, Marie disappears through the door.

"May I help you, dear?" Mrs. Ray offers as she meets Marie at the bottom of the stairs.

Without answering, Marie hurries up the stairs. Claude's instinct urges him to avoid Marie, but hormones overrule his intent. "I didn't see Angeline in Sunday School either, is she all right?" Claude asks.

"Didn't ya' hear her on the radio this mornin'? She sang on WOKE." Marie fakes disappointment with a pout as Claude shakes his head. "I reckon she forgot to tell ya'; shame on her. Anyway, I left her at home to catch up on sleep. We've all been up since four this mornin'."

Claude tucks his music folder under his arm, to exit the choir loft but he notices Brother John re-entering the empty sanctuary. "I'm very happy for Angeline," Claude says loudly, "Did you hear that, Brother John? Little Angeline sang on the radio this morning in Birmingham."

The preacher mumbles a benign acknowledgement without looking up. He retrieves his Bible and notes from the pulpit, pretending not to notice Marie and Claude together in the choir loft. Now desperate to separate himself from Marie, Claude walks past her, but she catches him by the arm.

"I have more good news about Angeline, Claude. Can I tell ya' now, or wait 'til later?" Marie flutters her thick eyelashes.

Claude quickly scans the sanctuary to be sure no one can eavesdrop. "What about now?"

"It's a long story, but if ya' got time…"

"I have someone waiting just now, but could you come back this afternoon after youth choir practice, say around six?"

Marie smiles, "O. K.," and gives his arm a quick squeeze, "I'll be here."

"What did the stage mama want this time?" Ray's wife asks as he sheds his robe in the choir room.

"The usual," he shrugs. "Angeline's making the Sunday morning radio circuit in Birmingham and her mother just wanted to update me."

"Watch your step, Ray, that woman acts like she wants to do more than just update you. I've been around horses enough to recognize a mare in heat."

"For God's sake, Ruthie, I'm just her child's teacher, that's all."

"Um huh."

Sunday afternoon drags on for Marie, but Claude's mind runs in high gear. Unable to concentrate during youth choir practice, Claude lets them go early. "All of you bring somebody with you next week and we'll begin planning our spring tour."

As predicted, Marie arrives and closes the door just as the last teenager wanders out. "Oh, I forgot something. Hang on, I'll be right back," Claude says. A few minutes later, he returns leaving the door open behind him. He had forgotten nothing; he wanted to open the door without being too obvious. "Now, Marie what news do you have about Angeline?"

"Well, Claude, it's both good and bad news," she twirls a ringlet of black hair with her finger. "She's supposed to sing on television Saturday for that telethon they do every year."

"That is good news," he responds. "Do you want me to help her with the songs?"

"Won't be no cause for that, my husband has to work Saturday an' we ain't got no way to git to Birmingham." Marie pauses, rolling her glistening black eyes upward. "I reckon Lil Angel's gonna miss her big chance on television." She drops her head in disappointment. "Unless…unless ya' know somebody who might be goin' that way, come Saturday," she adds.

Claude lifts her chin with his finger. Lingering on the cusp of triumph, Marie suppresses a smile. "That's nonsense, Marie. All you have to do is ask. I'll be glad to drive Angeline to Birmingham. My wife's been begging me to take her shopping anyway. I'm sure we can do it."

Marie shakes her head tentatively. "Oh, I can't impose on y'all like that. Ya' done too much for us already. It'd be too much trouble…"

"Not at all, not at all, what time shall I pick her up at the church?"

"Let's see, they want her at the station by eight o'clock."

"Wow, that's early. We'll need to leave by seven."

Before the last word leaves Claude's lips Marie slings her arms around him. But a tapping on the door causes her to suddenly push away from Claude. "Excuse me, I didn't mean to interrupt." A petite woman slips her silvered head around the doorframe.

Ray whips around and stammers, "Oh, come in Mrs. Peerce, I've been expecting you. Ma…uh Mrs. Shook was just telling me the good news, Angeline's going to sing on television."

"How lovely," the organist responds with feigned enthusiasm. "And I suppose you've arranged for an accompanist, as usual." Her tiny, sharp voice reflects the fermenting bitterness of having been passed over previously.

"I'm sure the station provides one, Mrs. Peerce," Ray answers.

"I reckon I better go," Marie makes her way toward the door.

"Tell Angeline not to forget Angel Choir practice Wednesday after school," Claude reminds Marie as she leaves. The diminutive organist paces to the piano with tiny measured steps and slides onto the bench, all business.

"I suppose you've been…uh, too busy to select the hymns for tonight's service," she quips, thumbing through the Cokesbury songbook.

"No problem," Claude responds, overlooking her thinly veiled sarcasm. "We sing the same old favorites anyway. What about twenty-two and forty-one?"

When Marie comes by the church Wednesday afternoon to walk Angeline home, she reminds Claude Ray of the Saturday morning outing to Birmingham. "I'll have her here by 6:30," she says, taking Angeline by the hand outside the choir room. "She's real excited about bein' on television, ain't ya' darlin'?" Angeline giggles and bounces her curls with a nod.

"Oh yes, she even announced it to the choir this afternoon," Claude chuckles. "I'm looking forward to witnessing a live telecast myself."

"That'll really be somethin', watchin' how they make pictures fly into people's houses," Marie exclaims, her face beaming like sunrise. "I'm gonna come downtown to General Furniture Store an' watch her sing her little heart out."

"Wait a minute. You don't have television at home?" Claude rubs his chin, but he dares not risk inviting Marie along for the trip to Birmingham, fully aware of Ruthie's suspicions toward the buxom *femme fatale* standing wide-eyed before him.

"That's all right, we're savin' up to get one soon," Marie says, forcing a smile. "Anyhow, we'll see ya' bright an' early Saturday. Come on Lil Angel, let's go git started on ya' homework." Angeline retrieves her book satchel from the hallway and skips out of the building.

On Saturday a heavy fog shrouds Mimosa in pre-dawn darkness. Claude Ray does not see Marie and Angeline waiting in front of the church until his car is only a few yards away and he spots Marie waving a flashlight. "Hey," she shouts as Claude pulls his Ford to the curb. "I was afraid ya' wouldn't see us in this fawg." She leads Angeline down the steps and opens the back door of the sedan. "Oh." Marie's eyes widen when she sees Claude is alone. "Where's ya' wife?"

"She decided not to come. Her mother and sister are coming for a visit. I was thinking on the way over. Marie, why don't you come with us so you won't have to spend the morning watching television at General Furniture?" Marie's face brightens at first, then falls.

"But jist look at me. I ain't dressed to go nowhere." She pulls her Army surplus coat tight to conceal the worn housedress she threw on to walk Angeline downtown.

"You look fine, Marie, nobody'll notice us, not with Angeline along," he laughs. "Come on, get in the front seat."

Marie closes the back door and climbs in front, shaking her head and mumbling, "I'm a pitiful sight, should've put on somethin' nice."

About halfway to Birmingham the fog lifts, except atop Red Mountain. Driving up the winding road to the station is like entering a cloudbank. "We're fifteen minutes late," Claude says after parking the car. "Let's hurry on in."

"No, ya' take Lil Angel inside. I hafta fix my hair an' put on some makeup. I'll be in later." So Claude and Angeline leave Marie fumbling in her purse as they walk through the blushing fog tinged red from the neon sign. Claude reappears ten minutes later and opens the driver's side door, "I thought you'd be getting chilly by now. Do you want me to run the heater until you're ready, Marie?"

"What about Lil Angel?"

"She charmed her way right into the main studio where they're rehearsing. The show starts in about thirty minutes. It's a madhouse in there." Claude cranks the motor and switches on the heater.

"I can't see worth a damn in this dim light," Marie complains. "Is my lipstick on straight?"

Claude clicks on the overhead light. "Let me see. Yes, you look very...attractive." Marie smiles. "I'd take you anywhere looking like that."

"I'm still worried about this old dress." Marie pushes the heavy khaki coat off her shoulders. "What do ya' think? And don't say nice just to please me."

It's the very same dress Marie wore the day she sent his hormones raging in the choir room. She accidentally pulls the top button loose exposing cleavage that turns Claude's face red as he stares at her ample breasts. She looks down, lips pursed, "Honestly, I have more trouble stayin' decent in this old dress." She slowly pulls it together. "I better check the other buttons before we go in." Marie parts the coat, pulls the dress down over her shapely legs, and buttons it at the bottom.

"I shouldn't say this, Marie, but every time I see you in that dress, I get goose bumps."

"Why, that's the sweetest thing anybody's said to me in a coon's age," she sighs. "That deserves a Yankee dime." Marie leans toward Claude and he turns his head, expecting a peck on the cheek, but she places her palm against his cheek, guiding his face toward her and touches her lips to his. Startled, Claude stiffens as if to back away, but Marie slides her hand behind his head and holds tight. Claude relaxes and gives in.

When she pauses for air, Marie whispers, "I've been wantin' to do that for a long time." She kisses him again, pulling him down in the car seat almost on top of her. He pulls loose. Marie pulls back the top of her dress and suggests, "Maybe ya' wanna kiss me somewhere else."

The temptation is so great that Claude struggles for strength to resist. "You have no idea, Marie, no idea at all," he utters shaking his head. "We should go on in before we miss Angeline's performance. Maybe...maybe some other time."

Marie pouts as she fiddles with a wayward button. "Ya' better wipe off the lipstick an' I better put on some more," she sighs, buttoning her dress and wrapping the coat around her. As she leads the shaken Claude up the steps to the studio, Marie turns and says, "Know what, I'm gonna hold ya' to that promise."

The long rehearsal and performing under the hot lights siphons Angeline's energy. Wiped out, she crawls in the back seat of Claude's car and falls asleep. "Poor darlin', all tuckered out," Marie observes as Claude maneuvers the car along Twentieth Street.

"They really put her through the paces; she sang her entire repertoire. Those people in the studio couldn't get enough of our angel," Claude brags, beaming as though he owns a share of the Angeline stock.

Marie slides her hand across the seat and pats Claude's leg. "That's so true."

"Marie," Claude says with a slight cough. "When we get back, maybe I can drop y'all off close to your house, you know, so you won't have so far to walk."

"That's all right. We don't mind the walk. It'll do us good."

Claude drops the subject until they approach the town limits, an hour later. "I hate to bring this up again, Marie, but we really don't need to go by the church. Somebody might see us and misunderstand."

"Oh?"

"You see, I didn't actually tell my wife about taking Angeline to Birmingham today. I guess it just slipped my mind. So when I invited you to come along, well that just complicates the situation.

"Ya' mean she'd be jealous," Marie smiles.

"Let's just say I don't want to have to explain anything to her, or to anybody else, for that matter, including your husband."

Angeline sits up in the back seat and digs her fists into her eyes. "Are we home yet?"

"Just about, Mr. Ray's kindly offered to drive us home. Won't that be nice?" Claude takes a back road around town and follows Marie's directions.

"Ya' can let us out here. There's the road to our house an' it ain't paved. Ya' might get stuck an' how would ya' explain that?" Ray stops the car and lets his passengers out. "Lil Angel tell Mr. Ray 'thank ya', sir'." Angeline does as she's told. Claude drives away as Marie leads her daughter gingerly along the weedy edge of the road.

Claude Ray goes through each day unable to erase from his mind the image of Marie lying suggestively on the seat of his car. His mind wanders during Angel Choir practice, anticipating the sight of her in that dress when she comes to pick up Angeline. The way he looks at Marie during Sunday services catches the attention of Elsa Elliot, the organist's bridge partner. A gossip vine takes root and spreads, wrapping its tendrils around the ears of most women of the church. Ruthie Ray is the first to mention the rumor to her husband after church service.

"Claude, people are starting to notice the way you drool every time you see Marie Shook," she says as she arranges her choir robe on the wooden hanger.

"Nonsense, Ruthie, we've been over this ridiculous bit before," Claude huffs.

"I watched you during church today and..."

"So," Claude interrupts, "instead of listening to John's sermon, like I did, you were tracking my eye movements."

"If you were listening to John, then why were you so surprised when he changed the last hymn? You were the only one on the wrong page when Agnes Peerce began playing the organ."

Claude glares at his wife with a look that terminates the discussion, but her message leaves no doubt—his relationship with Marie must be more discreet. It's a good thing Ruthie can't read his mind. Claude fantasizes being alone with Marie just once, to taste the sweet nectar of her appreciation for all he has done for Angeline. His fantasies slowly evaporate as he considers the possibility of getting caught, disgraced and losing his jobs at the church and at school, not to mention destroying his marriage. The angel of morality is more persuasive than the devil of deception, so Claude decides to clear his mind of all temptation. He definitely needs to divest himself of further responsibility for Angeline's singing career.

Claude wrestles with a plan to disconnect with Marie as soon as possible. Wednesday afternoon after Angel Choir practice, he announces to the elementary children, "No practice next week during spring holidays."

"Yay!" they shout and cheer.

"Now y'all don't get sunburned and I'll see you in two weeks." As usual, Marie lingers at the door, waiting for Angeline. Taking her daughter by the hand, Marie glances sideways at Claude and licks her upper lip slowly. Brother John appears from the doorway down the hall. He acknowledges the rambunctious choristers' greetings while casting a suspicious eye toward Claude and Marie.

"We need to talk, Marie," Claude whispers without looking at her. "May I call you later?" Marie smiles and nods in agreement.

"Afternoon, Mrs. Shook," says the preacher as he makes his way past her to the choir room, "and Miss Angeline." He turns to watch the mother and daughter leave the building before addressing Claude Ray. "Have a good practice today, Claude?"

"Pretty good considering spring is in the air," Claude answers, "but they'll be ready to sing by Palm Sunday."

John closes the choir room door and takes a seat on the front row. His furrowed brow indicates he's not making a courtesy call. "Have a seat, Claude. We need to talk."

"All right, Brother John, you sound serious." Claude pulls a chair out of line and sits facing his preacher.

"That depends on you, Claude. Would you care to tell me about what's going on between you and Mrs. Shook?"

"What? What do you mean?"

"I'll come to the point. There's a good deal of loose talk going around about you two. Now, I'm not one to add credence to every rumor I hear, but…"

"But what, Brother John?" Claude interrupts, knowing that gossip often greases the preacher's wheels. "It should interest you to know that Ruthie and I have discussed those ugly rumors and we've resolved the whole matter. There is nothing untoward going on and there never will be."

"Mrs. Shook is a mighty attractive woman, Claude, and she seems to be quite lonely. That's a potent formula for temptation."

"Her only interest is pushing her daughter toward stardom no matter what it takes."

"Ah yes, you said that before, but that adds yet another element to the formula—ambition."

Claude emits a nervous laugh. "Let me ease your mind. I decided today to withdraw any and all support from little Angeline's trek to stardom. Needless to say, it has not been an easy decision to make because I am still her teacher. At any rate, you have no cause for concern, Brother John. My talent scouting days are over."

"That's a wise decision, my boy, wise indeed," the relieved pastor gives Claude a benevolent pat on the shoulder and leaves.

Claude gives John ample time to disappear before crossing the street to the phone booth near the drug store. Calling Marie from the church office could possibly set off a new round of gossip. The phone rings only once before Marie's breathless voice answers. "Marie, this is Claude Ray."

"I know, I know," she gushes. "I mean, hello."

"I've been thinking about Angeline's future and I wonder if..."

Marie interrupts, her voice changes, "Ya' git off the phone, Nellie! This is private, ya' hear?" There is a click on the line. "Excuse me, Claude, I'm on a two-party line an' ol' nosy Nellie thinks she's gotta know all my business and hers too. What were ya' gonna say about my Lil Angel?"

Claude pauses, concerned that the eavesdropper may identify him and set off another wave of rumors. "I have an idea for coordinating future singing engagements that I'd like to discuss. Since school will be out next week, what day would be convenient for you and Mr. Shook to meet with me?"

Before hanging up, Claude agrees to meet Marie and her husband on Tucker's day off. "Ya' jist come on by the house Monday about ten in the mornin'. We live at the end of the dirt road where ya' dropped us off before, remember?" Her invitation surprises Claude because previously she had made every effort to keep him away from her house.

Claude spends the next few days rummaging through files searching for names of agents that specialize in booking religious performers. He plans to divert Marie's attention from him by giving her a list of agents to pursue. Despite the gusting turbulence of March weather, Claude sets out from the church on foot to avoid any suspicion if someone were to see his car parked at the Shook's house. His pace is steady, but he takes time to chat with a storeowner sweeping the sidewalk in front of his building. The sidewalk ends where a narrow dirt road veers off Main Street between rows of cedars. He stops, looks around casually, then scurries up the dirt road. As he rounds the curve, an unpainted shack appears at the end of the short road. *Ah, good, Tucker's pickup truck in the front yard, a good sign,* he thinks. Claude selects a path to the porch that avoids all the tools, engine parts and chains scattered about. He knocks on the door and clears his throat.

"Door's open," Marie shouts, "Come on in."

Claude pushes the door open and pauses, to adjust his eyes to the semi-dark front room. A whiff of lilac quickens his nostrils, a familiar fragrance. Marie stands in the doorway to the kitchen, a faint silhouette holding something in her hands.

"Coffee?" she asks, raising a metal pot in one hand and a cup in the other.

Claude moves close enough to see she is wearing the thin cotton dress he finds so sexy. "No, thanks," he sputters, "had my one cup for the day already." She turns and walks back into the kitchen as Claude follows, fixing his glare on her swaying hips.

After placing the pot on the stove, she twirls around, throwing her arms out and exclaims, "It's the dress ya' said ya' like."

Startled by her sudden candor, Claude jerks his head from side to side. "Where's Mr. Shook…and…and Angeline?"

She giggles, "Gone fishin'."

"Fishing?"

"Yeah, Tucker always goes fishin' on his day off. This time, he took Lil Angel to show her how to bait a hook."

"Then, they'll be back soon for our meeting?"

"Guess not, they're miles down the Sipsey by now."

"But, the truck…"

"Oh, Tucker wouldn't go fishin' in his precious truck. They went with his buddy from the mine. Anyhow, ya' said ya' wanted to talk about Lil Angel."

Claude takes a deep breath and spreads the brochures across the kitchen table. After he sits down, Marie slides a chair up close pressing her side against his as she takes a seat. Struggling against the overpowering scent of lilac, Claude explains about booking agents and points out one in Nashville who might be interested in taking on Angeline as a client. "Here, let me get the light, so you can read this," Claude says, reaching above the table to pull the chain. "There, now you can see." As Claude sits back down, he glances at the outline of Marie's breasts beneath her dress. She presses closer, pointing to statements on the paper and asking questions. "I'm sorry, but what were you asking?" Claude mutters, flustered and distracted.

Marie lays down the brochure and delicately plunges forward with the strategic skill of Delilah. Placing her lips provocatively close to Claude's ear, yet piously careful not to touch, she teases softly, "Maybe you got ya' mind on somethin' else."

Claude turns to answer her and wonders, momentarily, *how can my tender soul possibly descend to such divine depths of depravity?* The sultry parting of Marie's lips tests his golden primal passion.

"Come on, baby," Marie whispers, "Come on, a promise is a promise."

4

> *June 4, 1953*
> *Dear Mrs. Shook:*
> *Please sign the enclosed agreement allowing me to book Lil Angel for appearances to sing. As we discussed, my fee would be twenty percent after expenses. I have several potential engagements lined up already and will proceed with haste as soon as I receive the agreement with your signature.*
>
> *Best wishes*
> *Ben Sawyer*

"Paul, this is Claude Ray…Yes, I'm fine, and you? I'm in town for a while and wonder if you might have a few minutes this afternoon. I know you prefer to prepare your sermons on Saturdays, but I really need to talk…Yes, I'd like to come over, maybe buy you a cup of coffee…Good, I'll drop by your house around two."

That afternoon Paul Peterson watches Katy jump rope in front of the church as he waits for Claude to arrive. Before long Claude's sedan pulls up to the curb. "Kat-eee," he exclaims as he opens the car door, "my how you've grown. What grade are you in now, twelfth?"

"No…ooo, silly, I'll be in sixth grade," Katy squeals as she runs to wrap her arms around her old friend.

"It's good to see you again, Claude," Paul squeezes his hand, "How's your blushing bride?"

"Ruthie's fine, but she's not exactly a blushing bride. It's been more than two years since you tied the knot for us."

"Well, come on in and say hello to Lorna. She's made some fresh coffee."

Katy takes Claude's hand and leads him in the house. "I need to talk to you in private, Paul, if you don't mind," Claude whispers to Paul.

"I understand, we'll grab our coffee and go over to the church."

After a brief visit with Katy and Lorna, the two men go next door to a small conference room. "This is not very comfortable, but it's private," Paul apologizes as he switches on the overhead light. "You seem worried, Claude."

Claude sits druming his fingers on the heavy oak table. Paul waits patiently until Claude begins, "Do you remember counseling Ruthie and me before we got married?" Paul nods. "You said that at some point our marriage would confront a real test."

"Yes."

"Well, I faced the test a couple of months ago."

"And...?"

"I'm ashamed to say, I failed it."

"You failed?"

"Yes, and I'm not proud of what I did. My plan was to forget what had happened between me and this other woman...you know...I swore, I mean, I promised it would never happen again. Then, yesterday, she told me she's pregnant. Now, I can't let it go. If this gets out, there goes my marriage, my career and my reputation. I've been up all night thinking, worrying. I just don't know what to do."

"I see." Paul tries to recall what he'd learned in his single counseling course. He proceeds as best he can, guiding Claude to work through the agony by reflecting and accepting his feelings. Only moments later, the catharsis abruptly ends.

After a long agonizing silence, not knowing what else to say, Paul asks his friend, "How can I help?"

"There's nothing you can do, Paul, nothing at all. I suppose I'd better go back to Mimosa and face the music...ha ha," he releases a nervous laugh, "That was a bad pun." Claude stares at his tepid coffee and realizes his former pastor will offer no magic potion to ease his pain. "Thanks for listening, Paul, and for not insisting on hearing the details of my sordid episode."

"I'm sorry to have been of little help. Mind if I ask just one question before we pray about your dilemma. Is the woman you mentioned married?"

"Yes. She also has an eight year-old."

"Still with her husband?"

"Yep."

"I see. Have you told anyone else?"

"No, not even Ruthie, she'd be devastated."

Paul strokes his chin. "As your former pastor, I can only encourage you to pray for divine guidance and strength to address this problem. On the other hand, if I were a lawyer, I'd offer you a more direct piece of advice."

"What's that?" Claude lifts his brow.

"One word—wait."

"Wait? Wait for what?"

"Just wait. You see, a married woman making such an accusation has more at stake than someone who is single. Give her more time to think through her options and risks."

"I'm afraid that won't work. She's uneducated, but smart with the gall of a gypsy dancer. She wouldn't think twice about standing on Main Street and announcing her predicament if it would serve her purpose," Claude shakes his head.

"And what is her purpose?"

"Promoting her daughter's quest for stardom. She'll do anything to make her another Shirley Temple."

"Unfortunately, I know of whom you speak. Do you remember she brought her daughter to sing here in Coal City, twice."

"Oh yes, I'd almost forgotten."

"The advice still stands, Claude. Be patient; give it some time. It'll do no good to suggest you stop worrying, an impossible notion, but at least get your emotions in check. Wait a couple weeks then let's talk again. Meanwhile, I'll keep praying for you and Ruthie as well as for that ambitious Jezebel." Paul offers a brief prayer before adjourning their session.

"Thanks, Paul."

Claude picks up his cup and rises to leave. "Never mind, I'll take care of the cup,"

"Tell Lorna and Katy goodbye for me."

As he tops the hill and looks over the trees at the bell tower of First Methodist, Claude shudders. All the way from Coal City, his mind has played scenarios of being run out of town in disgrace. He turns the corner and parks on the side street. Resting his head on the steering wheel, he tries to gather his thoughts before going inside. Finally, he saunters in the side door and wanders down the dim hallway to the choir room, where he sits pondering his plight until darkness begins to absorb the thin twilight shadows in the room. The electronic chimes in the church tower strike the hour and the carillon plays the hymn, *It is Well With My Soul*. He must now head home and prepare to face a tenuous prelude to his impending fall from grace.

Claude rises earlier than usual Sunday morning, grabs a quick bowl of cereal and dresses for church before Ruthie stirs from her bed. "I'm leaving you the car, honey," he says as he kisses his wife on the forehead to wake her. "I'll see you in the choir room." Claude is anxious to avoid conversation. He expects the short walk to church will help shake the dread and despair that stifle his spirit. If he runs into Marie at church today, he must construct a calm reaction that will not betray his inner conflict to the gossip mongers.

"Good morning, Claude. I know you must be dreading this day, like the rest of us." Mrs. Peerce greets Claude in the choir room.

Oh no, she knows about Marie. The word's out already. Claude tries to hide his panic, to maintain control.

"Brother John's already been here looking for you. He wants to see you in his study." The organist clutches a stack of music against her chest and skitters past Claude. "Gotta go practice."

Claude's gut tightens and threatens to dispense his cereal as he trudges down the hallway to the pastor's study. The door is open; he walks in. "Come in, Claude. I just want to have a private word with you before we go our separate ways," Brother John says, getting right to the point.

"Sure," Claude responds, almost inaudibly. As he takes a seat across from John's desk, he struggles to appear casual and unconcerned.

John's swivel chair creaks as he leans back interlocking his fingers across his chest. "You've performed your duties well over the past few years, Claude, and despite our minor differences, I've been well pleased with the music program. I deeply regret that I will no longer enjoy the fruits of your labor." John rises and walks around the desk toward Claude. Claude's mouth goes dry and his breathing becomes shallow as he stands to take the bitter pill of condemnation. "I have one last favor to ask of you. I know how you detest last minute changes in the service, but Mary wants you to have the choir sing the *Sevenfold Amen* at the conclusion of the service today. It's her favorite."

Claude's spine crumbles taking on the shape of the chair. Taking a deep breath he sputters, "Of course...sure...I should've thought of it myself. I completely forgot this is your last Sunday. I feel so stupid!"

"Oh, I'm sure you've had plenty on your mind." The preacher reaches to grasp Claude's hand. "Just wanted to take a moment to say goodbye and hope our paths will cross again soon."

With a new spurt of energy, Claude bolts down the hall to the choir room and pulls out the *Sevenfold Amen* folder. He welcomes the reprieve and forgets about Marie Shook for the moment. A large crowd gathers in the sanctuary to say farewell to their beloved pastor who is retiring after six years at Mimosa. As Brother John begins his farewell sermon, Claude notices that Marie is not in her regular place on the back pew. He scans the congregation examining every female face to be sure he has not overlooked her. With a sigh of relief, he settles back to listen to the preacher and observes several women dabbing tissues against their moistened cheeks.

Marie Shook is eighty miles away from Mimosa not giving a second thought to the deception she perpetrated on the unsuspecting Claude Ray two days before. Telling him she is carrying his child was an insidious entrapment aimed at keeping him involved with Angeline's singing career, at least through the summer. The thought of Claude twisting in agony gave Marie a pernicious but short-lived high. A phone call after she had left Claude that Friday morning lifted her into an even higher orbit.

"Mrs. Shook, this is Melva Strong with Guideline Agency. We would like to schedule an audition for Angeline Shook as soon as possible, perhaps sometime next week." No, she couldn't wait that long. By the time she hung up the phone, Marie had arranged an audition for the next day at the Guideline recording studios in Muscle Shoals.

"Yes, we'll be there by one o'clock. Gimme that address...O.K., I got it."

Before Tucker's truck comes to a complete stop in the yard, Marie screams, "Tuck, Tuck, we're gonna make the big time, honey," She pulls open the cab door and continues rattling on as he wipes sweat-caked coal dust from his brow. "Angeline's got a' audition with a recordin' company in Muscle Shoals tomorrow. Ya' gotta drive us up there, you jist gotta!"

Tucker is too tired to respond with the enthusiasm Marie expects, but her jumping up and down like a barefoot kid on hot pavement draws a tentative smile. He slides out of the truck and takes her hand. "All right, all right, hon, calm down. I ain't seen ya' this worked up since ya' got pregnant with Angeline." Marie grows silent when he mentions pregnancy. Tucker leads her toward the porch, startled at her sudden loss of enthusiasm. "Now, set down on the step and tell me what's goin' on."

"I ain't gonna have a baby, Tucker," Marie blurts out, rubbing her flattened belly.

"I know, I'm jist funnin' ya'. We ain't done nothin' in a while to make a baby," Tucker says with a laugh as hollow as a dried up well.

Marie regains her composure and tells Tucker about the phone call from the agency. "The woman said we oughta come prepared to stay overnight in case Angeline gets a recall, whatever that is."

"Then, I reckon I'd better put the camper shell on the truck," Tucker replies.

"Aw, c'mon Tucker, can't we stay in a motel? I won't have no way to press our dresses. Lil Angel don't need to look like she slept in a truck."

"Don't push ya' luck, Marie. I ain't too hot on going to Muscle Shoals nohow." Tucker ventures into the house leaving Marie in the yard cursing under her breath.

They pull into Muscle Shoals the next day and Tucker finally locates the Guideline Agency Studio after passing the nondescript storefront twice. He parks the truck across the street and slides a nickel in the parking meter. "We got one hour," he tells Marie. "If y'all ain't back in time, I'll drive around an' find another parkin' place an' y'all hafta look for the truck."

Marie nods as she unties Angeline's head cover and combs her hair. Satisfied with her daughter's image, she climbs out of the truck and takes Angeline's hand. "It sure didn't waste no time gittin' hot quick," Marie complains as she helps her daughter from the truck. "I ain't sure them curls'll hold up in this heat. Let's hurry inside, maybe they've got air conditionin'."

Tucker pokes out his lips and shakes his head. "Do they wanna listen to Angeline or take her picture?"

Ignoring his insidious question, Marie practically drags Angeline across the busy downtown street, dodging cars and trucks. Looking in the painted plate glass window, she brushes at wrinkles on her dress and pushes open the door. A tinkling bell summons a platinum-haired woman from the back. "You must be the Shook family," she gushes. "My, my, what a darling child. I wish I had those curls. If she sings as pretty as she looks, we'll have no trouble placing her. Now, sit over here and let me get some information." The lady maneuvers her long fingernails around the ballpoint pen and begins filling in the blanks on a sheet of paper with tiny print. After extracting all the essential information from Marie, the lady turns the paper around for her signature. "This is a standard artist's contract giving the agency exclusive rights to Miss Angeline's bookings, should she qualify. As I mentioned over the phone, there is a fifty-dollar audition fee. How do you wish to pay, by check or cash?"

Marie's mouth drops open. "Ya' didn't say nothin' 'bout payin' for the audition. I...I don't have that much money on me right now."

"Oh, and that's a shame, too. Miss Angeline looks like she can write her own ticket to fame. Why don't we re-schedule the audition for another time when you can afford to invest in your child's future?" The lady folds her contract and gestures toward the door. Marie is reluctant to leave, but she has no choice. Even if Tucker has fifty dollars on him, he'll never turn it loose.

Tucker is surprised to see them coming across the street, so soon. "That was quick," he says, crushing his cigarette on the sidewalk with his boot.

Marie opens the passenger door and boosts Angeline inside. She turns to Tucker, "The bitch wants me to pay to let Lil Angel sing. I told her to 'shove it'. Let's go!"

Tucker starts the motor and merges into the line of other pickups and older cars. "I wanna head over to the river while we're here. I hear there's good fishin' on the Tennessee."

"Do like ya' want, Tuck, but stop somewhere and git us a hamburger. I'm starved." Marie crosses her arms and slumps down in the seat as if to snuff out the delusion she had created. On the way out of town, Tucker spots a burger-shake drive-in, pulls into the lot and parks. After giving their order to the carhop, he switches the radio dial to a country music station. The disc jockey announces the call letters of the station, snapping Marie back to the moment.

"There's WLOR across the road," she exclaims. It was like finding familiar ground in a strange town—she had taken Angeline to enough radio stations to claim kin to most of the Alabama disc jockeys. "Let's go see if they'll let Lil Angel sing a song," she bubbles over, fresh blood flowing through her veins. Before Tucker can object, Marie jumps out of the cab and tells Angeline to stay with her daddy until she comes back. She crosses the road and approaches the white frame shack centered on a gravel parking lot. A tall lanky man in a checkered sport coat bolts out the station door and barely avoids a collision with Marie.

"Can I help you, m'am?" he asks, raking his fingers through a shock of hair too perfectly black to be natural.

"Uh, I reckon," Marie says as the man's gaze suddenly makes her conscious of her appearance. Pressing the wrinkles in her dress, she asks, "Do ya' work here?"

"Yes m'am, if you can call it work, I'm the morning D. J., Station Manager and chief light bulb changer," he laughs. "Name's Ben Sawyer, better known as Brother Ben. What can I do for you?"

Marie collects all the charm she perfected at Claude Ray's expense to impress her child's new benefactor. "I was wonderin' if y'all need a singer."

"No m'am, we don't do live programs, just play records and report the news," the D. J. shakes his head.

"Oh."

"Except for Sunday morning gospel hour, but that's mainly for quartets and such. Are you part of a gospel group?" A new anticipation rises in the man's voice as he manages to prolong the conversation with his new flirtatious acquaintance.

"I don't sing. My little girl does. She's been on radio an' television in Birmingham an' I thought…" Marie hesitates and points across the road, "She's over there in that truck. I'll go get her…"

"That's all right…" the disc jockey's words trail off in traffic noise as Marie rushes across the road.

"Come on, Lil Angel, there's a radio star who wants to meet ya'," Marie gushes, breathlessly.

"What about ya' hamburger? Tucker asks, "It's gittin' cold."

Ignoring her husband, Marie drags Angeline to the station's parking lot. "This here's Lil Angel, Mr. Brother Ben."

Ben prepares to dismiss the insistent mother and her prodigy but he steps and kneels in front of Angeline. "I've seen you somewhere before, Miss Angel. Now where…were you on the big Telethon a few months ago?" Angeline cocks her head with her deep brown eyes fixed upward, deferring the question to her mother.

"Yeah, she was on television. Did ya' see her?"

"Not only did I see her, I was there helping with the broadcast. I was the clown in the crazy hat. What a wonderful voice you have, Angel. Is that your real name?"

Angeline steps back, recalling the clown at the T.V. studio had frightened her. "No, Lil Angel's her stage name. Her name's Angeline Shook an' mine's Marie."

Tucker grows impatient and honks the horn. He honks several times until Marie brings Angeline back to the truck. Before he can fuss at her, Marie exclaims, "We gotta stay overnight, Tuck. That man wants Lil Angel to sing on his show tomorrow mornin'. He's also a big producer. He can do great things for our little girl and it won't cost us nothin'."

"Ain't nothin' free," Tucker snorts. "Anyhow, I'll git some good fishin' in. Let's go find a good campsite by the river."

The next day, Angeline performs two numbers for Brother Ben's Old Time Gospel Hour squeezed between the Goodner Family Trio and the Moonlighters Quartet. When the program ends, Marie and Angeline return to the parking lot where Tucker waits in the truck. "Did ya' hear our darlin' singin', Tuck, did ya' hear her?" Marie exclaims. Tucker turns up the volume so she'll know he's tuned to the right station. "Listen!" Marie says, "Brother Ben's talkin' 'bout Lil Angel."

"Yes-sir-ee, folks, the ol' switchboard is all lit up. Y'all really liked today's show, especially Lil Angel. Brother Ben's proud to announce that the little singing angel will be a regular feature on Old Time Gospel Hour. And she's available for any of your singings or gospel conventions. Just call Brother Ben here at WLOR for details…"

"Didja hear that? Our girl's gonna be a star!" Marie shouts.

Ben Sawyer, impressed with Angeline's singing and drawn to Marie's seductive allure, uses his popularity in the tri-cities area to promote Angeline as the singing angel. Friday nights, Tucker, Marie and Angeline hit the road and do not return home until late Sundays. Marie sorts out the money Ben gives her, after keeping his share, and presses the bills into a cigar box she keeps hidden in a drawer.

Every Sunday throughout the summer, Claude Ray approaches church with incipient pain. Not encountering Marie temporarily relieves his anxiety until the next Sunday. The image of Marie appearing in church heavy with child and confronting him in the presence of church members dangles his soul on the end of a very thin string. To relieve the tension, he calls his friend Paul Peterson.

"Brother Paul, this is Claude…yes, I'm doing O. K…well, not O.K…Just wanted to say there is no good news…no bad news either…I have neither seen nor heard from the subject of our conversation since we talked…Just wanted you to know nothing's happened…It's driving me crazy…Give Katy and Lorna my love…See you soon…yes, I'll let you know if anything pops up…I mean…you know what I mean…bye."

The day after Labor Day, Claude, in his usual position in the front hallway of Mimosa School, checks off the names of returning students. He looks up and sees Marie on the threshold of the double doors, fiddling with Angeline's golden curls. Angeline kisses her mother and skips down the hall toward Claude's table.

Marie waves, but as her eyes adjust to the darker interior, her hand freezes in midair, eyes fixed on Claude. She lowers her hand, shrugs and turns to leave. Observing her profile, Claude sees no sign of pregnancy, the image that had tormented him all summer.

5

> May 4, 1956
>
> Dear Reverend Barron:
> I read your letter of April 30 with great interest; however, it would be inappropriate for me to lobby the Bishop and his cabinet on your behalf. Moreover, I am unaware of any church in the Birmingham District anticipating an opening on its staff for a seminary student. I trust your final year in seminary will be successful and you will be appointed to a church befitting your personal gifts in ministry.
>
> Yours in Christ,
>
> Paul Peterson

The phone rings as Marie returns home from enrolling Angeline in the third grade. "Hello...yes sir, it's me...what a surprise, Brother Ben...I saw ya' just yesterday...I know...I understand...yes sir, we'll be there...meet ya' where?...Florence High School...yes sir, Tucker'll find it...four-thirty...bye now."

With Tucker at work in Number Ten mine and Angeline in school, Marie has no one to share the good news with. She busies herself ironing her daughter's dresses, drawing a homemade calendar for September and pacing across the front porch wondering who will come home first. A few minutes past three Angeline's golden locks come into view over the rise. Marie resists the urge to run and tell her about Ben's call. She has to make sure Tucker will drive them back to the Tri-cities Saturday.

"Hurry on in the house, Lil Angel. I'll make ya' a sandwich while we wait for Daddy. I've got a surprise, a big surprise when Daddy gets home." Angeline knows the news is about singing somewhere; otherwise her mother would have called her "honey" or "darling."

"I hear Daddy's truck outside, Lil Angel. G'wan and eat ya' sandwich while I talk to 'im," Marie says, hustling to the front door. "Tuck, honey, ya' won't believe who called. Who do ya' reckon?"

Tucker lifts his work gear out of the truck bed and trudges towards the house. "I dunno, Marie. I'm too worn out to think."

"Brother Ben. He said Wally Farmer wants to hear Lil Angel sing. Ain't that something? Wally Farmer!"

"Who's he?"

"Jist the biggest name in gospel singin'. Can you take us to Florence Saturday? Lil Angel really wants to go. It's her big chance!"

"This Saturday? Cain't do it, Marie. I wasted every weekend this summer haulin' y'all here an' yonder," Tucker moans. "Angeline needs a break an' I need to go fishin'."

"Why don't ya' drop us off at the high school an' then g'wan to the river? We'll be fine 'til ya' get back," Marie suggests.

Tucker agrees to make the trip, unaware that after this Saturday his fishing excursions will extend across four states over the next three years. After hearing Angeline sing, Wally Farmer asks her to perform her trademark gospel medley for the opening of his All-night Singing Convention every other weekend. It becomes the hottest Saturday night show in the South, second only the Grand Ole Op'ry. Marie collects a substantial sum in cash after each performance, which she temptingly flashes in Tucker's face when he tires of chauffeuring, and accompanies it with the promise, "Next time, we'll go early so ya' can find a good fishin' hole."

The soft winds of May whisk the pesky mixture of cinders, coal dust and soot over Coal City's sidewalks as the eighth grade class of 1956 stands outside the school preparing to march into the auditorium for the last time. Lorna Peterson swells with pride as Katy leads the procession and takes her place on the stage behind her dad as he readies to give the invocation. Following Paul's prayer, the principal welcomes parents and laments the school's loss of yet another banner class of eighth graders headed for high school. Then he announces the class valedictorian and relinquishes the podium to Katy. Paul divulges his pride to Lorna with a wink, as Katy addresses the audience. As the message of her speech becomes clear, it is obvious that the audience does not share her parents' joy. Deviating from her prepared presentation, Katy concludes with a passioned plea for the community to reach out to colored students with open arms of Christian friendship.

"You caused quite a stir, Katy," Paul says, as the trio strolls through the piquant spring evening toward the parsonage.

"Everyone did listen to her," Lorna asserts. "That's more than one can say about most valedictorian speeches."

"All I did was suggest we obey the law. What's wrong with that?" Katy shakes her head. "Nobody spoke to me afterwards, not even my friends."

"What did Mr. Wells say?" Paul asks.

"He was not pleased at all. He said I should have stuck with the speech he had approved. I'll bet I'm in trouble now."

"You're not in trouble, young lady. You just graduated, he's not your principal anymore," her mother banters. "However, you and your dad are due to have a discussion about propriety."

"Pro—what?" Katy stammers. "What's that?"

"Let's just say there's a time and a place for everything, especially expressing your views."

"M-o-t-h-e-r-r-r," Katy drags out her voice in exasperation as she stomps across the porch and into the parsonage.

The next day, Lorna initiates a dialogue with Paul about Annual Conference. "The Bishop will read appointments for next year in a couple of weeks. Have you heard anything yet?"

"About what?" Paul teases, knowing full well what she means.

"About us, are we staying or leaving?"

"That's between the Bishop and the Lord. You know I'm not into pastoral politics. I'll go wherever I'm meant to serve," Paul delivers his final word on the subject.

"Excuse me! You also have two passengers on your drifting boat. I think it's about time you set a course for your ministry and let the Bishop know where you're headed. We've served our time in this soul-withering place. Four years in Coal City is long enough. You need to think about Katy and me for a change."

"What's that supposed to mean? I always include you two in my plans," Paul bristles.

"Katy will go to high school this fall. The school board doesn't bus students, so either she will ride a public bus or one of us will have to drive her to Fairmont and pick her up. We only have one car."

"I don't see that as much of a problem. If we're busy, she can ride the bus, actually it would be cheaper than driving. How far is it to the high school, five or six miles?" Paul fails to read between the lines of Lorna's concern. She takes a deep breath and makes a desperate attempt to explain.

"Katy and I rode the bus to the high school last month to pre-register her for classes. When we passed through the government housing projects at Downbeat Junction, I broke out in a cold sweat. Katy thought we were having quite an adventure, but the image of our innocent little girl being mugged on her way to school is giving me nightmares."

"I think you're blowing the situation way out of proportion. I've heard nothing about any muggings on the Coal City/Fairmont bus line, have you?" Paul asks. "Besides, Katy has a good head on her shoulders. She can take care of herself."

Lorna bites her lip and nods her head—not in agreement, but in exasperation. She proceeds with solemn determination. As Paul pursues his pastoral duties, Lorna calls and makes an appointment to talk with the presiding bishop.

"Come in Mrs. Peterson, is anything wrong? Is Paul well?" Bishop Landing asks as he offers her a chair in his office.

"Paul is fine, active as always, thank you. But I sometimes wish he would catch cold so he won't work so hard, he takes himself too seriously," Lorna says with a half-hearted chuckle.

"Oh, I've heard that complaint before...at my own dinner table. How may I be of service to you, Mrs. Peterson?" he smiles and forms a tent with his fingers.

The Bishop's inviting gaze causes her to squirm, racking her mind for an appropriate disclaimer for this impromptu visit to the head of the church. "I know this is highly irregular and if you say I'm out of line, I'll leave quietly, no harm done." Bishop Landing nods, eyebrows crunched together. "My husband is a wonderful compassionate pastor and he has served Coal City Methodist faithfully for four years. Our daughter Katy starts high school this fall and I am concerned."

"Oh?"

"I was wondering if you would consider moving Paul to a church near a high school. You see, we only have one car and Fairmont High is a long way from the parsonage." Lorna pauses, hoping she will not have to play the "fear" card.

"Have you discussed this matter with the District Superintendent?" Lorna lowers her chin, eyes still on the bishop. "You must understand," the Bishop continues, "he makes all recommendations concerning appointments."

"No I haven't, you see Arthur and Paul are such close friends, I'm afraid my husband would be upset and consider my voicing concern to be interference or dallying in church politics. As a matter of fact, Paul has no idea I'm discussing this appointment with you. He places complete trust in those who make the decisions."

"And that is as it should be, Mrs. Peterson. I appreciate your concern and I appreciate Paul's faithful performance as a servant of God. But the Bishop cannot respond to requests from pastors' wives, regardless of their nature. Please give my regards to your husband—oh, it slipped my mind, he probably should not know about our discussion." The Bishop rises from his chair to escort Lorna to the door. "I appreciate your taking the time to come by and I'm sorry I can't accede to your wishes."

Lorna forces a weak smile as she departs. The Bishop closes the door, returns to his desk, and pulls out a map which he spreads across the desk. Tracing his index finger along the main thoroughfares in West Birmingham, he draws a small circle around each high school within the district.

~~~

"I got my notice from Uncle Sam," Chad announces, waving an envelope toward Paul Peterson. "I'm headed for the Army in three weeks."

"That was quick," Paul replies, "you graduated only last week."

"I'm sorry, but my deferment ended with graduation. You'll have to find another boy to play with the kids and entertain the choir." Paul grins knowing it will not be his problem to find a replacement. The District Superintendent had called Paul the day before and advised him to prepare his congregation for a change of pastors. He knows the Bishop will announce specific ministerial changes on Wednesday.

Miss Bessie's arthritic fingers bravely hammer out a prelude as choir members ease into the choir nook, bemoaning Chad's announced resignation. The ladies pick up funeral home fans to stir the thick June air suspended in the heat of the sultry midday sun penetrating the windows. One of the bass singers pushes open a window with a loud squeak, piercing the insipid atmosphere. Paul approaches the pulpit from the side door, startled to see J. B. Colley seated in the pastor's chair. "Good morning, Brother Paul," J. B. extends a hand to his pastor, "I'd like to make an announcement before the service begins."

"Surely," Paul responds.

When the choir finishes singing the call to worship, J. B. stands behind the pulpit and raises both hands. Then donning a somber façade, he lowers his hands and proceeds, "Before we sing the opening hymn, I'd like to have your attention, please." A hush falls over the congregation, broken only by subtle sniffles drifting from the choir nook. "It is with deep regret I must report that our beloved Brother Paul will be leaving us for another church." Gasps and utterances of dismay rise from the congregation. J. B. raises his hands to quiet them. "As much as we hate to say goodbye to Brother Paul, let me remind you that we are part of the Methodist system. We will prepare to welcome a new pastor week after next." Stunned by the church's self-appointed mogul stealing his thunder, Paul can only acknowledge the gracious applause. J. B. shakes Paul's hand and winks before leaving the dais.

"Did you tell J. B. that we were moving?" Paul asks Lorna after the service.

"Of course not, I didn't tell a soul, not even Nora Belle."

"What about Katy?"

"No, she didn't know Chad was leaving either. She's pretty upset."

"About our moving?"

"About Chad, she thinks he'll be killed in Korea."

"Doesn't she know the war ended three years ago? By the way, where is she?"

"In her room, crying."

~~~

The Bishop, in an unexpected move, assigns Paul Peterson to West Park Methodist, across town just two blocks from Lincoln High School. On the day the Petersons move in the West Park parsonage, their new parishioners file into the kitchen and deposit sacks of food on the table, counter and in the pantry. "What a "pounding!" Lorna declares with delight, after the last bearer of gifts leaves. "A pound of this, a pound of that, it's more food than we can eat in a month. I think we're going to like it here. What do you say, Paul?" Paul, preoccupied with sorting out the boxes of books piled in the living room doesn't respond. "Honey, I asked if you like our new home."

"I'm sure I will. The Lord sent me here and I'll make the best of it," Paul replies, pre-occupied with studying spines of the books stacked on his desk.

Lorna covers her mouth and smiles. *The Lord's will be done.*

~~~

Oliver Barron rips open the envelope bearing the Coal City postmark and scans the letter anxiously. "Damn!" he exclaims. A hush falls over his fellow seminary students retrieving their mail from the numbered boxes in the student center. Startled by the awkward silence, Oliver's face turns the color of his hair as he hurries out the door. A fellow seminarian follows and catches him up with him.

"What's wrong, Brother Ollie, bad news?" he observes with concern.

"You'd think our elders in the faith would reach out and help us, wouldn't you? But, no-o-o-o, they've got it made in well paying churches and don't give a shit about us new guys. I am sick and tired of being kicked around by those self-righteous bastards that weasel their way to the big churches and then pull in the damn welcome mat."

Startled by the sacrilegious language, the student shakes his head. "I'm sorry you feel that way Ollie. See you later." He leaves Ollie ranting to himself.

Ollie opens another letter, this one from the Birmingham District Superintendent, is not as disappointing as Paul Peterson's message, but not the good news he expects:

> *Dear Reverend Barron:*
>
> *In response to your letter, I do not anticipate any vacancies among associate pastorates in my district. Would you be interested in starting a new church? There is a small group of Methodists willing to accept a seminary student as their part-time pastor for one year. If you would consider this opportunity, please let me know as soon as possible. As you know Conference begins next week.*
>
> *In His name,*
>
> *Arthur Olds, District Superintendent*

Ollie has no choice; he wants a church in Birmingham so he can be near his fiancée on weekends. The Bishop appoints Oliver to a fledging congregation among the wooded hills of Cliffside Park, a Birmingham suburb. "There's no church, no property and no parsonage," Ollie complains to his District Superintendent.

"I disagree, my son. A church already exists there, made up of two-dozen families—good people with children. God has put you in the middle of a community with the greatest potential for growth in the county." The District Superintendent shows the young pastor a hand-drawn map. "Your congregation will meet here in the Cliffside Park School gymnasium beginning this Sunday. Allied Real Estate has offered to give the church this piece of property," the D. S. points to an "X" on the crude drawing. "As soon as the county puts in a road, it'll be up to you to initiate a building program."

Although unhappy with his assignment, Oliver Barron charms his way into the hearts of his fledgling congregation. Without a sanctuary in which to preach, Oliver decides to try some innovative approaches to worship. He hoists his guitar and breaks into song in the middle of sermons. He often preaches costumed as Biblical characters or historical figures. His risky experiments reap amazing results. By Christmas, over a hundred families have joined his flock. Oliver Barron takes all the credit for Cliffside's escalating membership, ignoring the fact that builders crammed expensive houses among the boulders and giant oaks along the ridge near the church attracting upward mobile families by the dozens. As the 1957 Annual Conference approaches, the leaders of Cliffside Methodist Church make a deal with the District Superintendent. "Leave Brother Ollie with us and we'll buy him a house, pay him a decent salary and start construction on a sanctuary."

The bargain far exceeds Ollie's expectations. He graduates from seminary and moves his new bride into an apartment until their parsonage is cleaned and repainted. Cliffside Methodist experiences phenomenal growth in membership and financial support for the next two years. Oliver Barron enjoys his meteoric rise as pastor of a new church that welcomes several new families into its membership every Sunday. His colleagues often refer to him as the "Red Barron", befitting his aggressive manner of shooting down traditional approaches to ministry.

But the Red Barron's combat wings soon begin to tarnish in the heat of controversy. During his third year at Cliffside, some church leaders raise concerns about his unorthodox methods. Bert Sharp, Chairman of the Official Board, meets in secret with the District Superintendent. "I've come to request that you send us a new pastor next year," Bert says. "Someone more experienced, more, shall we say, 'mature'."

"But I've heard nothing but good things about Reverend Barron. What seems to be the problem?" asks the D. S. as he leans forward to listen.

"We don't mind Brother Ollie's rather creative ways of delivering sermons. We've tolerated his driving around in a Thunderbird convertible wearing a clerical collar, but we are not making any progress toward constructing a sanctuary for our expanding congregation."

"I approved your plans almost two years ago. What's the hold up?"

"Brother Ollie scrapped that design and substituted a plan for a round sanctuary with the pulpit in the center. We gave him a few months to see the folly in such a design, to realize it's not appropriate for what may become one of the largest churches in the district, but he has dug in and won't budge."

"Mmm, I see, you're saying Ollie's vision is limited to a small congregation. Is that correct?"

"That's an interesting observation, Reverend. On the contrary, we see Brother Ollie as having grown too big for his britches, so to speak. He's a performer who wants to be the center of attention. Our architect explained that a round building is the least practical of all designs for growth and expansion. Brother Ollie responded by suggesting we hire another firm."

"Thank you for your insight, Brother Bert. You are aware that Brother Ollie and Betty are expecting their first child this spring. We normally don't like to add to pastors' stress by moving them at critical times. Considering the situation, I'll try to work out a mutually satisfying solution."

"I understand Reverend, but the bottom line is, Ollie must go before it's too late."

6

> *January 21, 1960*
>
> Dear Mr. Ray,
>
> I would love to hear the choir sing some of the songs done by Wind and Flame. I don't think the foundation of the church would crack if you did. This suggestion is not because my daughter sings in the group.
>
> Sincerely,
>
> Paulette Goddard

The popularity and recognition that powered Angeline through childhood suddenly backfires as she enters junior high school. Her fame becomes a grindstone for honing barbs of jealousy with which classmates puncture Angeline's over-inflated ego.

"Show us your wings, Lil Angel," sneers a ninth grade classmate.

"And where's your golden harp," scoffs another.

Despite the malicious intents to bring her down to size, Angeline conceals her anger with a saccharine grin plastered across her face until the end of the first day of school. The simmering resentment builds as she walks home, finally reaching a boiling point, and explodes when she enters her front door.

"I'm never going back to that school again," she screams, slamming her books on the kitchen table. "Those bitches don't know who they're talking to!"

"Now baby doll, don't tear y'self up inside. Tell mama what happened." Marie puts her arm around Angeline to soothe her.

Angeline jerks away, tears flooding her eyes. "I hate school! I hate them girls! They call me ugly names." She wipes her eyes with the hem of her dress as Marie reaches out again to console her.

"Pay 'em no mind, them's jist words from uppity bitches," her mother coos, brushing Angeline's damp curls back off of her forehead. "They're jist jealous 'cause ya' look more like a grown woman than they do. But ya're still my Lil Angel."

Angeline shoves her mother's hand away and yells, "Don't ever call me Lil Angel again! Lil Angel's dead and gone on to heaven where she belongs. From now on I'm Angie from hell."

Diverging from the trail Angeline's mother has blazed for her, Angie from hell plunges recklessly down a different path at breakneck speed. She refuses to let Marie continue bleaching her signature blond curls, and they gradually fade to their natural auburn. Sneaking some of her daddy's cigarettes, Angie finds refuge among daughters of other coal miners at school. Although Tucker suspects his girl has taken up smoking, he keeps it to himself. He sees her rebellion as the first sign of breaking the bonds of Marie's influence and drawing closer to him. She identifies with the grungy miners' kids Marie taught her to despise. Tucker celebrates in secret, *Finally, my girl's gonna break out from under the spell of them high falutin' city kids.*

Angie's singing continues to be a thin tether to the church; however, her refusal to participate in the youth choir leaves Claude Ray in a quandary. Although she is clearly the best soprano in town, Claude, attempting to avoid criticism and further contact with the wily Marie Shook, rarely calls on Angie to sing solos. In June of '59 when a new pastor is assigned to Mimosa First Methodist, he unknowingly removes this burr from under Claude Ray's saddle.

T. Oliver Barron strikes Mimosa First like a refreshing summer thunderstorm, the first pastor under fifty to serve the historic downtown church. The congregation does not necessarily prefer their pastors to be elderly, its just that their choices are dictated by the size of the parsonage—a two bedroom bungalow being suitable for only a small family. With the aging congregation beginning to shrink in number, the church leaders opt for young blood in the pulpit for a change. They want to buck the trend of older pastors using their church as the last pit stop on the downhill grade to retirement.

A bit peeved over being assigned to a sleepy mining town in West Alabama, Ollie decides to use the disappointment to fuel his ambition. After settling his wife and newborn into the antiquated parsonage, Ollie sets out to prove he can transfuse new life into Mimosa First Methodist the same way he had built Cliffside Methodist into a vibrant congregation. Expanding the membership base becomes Ollie's top priority, by reaching out to young families, children and youth. His square jawed determination and clean-cut face win the trust of older church leaders, previously suspicious of any long haired, bearded and beaded preachers. Beyond his apparent youth, Oliver Barron's appearance does not fit their rebel image. He charms the youth with a guitar on his knee and a folk song on his lips.

Angie is among the first to succumb to Reverend Barron's persuasive spiel. He wins her over the first Sunday evening when he leads a youth sing-a-long. Angie is attracted to the gathering intending to show off her voice for the new preacher, an idea Claude Ray had planted in hopes of involving her in the youth choir again. Brother Ollie invites the teens to plop down on the floor around a large beanbag chair where he sits with a twelve-string guitar slung across his shoulder. One by one the youth introduce themselves to the new preacher. As each stands, Ollie strikes a chord and improvises a brief tune using the youth's name. When it comes his turn to parody his own name, Oliver Barron sings about Red Barron, a WWI ace, an obvious reference to his shock of bright red hair, neatly combed and sprayed in place. He ends the song with a warning, "Please don't ever call me 'Red' unless you want to see your pastor go down in flames. My friends call me Brother Ollie, and I consider all of you friends." He teaches the youth a few choruses and they sing along with him before he concludes the meeting with *Kum Ba Yah*.

"You know, Angie, you remind me of someone," Ollie says as he nestles the guitar in its case. "Have we met before?"

"No sir," she answers trying not to expose the heated sensation in her face that his attention arouses. "But I've been on radio a lot, even on television."

"That's interesting, maybe that's it. If you'll come by my office tomorrow, I'd like to share with you some plans I have to liven up the music in this church. What do you say?"

"O. K., I guess," she says, unaware Ollie would approach Claude Ray about forming a select group of youth singers, a discussion that goes awry for the choir director.

"Mr. Ray, I want your help to put this church on the map. I need a group of eight or ten good voices to market Mimosa First to the rest of West Alabama. Also, see what you can do to arrange some free radio time, say once, maybe twice a week."

"Right! Super idea! I'll gather some folks and start rehearsals right away." Claude's enthusiasm bubbles over until Ollie Barron raises his hand.

"Hold on, I'm afraid you misunderstand. I don't see this group doing traditional sacred music, Mr. Ray, only praise songs, folk tunes; you know the stuff that reaches out to the un-churched. Your formal training might not be suitable for teasing out a contemporary sound from my back-up group." Swallowing the insult to his conservatory education and years of successful teaching, Claude Ray backs away from this *prima donna* pied piper of the pulpit hoping to give him enough rope to strangle his ego.

On Monday morning each chosen young person arrives at the church early for an appointment with Brother Ollie, anxious to learn what adventures this troubadour has in store. Each is disappointed to discover the preacher's invitation is not exclusive. In no rush, Angie ambles up to join the early birds gathered at the office door. Finally, the secretary arrives, shocked to find eight teenagers waiting for her to unlock the church office on a June morning when most high school kids are sleeping in.

"Brother Barron is not here," the secretary peers over her half-moon glasses, perturbed by the invasion of teenagers. "You all know he's new and I don't have any idea what his office hours will be. It won't do any good to wait because I don't know what time he's coming in, or even if he plans to be at the church today."

While she explains, one of the older boys slips away from the group and goes next door to the parsonage. He knocks on the door twice before the preacher's wife comes to the door holding her baby girl. "Is Brother Ollie in?"

"No, he's making hospital calls in Birmingham. I don't expect him to return until around noon." The disappointed messenger runs back to break the news to his companions. Dismissing the grumbling kids, the secretary suggests they call back later for an appointment. She needs time to take charge of the new pastor's agenda and let him know that she supplies the grease that keeps the church machine running smoothly.

Pissed off, but not put off, Angie cleverly borrows a page from her mother's book of persistence. Watching her dejected companions drift off in several directions, she slips across Main Street to the drug store. After glancing in the mirror on the weigh scale near the door to be sure she has ironed all the curls out of her silky auburn hair, she goes inside. She orders a chocolate soda, planning to nurse it at a corner table that provides a clear view of the church office door. An hour later, a light blue Thunderbird drives up and parks on the street between the church and the parsonage. Angie watches as Ollie combs out the damage the wind has done to his wavy red mane before he steps out of the convertible. She pushes her chair away from the table, preparing to intercept the preacher before he disappears inside the church, but to her surprise he heads to the drug store. She sits back and waits as he goes straight to the counter and orders coffee to go, not noticing his ogling admirer. He then turns and traps her in a stare.

"Well, look who's here. It's Angie, isn't it?" he says walking toward her with arms extended as if inviting an embrace right in front of all the customers. Angie is petrified as the handsome preacher with the blue convertible approaches exuding the enthusiasm of a life-long friend. She keeps both hands at her side, unsure how to react. Instead of the expected hug, Brother Barron reaches down taking her right hand in both his hands and offers a polite handshake.

"Yessir," she says trying to suppress the flushing she knows is creeping up to her face.

"Mind if I join you?" he asks, pulling a wire-backed chair away from the marble top table.

"Hey mister, your coffee's ready," yells the lady behind the counter. "Thought you said 'to go'," she adds.

Brother Barron retrieves his coffee and lays a dime on the counter. "That I did, Miss...?"

"Clara."

"Miss Clara, I'm Reverend Barron, the new pastor at the Methodist Church across the street. And I'm afraid I'll be bothering you often because I love good coffee. Word around here is you make the best."

Writhing in frustration, Clara wipes her hands on her apron and reaches over the counter to shake his hand. She pushes his dime back. "Gosh, I didn't mean to holler at you like that, sir. You don't look like a...I mean, I didn't know they had a new preacher over there. First cup's on the house."

"Thank you madam, next time I'll be in uniform," Ollie chuckles, circling his finger around his bare neck.

Reverend Barron returns to Angie, her face still flush with anticipation. "Looks like you've finished your drink, so why don't we walk on over to my office and chat, that is, if you have time."

Time is Angie's slave that warm June morning. She would even agree to go for a spin in his T-Bird convertible if he offers.

"Oh, I love your car," she hints, gently caressing the hood emblem.

"People at my other church think it's too sporty for a preacher," he says and waits for the prompted response he expects from the infatuated teen.

"Oh, no," Angie stammers, "It's really groovy, I mean neat, I mean..."

"Yes, I know what you mean."

As they walk through the office door the church secretary's dour expression greets her new boss. "Good morning, Mrs. Stripling, is there something wrong?"

"Not really," she rolls her eyes. "It's just that I didn't know where you were and all kinds of people have been looking for you. The movers have already delivered your books, so I told them to stack the boxes in your office." Her eyes dart to Angie and back. "I told her and the other kids to call back for an appointment after you get settled in."

"It's all right, Mrs. Stripling, I stepped into the drug store for coffee and ran into this young lady."

"Then I suppose there's no need for me to make coffee every morning," Mrs. Stripling grouses. Ollie shrugs off her comment, pushes open his office door and invites Angie inside.

"I'm still scouring through my memory to recall where I've met you before, Angie," Ollie weaves his way through a maze of boxes on the floor. "Did you ever attend a service where I preached?"

"No sir, not that I remember." She waits until he is seated behind his desk before settling into the polished maple chair.

"That's all right. My mind must be playing tricks on me." As Angie silently admires Ollie's red hair and eyebrows, a memory flashes through her mind and vanishes just as quickly. She would not recall that childhood Christmas Eve service when Oliver was student pastor at Gallant Heights. After singing that evening, she had slept through the sermon. Ollie's recollection is thwarted by Angie's sleek auburn hair, the signature of her new image, far removed from the golden blonde curls of the eight-year-old Lil Angel seven years earlier.

"Angie, I want you and a few of your friends to help me put Mimosa First on the cutting edge of a new revolution in church music, songs that young people love to sing instead of stodgy, antiquated hymns. We'll have to commit to daily rehearsals for the summer. Are you interested?"

"Oh, yeah, I mean, yes sir." Angie jumps at the promise of meeting with this handsome young pastor every day.

"Good, I'm glad I can count on you. Let's begin right away, say this Wednesday afternoon around three o'clock?"

Ollie invites four other girls and four boys to join the group; however, only two male singers can squeeze rehearsals into their summer work and baseball schedules. Ollie names the seven-member ensemble Wind and Flame; Wind representing the youth and Flame their redheaded leader, the guitar-picking preacher with a voice akin to Pat Boone's. Before school starts in September, the group has worked up a number of popular folk songs that are loosely connected to religious themes. It isn't long after singing on the weekly radio devotionals that Wind and Flame receive invitations to entertain at civic clubs, youth rallies and Friday night football games.

Mimosa is a small town, so when football season ends, opportunities for Wind and Flame to perform are exhausted. Performing for the weekly devotional radio programs wears down the group because of their limited repertory. Wind and Flame's brief brush with fame concludes with a Christmas season appearance on a Birmingham television station.

After the holidays, the chairman of the Official Board meets with Brother Barron for his mid-year review. "The congregation is pleased with your work," the older man reports, "but there are a few concerns."

Ollie raises his red eyebrows. "And they are...?"

"While we appreciate the time you spend with the youth, there are other pastoral care needs you should devote more attention to."

"Such as...?"

The chairman unfolds a paper and reads a list of items of neglect. "For example, Mrs. Jackson lost her niece and you did not visit her in her time of grief. Widow Grace Bowen hasn't had a visit from you since you arrived last June. She has always taken communion at her home once a month. You have been to only one Men's Club meeting." Brother Barron listens patiently while the chairman continues to recite complaints from mostly older members of the church. When he finishes, the chairman rips the paper apart and smiles. "There, I've done my duty and relayed these gripes from a handful of whiners. You can respond anyway you see fit, preacher, but on the whole, the Board thinks you're just what this church needs. A word to the wise should be sufficient. Reach out with some strokes for the older folks—to keep the peace—if you can do it without losing that great energy you bring to our worship services. There is no doubt we made the right choice in bringing you to Mimosa and I hope you and your wife will enjoy a long stay."

As the chairman leaves the room, Ollie tries to determine whether he was reprimanded, condemned or praised. He has six more months to prove himself worthy of an additional year or more at Mimosa. His ego still smarting from Cliffside's rejection, Ollie vows never again to be asked to leave a church.

Pressed to turn his attention to more pastoral matters, Ollie begins to neglect his back-up group of teen singers. Two members of Wind and Flame make the basketball team, devastating the baritone section. Those remaining respond to Ollie's lack of leadership with apathy, except for Angie. She dreads facing three more years of high school without the exhilaration that Wind and Flame pumps through her blood. It's as though she's addicted to performing and cannot let go. She thrives on the demands of rehearsing and performing as well as the attention of an older man.

Angie finds a fix for her obsession when Claude Ray stops her in the hallway at school just after spring break to make a request. He garners his most desperate expression and asks if she will please take over the lead in the spring musical, *Annie Get Your*

Gun. He explains that the girl chosen to play Annie has been seriously injured in an automobile accident. "We're just two weeks away from opening night and you're the only one who can make it happen," Claude begs. Angie's addiction to performing overcomes her pride and she sets aside her prior conflicts with Mr. Ray, plunging into rehearsals with reckless abandon.

Each dress rehearsal elevates Angie's level of excitement a notch higher. By opening night, she is no longer just Angie. She has become Annie—the spirited rough talking independent Annie Oakley. She gains a further boost to her confidence when she tries on the costume that had been ordered for the older girl whom she replaced and it fits perfectly, with no need to pad the top. Her transition from Lil Angel to Angie is complete. Tucker Shook likes Angie's description of her role so much that he agrees, for the first time ever, to come watch her perform.

After the final curtain and customary bows, Angie bounces around backstage holding the bouquet of roses her mother had thrown on the stage as she scans the crowd of well-wishers to catch a glimpse of her daddy's face.

"Where's Daddy?" she asks Marie.

"Don't fret, honey, he ducked outside for a cigarette. He's real proud of ya' I know."

They find Tucker sitting in his pick-up sucking on a Camel. "Guess ya' did y'self proud, sweetheart, it 'pears everybody liked ya'."

"What about you Daddy, did you like me?" Angie pleads for her father's affirmation.

He takes a long puff of the cigarette and coughs several times before answering. "Better'n most, I reckon. Better'n most." That's the closest her daddy can come to a compliment in Marie's presence. He fears his compliments will be misinterpreted as validation for all the years that Marie has devoted to developing Angie's talent. Perhaps Angie knows her daddy's proud of her. Perhaps she understands that he can't bring himself to show it in front of Marie. She accepts his broken bits of praise and hugs him, unaware he missed her performance altogether.

~~~

When school lets out for summer of 1960, Angie is anxious to know if Brother Barron will revive Wind and Flame. "I would love to, Angie," he says, scrunching his face, "but I'm enrolled in a doctoral program at the seminary and don't have time. Maybe Mr. Ray would be interested in doing something with a group."

Realizing her idol has finally nailed her group to the cross, Angie reluctantly asks Claude Ray to revive Wind and Flame. He makes excuses in order to avoid future entanglements with the obsessive Marie Shook. Neither can Claude bring himself to play second fiddle to Ollie Barron. He has a better plan in mind.

"Angie, right here at Mimosa Junior College is a wonderful voice teacher who also produces summer musicals. Here's her number. Call and tell her I sent you."

Angie arranges for weekly voice lessons and takes a job at the Pizza Palace to pay for them. Claude invites Angie to sing in the adult choir at church for the summer to complement her lessons. The voice teacher selects more and more complex, challenging solos for her to learn, works that require organ accompaniment instead of Brother Barron's guitar.

Angie enters her sophomore year of high school possessing a voice with the range and timbre of a young woman twice her age. Her personality and poise are well-developed dividends from those childhood years of grooming by her mother. Marie's hovering omnipresence provokes resentment from Angie as she tries to cut the apron strings. The two quarrel more frequently with increasing intensity. Tucker, suffering the debilitating effects of nearly two decades in the mine, retreats from the contentious duo by going fishing every chance he gets.

Frustrated by Angie's independence, Marie tries to reconnect with her with appeals for sympathy. Citing her litany of sacrifices, she complains of arthritis in her fingers from making dresses and costumes during Angie's appearances with Wally Farmer's All-night Singing Caravan. "Didn't I buy us a car so ya' wouldn't have to ride in daddy's truck no more?" She recounts the hours spent on the road with Angeline, making sure her little girl took advantage of every opportunity. Marie artfully avoids mentioning the flirtations with promoters that she used to fan the embers of Angie's career.

"I didn't make you do all those things for me," Angie screams in response, covering her ears. "I don't wanna hear anymore!" Angie ends every fray by running out of the house to escape the monotonous saga of her sacrificial mama.

~~~

It's a cool October night that Brother Barron brings his wife and baby girl to Pizza Palace and Angie serves their table. She deliberately flirts with Ollie in an attempt to irritate Betty Barron. When Ollie goes to pay the bill, Angie rushes to meet him at the cash register. "How are things going with you, Angie?" he inquires politely. "I haven't seen you in the choir lately." She rolls her eyes and shakes her head. He reads the lines beneath her troubled expression, "I'm having coffee at the usual spot in the morning. Stop in on your way to school, if you need to talk." He hands her a large tip and follows his family out the door.

"That girl's got trouble written all over her sexy body," the preacher's wife warns as he helps her into the Thunderbird. "Isn't she one of the girls from Wind and Flame?"

"Yep, she's trimmed her hair and dyed it black. Angie's all right, she's just experiencing the usual conflicts with her parents, like most sixteen year olds. All she needs is a good listening to," Ollie chuckles, trying to lighten the conversation.

"Is that why she didn't take those bedroom eyes off you the whole evening? It's a wonder she didn't dump pizza in my lap." Ollie changes the subject and sloughs off his wife's observations as he had done many times before.

Early the next morning, Angie is waiting at the usual table diddling a straw in a chocolate soda when Ollie walks in the drug store. He goes straight to her table and sits down without a word.

Clara interrupts the long silence when she brings Ollie's coffee with extra cream and a smile. "Morning, Brother Barron, gonna be a hot 'un today, not good football weather."

Ollie nods and stirs his coffee as Angie fixes her eyes on him. He looks up and speaks in muted tones, "I know you're bearing a heavy burden, Angie, I'm just offering to share it with you." She releases a faint smile and nods ever so slightly, still gazing into his eyes. "But, this is not the place to talk," he continues, glancing around to see if any of the other customers are eavesdropping. "Are you coming to choir practice this Wednesday?" She nods again. "Come by my office before practice, say around six, and we'll talk." He finishes his coffee and slides a quarter across the table. "The soda's on me this time." He hurries out the door of the drug store and across the street to the church. Angie still has not uttered a word, but her insides are aflame at the thought of meeting Brother Barron alone in his office in two days.

All the way to school, during every class, and all the way home, Angie's thoughts are consumed with what she will wear to please the preacher. She tries to think back to any comment he has made during their appearances of Wind and Fire, but he always said nice things about all of the girls' outfits. She needs to stand out in a way that transforms her into to an attractive, alluring woman rather than another cute teenager. She can now fit into her mother's dresses, but thumbing through her mother's closet is a waste of time—much too plain and dowdy. When Wednesday afternoon finally arrives, Angie puts on her best Sunday dress, lots of lipstick, rouge and eye shadow and heads for the church.

"Ain't ya' gonna eat ya' supper?" Marie asks as Angie starts out the door.

"No, m'am, gotta go early and…and practice something special," she replies as she releases the screen door behind her. Her mother's offer to drive her downtown gets lost in the rustle of her dress as she hurries to meet her idol. Daylight has almost faded by the time she reaches the church office. She opens the door and steps into the semi-dark room. Brother Barron swings open his office door to illuminate the outer office.

"Please come in, Angie. I didn't realize that it had gotten dark already." He closes the door behind her, snaps off the overhead light and moves slowly around the large mahogany desk easing into a thick leather chair. She sits on the edge of the nearest chair gazing at one of the shaded desk lamps that creates a soft, warm intimate glow. Brother Barron leans into this light to initiate the conversation; "I trust you've had a good day at school, Angie."

"I reckon, nothing to brag about."

They engage in small talk for a few minutes before he leans back and says, "I've just noticed how grown up you look lately, Angie." The compliment she had invited by pushing out her chest draws a coy smile across her face as she lowers her eyes and blushes. "Oh, I don't mean to embarrass you, dear. You know how I am. I just blurt out what I think sometimes without…you know, without considering how others might take it."

"That's O. K. You made me feel good."

"That's what I'm here for, anything to relieve your burden. I sense your parents are less than understanding." His opening that would have hit home with any teenager in his parish, releases a flood of anguished grievances that gush forth from deep inside Angie. He listens with occasional nods and utters affirmations until she is empty. She sits in relieved silence for several minutes. As her eyes begin to glisten with soft unbridled tears, Brother Barron pushes a box of tissues across the desk toward her.

"I wasn't going to do this, I'm sorry," Angie sniffles, "I guess my makeup's all smeared." She springs to her feet and turns away, ashamed of the tears. Cautiously, he rises and moves to her side.

"Here, let me help." He dabs a tissue around her eyes as she looks up. A piquant spice of aftershave accentuates the closeness of his face. "There, that should hold you for a while," he says, without moving away from the nubile angel. "I think all you need now is a little hug." He slips his hands into the curve of her back as he pulls her close. The arms of the man-of-God encircle her body, his holy hands meeting, interlocking in the small of her back, and with a blinding bolt of lightening the fusion has occurred—a halo descends on this innocent, vulnerable angel. Grand thoughts swirl in Ollie's head tinged with temptations of the flesh. *My sacred duty is to protect the helpless, save the lost, comfort the suffering.* His thoughts spin, accelerate, then combust. *Yea Lord, I walk though the valley in the footsteps of the exalted saints. I am your obedient servant. I embrace this lamb. I will guide this lamb into the fold. My strength will be hers.*

The fury of the flames burns as red as the waves of locks on his head. The heart of the angel, in the midst of the fire, melts in exultation—it runneth over and fills her empty soul. Her body goes limp. Aroused, the ethereal minstrel relaxes his arms and steps back. *Holy, holy, holy, Lord—grant me your amazing grace and forgiveness as I stand here—your lost child.*

"I almost forgot, I have something to give you." Hands shaking, Ollie returns to his side of the desk, opens the top drawer and retrieves a multi-colored paper sack with gold lettering across one side. "Here, it's a little token of my appreciation for all you've done to help me." She fishes a thin white box from the sack and removes the top. The tiny delicately etched angel set against the velvet lining of the box seems to be singing a silent song.

"Oh, it's so pretty," she sighs. "What...?"

"It's a little singing angel—a crystal angel. When I saw it in the shop, it reminded me of you, so I had to get it."

"Oh, it's so cute. Should I put it on?" she says lifting the silver chain from the cotton pad.

"I'd rather keep this between us, Angie. You're the only member of Wind and Flame that hung in there and didn't want to give up. This is a special reminder of the bond we share. So, why don't you keep it in the sack until you get home?" he cautions, making his point by closing her fingers over the angel with his hands.

"I'll always wear it when I sing, it's my guardian angel," she says, moving her face closer to his and pressing her body against their locked hands.

Looking into her face Ollie recovers his granite voice, "Look at the time. I must let you go to choir practice now. I don't have any simple solution to your problem, Angie. Let me think about what you've said and we'll get together again. I'm confident we can work through your dilemma together." He kisses her lightly on the forehead and walks to the door.

As he switches on the overhead light, Angie exclaims, "Oh Brother Barron, I got makeup all over your white shirt." She reaches over to clean it with her tissue, but he springs back and looks in the mirror behind the door.

"O my heavens, that looks awful.

"I'm sorry."

"Don't worry, dear, I'll fix it. I'll meet you here next week, same time?"

She answers "yes" and walks out into the night. She has too much on her mind to go to choir practice, so instead heads down the street to Pizza Palace clutching her gift and fantasizing over and over those brief moments of intimacy she had shared with the compassionate preacher. Clutching the door of the pizzeria, Angie has one last thought before going inside: *If only Brother Barron's wife will notice the makeup on his shirt, she may figure out that it's mine.*

7

> *January 10, 1963*
>
> *Dear Choir,*
>   *Please don't sing last Sunday's anthem again, PLEASE! I happen to know the song is the Negro national anthem and I don't appreciate the way our new choir director is sneaking Negro music into our church. We live in troubled times and we don't need to encourage Negroes to start coming to our services. We have enough music of our own and that's what I want to hear at St. Francis.*
>
> *In the name of Jesus,*
>
> *Harvey Pendergast, III*

"Tell me Mr. Willis, what's a nice young man like you doing teaching music in an elementary school?"

"Ma'm?" Chad isn't sure the oldest teacher at the lunch table is serious, but the curious stares of the other females command an answer.

"Of course I don't mean any disrespect, son, but the only men music teachers in Birmingham are in the high schools."

Chad puts the empty milk carton aside and dabs his lips with a napkin. "I know, Mrs. Rowlfe, perhaps my supervisor thought that a stint in Korea was insufficient training for taking on a high school bunch." Some teachers at the table giggle. "Anyhow, one takes what's available in the middle of the year. But, I'm not the only man on the faculty. What about Mr. Strong, doesn't he count?"

"We never see him. He keeps to himself in the woodwork shop," Mrs. Rowlfe replies.

"Yes, we don't need a Neanderthal eating with us women," another teacher chimes in.

"A what?"

"Never mind Mr. Willis, finish your Jell-O."

"O.K., I hope my presence at this table won't crimp your conversations too much."

"Not if you don't blush easily."

Insulated in the basement music room, Chad directs his attention to using music as a medium to instill patriotism, honor and respect in his young charges. All goes well for the first couple of months until that blustery March day when Bart Strong lumbers into Chad's music room huffing like an out-of-shape linebacker. He removes his cap with one hand and brushes maverick strands of blond hair back over his bald spot with the other. Bart jerks a rolled up magazine from inside his navy surplus pea jacket. "What d'ya think now, Mr. Willis?" he says fumbling to open a copy of *The Saturday Evening Post.* "What d'ya think?" he repeats, thrusting the magazine towards Chad. "The shit has really hit the fan now," he says jerking his head around to make sure no children heard his intemperate expression. Chad follows Bart's calloused finger down the page to the sentence that reads: *I shall refuse to abide by any illegal Federal Court order even to the point of standing in the schoolhouse door.* "There it is in black and white, if you'll excuse the expression, a pledge from George Wallace to keep our schools segregated."

"Surely, he won't get elected. There're too many decent citizens to elect that clown." Bart gasps in horror and looks up as if Chad has just wiped his feet on the American flag. Before he can chastise his younger colleague for uttering those blasphemous remarks, the intercom crackles overhead interrupting their conversation.

"Attention all students and teachers," the principal's voice sounds taunt, on the edge of panic, "This is a fire drill. Please vacate the building immediately!" Several short rings of the bell punctuate Mr. Ewing's terse instructions.

Once they are safely on the playground, Mr. Ewing walks over to form a huddle with Bart Strong as if calling a play. Both had been high school coaches in their prime, but loosing seasons and age relegated them to the elephants' graveyard for gridiron mentors—elementary schools. Ewing mutters out of the side of his mouth to Bart, "Soon as I got to my office somebody called and said he planted a bomb in a closet set to go off at 9:00."

Bart Strong looks at his watch. "It's eight-thirty now. What do we do, just wait it out?"

Mr. Ewing shrugs his shoulders. "It's not my job to go poking around in closets looking for bombs," he says in the crusty style of a football coach.

Chad overhears their conversation and says, "We can't just stand here and watch old Fairway get blown up." Then he turns to a group of second graders and starts to sing *This Old Man.* "Come on boys and girls let's all join in." He waves his hands high to reassure the children and to prevent the inevitable rowdiness of three hundred students herded together on a playground with nothing to do. While he moves among the singers, Chad wonders if he is witnessing the first political shot fired in the battle to integrate the public schools.

By ten o'clock police declare the bomb threat a hoax and the students return to their homerooms. Chad and Bart wait in the basement hallway watching students file into the building. "I wonder how many times we're going to repeat this routine now that schools are dragged into this race mess." Bart wonders aloud.

"I don't know, but I suppose I'd better teach a lot more songs to the kids." Chad's light hearted response doesn't reflect his deeper concern. *Should I consider a career change before our schools become racial battlegrounds?*

~~~

The Democratic Party nominates George Wallace to run for Governor in the April primary—tantamount to being elected in

November. The day after the referendum Chad calls on his friend Paul Peterson to inquire about possible openings for a full time church choir director.

"My word, it's so good to see you again," Paul greets Chad with a vigorous hand shake and then a hug. "Mrs. Green, this is my good friend, Chad Willis. He and I worked together at Coal City, how long has it been, seven or eight years?"

"Seven, I think," Chad replies.

"Come on in my office and let's...no, let me show you around the church first. St. Francis is very old but elegant." They climb the darkened staircase to the vestibule. Paul switches on a light and points to the marble inlaid entryway with the date "1912" set in darker tiles. "We'll celebrate our fiftieth anniversary next month," Paul says. He pushes open a pair of mahogany doors and leads Chad down the oriental carpet runner on the middle aisle. "Does this look familiar?"

Chad's gaze is drawn to the light filtering through the tinted windows made to give the appearance of stained glass. He cranes his neck to view the balcony suspended over the back seven rows. "Yeah, it's like a king sized version of Coal City First Methodist."

"That's what I said to Lorna the first time we set foot in this sanctuary, only the choir loft is behind the pulpit and those organ pipes are real."

"And there's no weird painting of Christ holding a sheep," Chad chuckles. "I suppose you don't have an artist who paints on velvet in your congregation."

"I'm thankful for that, but even though Mrs. Muller was no artist, she had a big heart."

"And her Jesus has big ears," Chad remembers when he learned not to be critical of a gift to their church no matter how tasteless it appears. One of the choir members at Coal City had presented Chad with a shimmering hand-stitched robe to wear one Easter Sunday. When he refused to bedeck himself in that homespun vestment for the most visible worship service of the year, the seamstress lobbied for his dismissal. Fortunately, her voice in the church was one only to be tolerated and forgotten. Chad takes a deep breath, "Smells like the Coal City sanctuary too, like old wood, furniture polish and..."

"And flowers," Paul suggests.

Chad laughs, "I was thinking...a funeral home."

"Perhaps, but I perform more wedding ceremonies than eulogies in this sanctuary. Speaking of weddings, is there a Mrs. Willis yet?"

"Not yet, but I came very close right after college."

"Oh?"

"My draft deferment expired and the army opted for two years of my life."

"And she didn't wait for you?"

"Nope."

"That's too bad."

"Speaking of Coal City, what's Katy been up to since we left?"

"You'll be proud of my girl, Chad. She'll be a senior this fall at our Alma Mater, majoring in psychology."

"A senior already?"

"Yes, she went summers to get ahead."

"That's great. Is she, uh..."

"Married? Not yet, but she has a nice young man in her sights." Paul walks to the front pew, sits down and pats the seat next to him with his hand. "Have a seat. Actually, I wanted to get away from the office to talk. Those walls have ears." Paul wheels his head around before continuing the private discussion. "How would you like to work with me again?"

"Oh, Paul, I'd love to, but I'm looking for a full-time position so I can quit teaching. I already have a part time choir job." Chad is frustrated that he has not made the purpose of his visit clear to his old friend.

"Hear me out, Chad, before you jump the gun. I've been here only a year and already we've taken in more than twenty new families, all with children and a few young people. New houses are going up all over Redmont. Here's my plan. I want to combine two part-time positions, youth director and choir director. But, to get the board's approval I'll need to include one other job in the position."

Chad squirms on the pew and cocks his head toward Paul. "Janitor or sexton?" He curls one side of his upper lip.

"No, we've got those covered," Paul laughs as he meanders toward the altar. "I need somebody to go out and visit these new folks and invite them to the church. The power company is installing new meters weekly in the Redmont community."

"Recruitment? You must be joking!"

Paul whips around to face his young friend again. "You'll be perfect for the job. I witnessed your on-the-job training at Coal City plus you spent two years in the army and have taught school. That's more than enough preparation. What about it, Chad?"

~~~

Paul takes a while to work out the details for his proposed staff position and phones Chad in the middle of July. "My friend, the good news is the Board approved the new position, but the bad news is they don't go along with the salary I recommend."

"Oh?"

"Well, we're extremely close to what you're making as a teacher, but not when you add the stipend from your church job. Just give me a few more days to work on it, Chad, because I'm very anxious to have you on my staff again."

"Frankly, Paul I've given the school board notice that I won't return in the fall. I've also contacted a new private school and an insurance company, in case I don't find a church position. How much time do you need?"

"Maybe a day or two, or possibly until the weekend," Chad agrees, knowing he might accept Paul's offer anyway. He reasons he could take the job until something better opens up at another church later. The next day, Paul calls Chad to meet him at the church that afternoon. Chad arrives to find Paul waiting for him on the street in front of the sanctuary. Paul opens the car door.

"Let's go for a ride." he says climbing in the front seat.

"Don't tell me I'm parked illegally," Chad jokes.

Paul directs Chad around the corner to the next block. "Turn right and stop at the alley."

They get out of the car and Chad looks down the alley. "Isn't that the parsonage at the other end?"

"That's right, the church owns this entire half block, all the way to the corner," Paul sweeps his hand in the air. "We plan to tear down the houses from here to that corner and build a new educational building." Chad allows Paul to continue the tactic he has cleverly devised to lure him into a lower paying job. As Paul describes the floor plan of the proposed building, a Lincoln Town Car drives into the alley. "Oh, here's H. R. now," Paul waves to the large man behind the wheel. A tall thick-boned man in his sixties emerges, flashing signs of success—a tailored suit, alligator shoes and a Shriner's ring studded with diamonds. He greets Paul with the aggressive handshake of a salesman.

"Good afternoon, Brother Paul, this must be the young man you told me about. Glad to meet you, son, I've heard a lot about you."

"Chad, this is Mr. H. R. Wood, Chairman of our Finance Committee and owner of Wood Realty Company, the one who's selling most of the new houses in Redmont."

"Now that's a rumor I want to keep in circulation," the ruddy-faced realtor quips. "Let's go inside, shall we? Probably needs more fixing up than we can afford, but I did promise to give it a look." Chad is puzzled as though he is trapped in some kind of transaction he knows nothing about.

"Oh, I haven't said anything to Chad yet, I'm waiting for your input," Paul explains to his parishioner who proceeds to unlock the door of the bungalow next to the alley. The door squeaks and drags against the uneven floor as he pushes it open. Paul and Chad follow him inside as the empty room echoes their footsteps. H. R. flips a light switch a couple of times.

"I guess the power company's already shut off the juice," he says. Then he inspects the two adjoining rooms before walking back to the kitchen. H. R. mumbles to himself as he pounds his open hand against several places along the walls. He bounces on the linoleum-covered floor as it creaks even louder.

Chad whispers to Paul, "What's he looking for?"

"Hold on, he'll tell us in a minute, as soon as he's through."

The real estate magnate comes back to the front room and announces, "The house is in better shape than I thought, preacher. I figure we can get by with some minor repairs, a windowpane in the kitchen, new locks and shaving off the bottom of that front door a little. I can send a man over tomorrow to take care of that." H. R. notices Chad's puzzled expression. "I know you're wondering what's going on, son. Well, we're trying to decide if a body could live in this old house until we decide to tear it down. If you'll agree to take the new position that Brother Paul's offering, we'll throw in this house, rent-free. All you'll need to pay for is utilities. How does that sound?"

H. R. has the same facial expression as J. B. Colley when he asked Chad to name a salary during the Coal City interview. A shiver runs down his spine, but this time the deal is different; H. R. and Paul are in agreement. Still, Chad reserves a small measure of distrust for any man who controls the purse strings of a church. He looks at Paul and breaks into a spontaneous smile.

"I'll take that happy grin as a 'yes'," Paul says as he seals the deal with a handshake. "I'll get busy rounding up whatever furniture you'll need to move in."

Paul sends Lorna and two other ladies shopping for used furniture at the Salvation Army store. Chad's apartment is a quintessential bachelor pad—a bed, a dresser, a beanbag chair, a television set and a reading lamp. The Finance Committee kicks in enough money to buy bare essential furnishings for their new Assistant Minister at St. Francis Methodist. Although Chad prefers the title Director of Music and Youth, he goes along with

Paul's ecclesiastical designation to avoid further delay in starting the new job.

The previous choir director had taken a month's leave before resigning and left the adult choir in disarray. Chad has his work cut out pulling the disparate group back together. Word that St. Francis has a single, under thirty Assistant Minister spreads like wildfire throughout the Redmont community. Young people flock to the church in droves. Seizing the opportunity to integrate music into their activities, Chad organizes a youth choir to sit in for the adult choir until after Labor Day.

At the end of three months, Paul cannot decide who is more pleased with the new spirit in the church resulting from his new partnership: H. R. Wood, the District Superintendent, the youth, the adult choir, or Ruth Russell. Paul stands before the Quarterly Conference in November and presents a glowing report to his constituents and the District Superintendent. Following a factual summary of increases in attendance, financial gifts, new members and baptisms of infants, Paul concludes his remarks. "My fellow travelers on the uncertain journey of faith, please bear with me while I lift up one among us whose dedication and hard work have revived the slumbering spirit of old St. Francis to once again make it a vibrant force in Redmont. Ruth Russell, please stand. Miss Russell took charge of the new Visitation Task Force and spread love throughout this community with her homemade loaves of bread, personally delivered to all newcomers."

The next morning Paul takes his coffee cup upstairs to Chad's corner of the choir room. "It was a good meeting last night, Chad, the best Quarterly Conference I've ever had." Chad nods his head and swells with well-deserved pride. "And do you know who's responsible for mining the resources within this old church to induce new life?" Paul points a finger at his partner as they both indulge in shameless joy, celebrating their successful revival of the aging St. Francis church. Finally, Paul puts his hand on Chad's shoulder and squeezes. "Nothing can stop St. Francis from surging ahead and becoming a great church, nothing."

Just six weeks after Paul prophesizes prosperity for St. Francis, the phone on his desk jingles. He puts aside transferring information from the Methodist Publishing House date book to the fresh 1963 edition. Mrs. Green has the morning off to exchange some Christmas gifts, so he picks up the phone. "Good morning, St. Francis Methodist Church." The voice on the other end has a northeastern accent similar to that of President Kennedy. "Yes, this is the pastor speaking, how may I be of service?" Paul listens to a series of questions that has the earmarks of reading from a prepared script. Intermittent beeping sounds in the receiver warn Paul that this is no ordinary call, but he dismisses them as line problems. "Of course, we would love to have you and your family to visit St. Francis this Sunday. May I have your name, we can look forward to greeting you in person Mr...?"

There's a brief pause on the other end of the line before the articulate New Englander continues, "Thank you Reverend sir, I'm a college student and my classmates and I will see you at church Sunday." He hangs up leaving Paul still holding the phone to his ear. Without putting the receiver in the cradle, he pushes the button to disconnect and starts dialing.

"Happy New Year, Bishop Grand's office, may I help you?" the cheerful voice chimes. "Oh, hello Brother Paul...No, the Bishop's still in Florida, would you like to leave a message?"

"No, thanks anyway, I'll phone him when he returns." The uneasy feeling that has crept over Paul is encased in a sense of emergency to discuss the odd telephone conversation with someone he can trust. After several failed attempts to reach fellow pastors, Paul decides the strange phone call is probably no cause for alarm. He strolls over to the window and warms his hands over the iron radiator. Yet the snowflakes brushing against the holly shrubs outside send a chill down Paul's back.

What a way to begin the New Year: no meetings this week, no choir practice, no Wednesday night supper. Nothing's more lifeless than an empty church building, or more conducive to study and reflection—all the more reason to stay inside and curl up with Dr. Bonhoeffer."

~~~

Meanwhile, a beehive of activity buzzes across town at Carver, the African Methodist Episcopal College. Some Harvard graduate students are conducting a briefing with a room full of local students preparing for Sunday's push to integrate Birmingham's white congregations. Jesse Shuman, a law student from Boston, unfolds a large map of the city and tapes it to the chalkboard. Then he places a sheet of clear plastic over the map and draws small circles until he has an even dozen. "Listen up please," he calls. A hush descends over the room of squirming students. "Here are the target churches for this Sunday's kneel-ins, five Methodist, five Baptist, one Catholic and one Episcopal." He points a ruler at each small circle. "These churches have the largest all-white congregations in the city where our efforts will have the greatest impact."

"Hey, there's a real big Jew congregation downtown," a Carver student shouts.

"And Presbyterian, too," says another.

"Our Jewish brothers don't hold services on Sunday and we'll get to the others in good time. Meanwhile, our plan is to have one of us," he sweeps his hand across the line of white Harvard students standing by the windows, "go with two or three of you guys," waving his other hand over the sea of darker faces seated in the desks before him.

"It's like twelve disciples taking the word to the Pharisees," a Carver student suggests.

"Amen!" the others shout in response.

"I wonder which one of us is supposed to be Judas?" one of the Harvard dozen whispers to another.

"I've already called the pastors of all these churches and received invitations to attend their worship services, so we anticipate no trouble," Jesse says.

"Uh huh," a student responds measuring out the expression of doubt like the chorus of a spiritual, "did you tell them we'd be coming too?"

"I said the same thing to each pastor," Jesse responds as he flips the pages of the clipboard. "The last statement I made after being invited to their churches is: *Thank you reverend sir, I am a college student and my classmates and I will see you at church this Sunday.*"

"But you didn't tell 'em what color we are, did you?"

Jesse tucks the clipboard under his arm and tells the student, "No, but they'll discover that when we walk through their doors this Sunday."

8

> *January 22, 1963*
>
> *Dear Brother Paul*
>
> *I just want you to know that there is at least one member of St. Francis who agrees with you. The doors of our sanctuary should remain open to all. I regret very much that I cannot take a public stand by your side because to do so would drive my customers away. Please keep this letter as a reminder that someone believes you did the right thing.*
>
> *May your courage be rewarded in Heaven,*
>
> *A special friend*

Paul Peterson looks hopefully around the sanctuary for new faces among the faithful few who braved the icy rain to show up for worship. Seeing none, he glances briefly at the darkened translucent windows, acutely aware that a full-blown wintery storm may be brewing outside—then greets his parishioners, "Happy New Year and may God continue to pour out his richest blessings on you all year long." Paul proceeds with the order of worship, unaware that a storm far more menacing than the one he expects could disrupt his service before the sermon begins.

A white woman and two black males measure their paces as they make their way up the sleet-coated steps of St. Francis Methodist Church. Charlie Winkman, surreptitiously guarding the doors, does not see the anomalous trio approaching until they are halfway up the steep front steps. He glances through the tiny porthole window and shakes his head in disbelief.

Although he had attended a clandestine meeting of the Methodist Laymen's Council only a month ago, Charlie never expected a confrontation at St. Francis. Judge Harmon, a local judge who teaches Sunday school at a large downtown church had rallied segregationist laymen determined to thwart all attempts to integrate Methodist churches. *Our cowardly bishop and spineless pastors refuse to take a stand opposing amalgamation of the races as dictated by the Holy Bible. Nigras can go to their own Methodist churches and worship. Therefore, we have a legal and moral obligation to stand in the doors of our churches and invite them to go where they belong. I want y'all to return to your congregations and recruit like-minded ushers that will pledge to refuse nigras entrance to your sacred places of worship. One more thing, keep your intentions under wraps in case you are unfortunate enough to have a liberal pointed-headed preacher in your pulpit.* Charlie had left the meeting apprehensive about keeping the judge's charge a secret from his pastor and friend, Paul Peterson, but he felt justified in maintaining the racial purity of his church.

Without alerting the other ushers, Charlie slips out the door into the sleet and crunches a path across the stair landing to meet the unwelcome visitors. They stop on the top step in front of Charlie. He confronts the trio, "Where y'all going?"

"Good morning," says the white woman who is a few years older than her two companions. "We've come to worship at your church today," she recites the well-rehearsed litany. "May we come in...out of the cold?"

The burly guardian of the entrance remembers the judge's instructions for *greeting* potential troublemakers at the church entrance. "This is private property and only those who come to worship are admitted."

"Well sir, your pastor invited us to worship here at..." she glances over her shoulder at the sign on the corner near the street, "...St. Francis Methodist."

Invited by Paul? Charlie is not prepared to turn away invited guests. He has to think quickly. "I guess one of you boys can tell me the name of the pastor who invited y'all."

The woman slips off a mitten and retrieves a note from her coat pocket. "His name is…"

"I didn't ask you Miss, I asked them," Charlie grasps her hand, covering the information on the note. The two young men look at each other in silence as pellets of sleet bounce off their heads. They don't think to look back at the sign on the corner with Reverend Paul Peterson's name printed at the bottom.

"Just what I thought, y'all don't even know who's preaching today. You're welcome to come in, Miss, but these two young bucks can go to their own church over yonder." The black men bristle. Being addressed in degrading terms is not new to them, but the place they least expect such treatment is at the portal of God's house. Bud, another usher, struts outside the church doors and stands resolutely with arms crossed.

The woman reminds her incensed companions that they come in peace. She stiffens her back and addresses the ushers with a strained smile, "Sirs, I assume this is a Christian Church open to all people…"

"But not troublemakers," Bud warns.

"…and if my friends are not allowed to enter, then I shall remain here and kneel in prayer with them."

"Suit yourself, Miss, but nobody's allowed to block the entrance. Like I said, it's private property."

"We must ask y'all to leave immediately," echoes the second usher. The steely eyed crusader pulls her coat tighter around her as the two black men begin to shiver from the cold wind whipping their neckties back and forth. The sleet intensifies—a barely perceptible but insipid whisper as it hits the shrubbery, like someone dropping tiny grains of salt into a wound, over and over. And, the standoff continues.

Bud ducks inside and reappears with two additional re-enforcements. As the four sentinels stand in the cutting wind, Bud realizes that Charlie, not wearing an overcoat, won't last long in the cold. "You go on in, Charlie, and call the police. I'll take care of things out here," he spouts, smacking his right fist into his other hand. The other two ushers move forward to form a barrier between the would-be worshippers and the door of the church.

"No, somebody just hand me my topcoat from inside. I'll be all right," Charlie assures them, aware that his companion's short fuse might ignite and blast their church's name all across the front pages of the New York newspapers. Ice pellets form on the woman's coat as she continues to stoically recite the rationale for allowing them to enter the church. Charlie's only response is to shake his head and brush ice from his eyebrows. The two young black men shiver more violently as they cross their arms over their chests craving warmth. One of the young men steps backwards to leave, but the woman motions him to persist. Grabbing the coat sleeve of his companion to prevent his departure, the second man loses his footing. As he tries to stabilize himself on the icy steps, both men tumble down the concrete steps to the sidewalk. The woman screams and slips on the ice, trying to descend to their rescue.

Charlie instinctively reaches to catch the woman, but his reaction comes a moment too late. The other ushers observe with muted delight as the standoff ends with self-inflicted tragedy. But the sight of a woman's crumpled body oozing blood on their church's sidewalk shocks some sense into Charlie and he rushes to her aid.

The scream has interrupted the service and members of the congregation now spill out the doors, followed by their pastor in his black robe and Epiphany stole. Charlie covers the injured woman with his coat as Paul descends the treacherous steps. When Charlie offers an apologetic version of the incident, Paul fumes in horror, "You did what? I can't believe you...never mind, we need a doctor." Seeing no doctor among the shocked spectators who are observing the tragedy from a safe distance, Paul asks one of the ushers to hurry around the block and summon help from the fire station. Paul takes charge of making the accident victims comfortable. "Charlie, see if you can help those fellows," he orders, pointing to the two young black men sitting on the sidewalk. After Charlie helps them to their feet, they jerk away and limp a safe distance from the gaping crowd that has begun to move closer.

"They seem O. K. to me, preacher," Charlie sighs, relieved that they do not require his assistance.

Paul places his fingers beneath the woman's ear. "She's still alive, thank God." He draws his hand back and notices his fingers are covered with blood. "O my gosh!" Paul jerks his stole from around his neck and presses it against her head to stop the bleeding.

"I can't believe you let this happen, Charlie. Blocking the door of the church is not our policy."

"But, preacher, I told the woman she was welcome."

"Who authorized you to...to...?" Paul's angry outburst is interrupted by the wail of an approaching siren. "We can't deal with this right now. After we make sure these folks are all right, I want to meet with you and the other ushers."

Paul rides in the ambulance with the injured woman. Placing no trust in these white Christians who denied them entrance to the church, her two companions refuse treatment for their minor bruises, and they drive away as the ambulance departs. The woman begins to mumble beneath the wail of the ambulance siren. Paul bends closer trying to make sense of her semi-conscious utterances.

"You're going to be all right, Miss. We're taking you to the hospital," Paul tries to comfort her. She begins to roll her head from side to side, crying out from the pain exploding in her head. "Just a few more blocks," Paul holds his hand on the bandage that has replaced his blood drenched stole.

"Where are the students? Are they all right?" she moans, trying to see if they're in the ambulance with her.

Paul assures her, "They're fine. They drove off as soon as we put you in the ambulance."

At Birmingham's Methodist Hospital an emergency room nurse cleans the head injury and instructs Paul to roll the patient in the wheelchair to one of the cubicles lining the hallway. The lengthy wait for an available doctor on a busy weekend affords Paul time to coax from her glimpses of the morning's unfortunate events until he is satisfied with at least a fair sketch of the entire drama. About to add one final confession to the testimony—revelation that her mission is to change the Jim Crow laws of Birmingham—the victim suddenly begins waving across the sea of people. She calls out a strained, "Jesse!" but her weak, raspy voice is lost in the clamor.

The short man with long brown hair finally catches sight of her waving and limps through the crowd toward them, in obvious need of medical attention. His face is badly bruised and his swollen eye has turned purple.

"What in God's name are you doing here? Are you all right?" he kneels beside her chair, gently touching her on the cheek. The woman glances up at Paul.

"Excuse me, I'm Paul Peterson. Who…?"

Ignoring Paul's extended hand, Jesse begs answers from the injured woman. "Who did this to you and where are Tyrone and…who else went with you?"

"Merlon, they're O. K., I guess…" she labors, her voice raspy from trauma and shock. Then without warning she blacks out.

Jesse shakes her gently, but gets no response. Panic-stricken, he springs to his feet wincing in pain and cries out, "Doctor, we need a doctor here," searching the busy waiting room for a white-coated male.

Paul reaches out and places a calming hand on his shoulder. "It's O.K., she's just passed out again. It happened several times in the ambulance."

Jesse's eyes advance slowly upward until they fix on Paul's face, *If this minister has accompanied my fellow protester to the hospital without even taking time to shed his robe, I should allow him a modicum of trust.* "So you're the one who brought Grace here," Jesse rises to face Paul. Hearing the injured woman's name for the first time, Paul smiles and nods. "At least you didn't just drop her off and then leave."

"Leave? I wouldn't think of it. Seeing the shape you're in how did you manage to get yourself here?"

Jesse winces as he unintentionally moves his injured arm. "A cop drove me to the entrance, but it's a long story."

"I take it you and some Negroes went to another church today, which one?"

Grace opens her eyes and moans. Jesse reassures her that relief will come soon. "You asked about the church, Reverend…"

"Paul."

"…Reverend Paul, it was Calvary Baptist downtown."

"Did the ushers beat you up or…?"

"No, no everything was peaceful until a bunch of thugs showed up after the service armed with baseball bats."

"So, you and your associates were allowed to participate in the worship service?"

"On the contrary, dear Reverend, we were summarily dismissed at the front door and despite our honest intent to enter and worship, we retreated to the icy sidewalk and knelt in prayer. As the congregation streamed out after the service, we stood and chanted 'Freedom of worship denied.' That's when a car drove up and dispatched its passengers—four thugs wielding baseball bats. Before I could react, a bat crashed down on my shoulder and split my ear open. I remembered our well-rehearsed strategy intended to reduce our vulnerability. The three students and I immediately put it into practice and knelt in a tight huddle on the sidewalk, protecting our heads with folded arms as those goons began pounding on us, punctuating each blow with curses."

"You're lucky you weren't killed by those idiots," Paul grimaces, shaking his head. "Were the others hurt?"

A nurse interrupts Jesse's account of the kneel-in to wheel Grace to a treatment room. Paul and Jesse's eyes follow the wheelchair until it disappears through swinging doors.

Paul repeats his question "So, was anyone else injured?"

"You may find this hard to believe, Reverend, but a gunshot rang out not long after the beatings began."

Paul shudders, "A gunshot? Was anyone hit?"

"No, it turns out an off-duty cop, one of the ushers that denied us entry to the church, had fired the gun in the air. He threatened to call the Black Mariah, whatever that is, and send the assailants to jail if they didn't get out of there."

"Black Mariah is Birmingham's notorious police van, a paddy-wagon."

"Anyway, the men refused to budge until the cop flashed his badge and aimed his gun at one of them."

"Oh my goodness! Did he arrest them?"

Jesse laughs, "Are you kidding? Staring down the barrel of a thirty-eight is a powerful motivator. They wasted no time retreating to their car. As their tires squealed down the street, the cop told the gawking crowd to go on home and enjoy Sunday dinner. Then he holstered his gun and helped me to my feet. When I thanked him for coming to our rescue, his response was, 'I ought to be taking you folks to jail for causing this mess in the first place.' I told him all we wanted to do was to go inside and worship peacefully."

"And what was his reaction?"

"He railed at me for breaking the law by interfering with public worship and threatened to lock us up and throw away the key."

"Interesting, apparently he changed his mind. How come?"

"I suppose because I was the only one of my group seriously hurt, he dismissed the Carver students and drove me here."

"A change of heart, huh?"

"It's possible, but something he said on the way to the hospital still haunts me despite all this pain."

Paul arches his eyebrows, "And…"

"He said, 'Those Negro friends of yours might've taken you to some back alley *auntie* who'd just as soon let a white man die as look at him.' Is that true, Reverend?"

Before Paul has a chance to respond, Jesse is summoned to the x-ray lab. Paul walks with him but is turned back by an attendant.

Early winter twilight settles in as Paul sits in the waiting room munching on a sandwich that Lorna and Katy have brought, both clamoring for details of the incident, Lorna chastising him for placing his life in danger, but Katy admiring her dad's courage in taking a stand for a cause she also embraces.

An hour later, Jesse, the first to be released, saunters into the waiting room, brandishing two small bandages on his ear and forehead, his left arm in a sling. Paul crosses the lobby to meet him. "Your arm, is it…?"

"Broken," his eyes scan the crowd, "but where's Grace?"

"I've had no word since they took her back. Come over and take my chair. I want you to meet my wife and daughter." Paul turns and bumps into Katy, unaware she has followed him across the room.

"Jesse! What happened to you?" Katy exclaims, not noticing the shock that breaks across Paul's face.

"It's a long story, Katy, but first I need to check on Grace."

"Grace? Is she hurt too?"

Jesse limps to the receiving desk. Paul, having seized these few moments to recover from shock, now asks his daughter. "How in the world do you know this man?" Katy's tearful eyes follow Jesse as she answers her father.

"Jesse's my tutoring mentor."

"Oh?"

"It's my senior project, tutoring freshmen."

"Does he teach at Methodist College?"

"No."

Straining to conceal his rising aggravation with the brief clueless responses from his daughter, Paul asks, "Could I trouble you for a full explanation of your relationship with that man, without playing twenty questions?"

Katy glances at her mother to be sure she is still preoccupied with repacking the lunch basket. "I didn't want you and mother to be worried, so I didn't tell you about my project," she whispers to her dad. "I've been tutoring freshman at Carver College one night a week since September."

"At night? My heavens, you've been going over to that neighborhood after dark?"

"Not to worry, Dad, there are four of us and we've really been careful."

Paul teeters on the verge of condemning his daughter for following in his footsteps—taking risks in the name of justice—when the double doors from the hallway swing open. An orderly wheels Grace into the waiting room, her head bandage leaving only her face exposed. She forces a smile when she sees Katy and Jesse. The orderly pushes the wheel chair to the entrance and stops. When he announces to no one in particular, "Somebody needs to bring a car around," Paul volunteers.

When Paul walks out of the emergency room, he faces a wall of young black people lined up along the sidewalk. The crowd spots Jesse behind Paul and bursts into cheers and applause. A young woman begins to sing, *We shall overco-o-me.* Others swell the chorus, *We shall over co-o-me, We shall over come, some da-a-a-a-ay.*

"Brother Paul," Jesse yells loudly over the singing, "thanks for your help. But my people are here now, they'll see us back to the campus."

~~~

Paul returns to the parsonage and phones Charlie to call a meeting of the ushers for Monday evening. Word spreads like kudzu that Brother Paul is really steamed over the incident on the steps of his church. Almost every man in the church attends the meeting to support Charlie and the other ushers involved. They show up in the fellowship hall bristling with lynch-mob furor. Paul, somewhat shaken when he faces the four score pairs of simmering stares, begins by breaking the mood with humor. "Gentlemen, I could only pray for such an attentive congregation as this for my next sermon," he says with a timorous chuckle.

"If there is a next sermon," a heckler in the back retorts. There is no laughter, but a few grunts of "amen" and "yeah" from the group.

"All right gentlemen, let us proceed. Yesterday, three visitors appeared at the threshold of our sanctuary pursuant to my invitation to join us in worship, however..."

"We all know what happened, preacher, and you don't need to dress it up. Some outside agitators tried to break the law and we stopped 'em, that's all, except they slipped on the ice and fell, which wasn't our fault. We didn't lay a hand on 'em." The usher who has interrupted Paul turns to seek confirmation from his buddies. All, including those who had not witnessed the disastrous incident, nod in agreement.

Paul starts to counter the man's summary, but Charlie stands and motions for his friend to sit down. "First of all, I'm really sorry those people got hurt, truly I am. And I agree with Bud, except for one thing. In all honesty, I have to admit that I did reach out and touch that woman's hand, but that was way before she fell down the steps."

"We didn't see you do that, Charlie."

"Thanks Bud, but we're still Christians and we must be honest..." The men moan as if Charlie is about to desert those who came to support him. "...in case we get sued by the N.A.A.C.P." The moaning subsides.

Paul seizes this opportunity to quickly get his word across. "Thank you, Charlie, for that affirmation, it's what we are all about—honesty. The only reason I called this meeting tonight is to make sure that the tragic mistakes made yesterday never happen again at St. Francis." Again the men moan and groan in response. "I received a phone call last week—some guests wanting to visit our worship service yesterday. In the spirit of Christ, I welcomed the caller to our church. I was never granted the courtesy of being informed of plans to deny entrance of anyone to our church."

"And you didn't give us the courtesy of warning us that St. Francis was about to be integrated either."

"That's quite true, Bud. The fact is I did not ask the caller the color of his skin just as we don't ask any visitors the complexion of their faith. Our denomination is inclusive, we welcome anyone to enter our doors for worship."

"How do you know they came to worship? Those people had only one thing in mind—to cause trouble by mixing with us white folks."

"You know, Charlie, I learned long ago that I'm not a mind-reader. If I were, I might not be able to finish a single sermon, knowing what you folks are thinking while I'm preaching. Let me conclude this meeting with a brief statement of my position, if you have not guessed already. As long as I am pastor of this church, its doors will remain open to anyone regardless of their race, color or creed. Ushers will greet all comers with the same courtesy and dignity that Christ bestowed on us in His death and resurrection. That is my position and it is immovable."

The men grumble among themselves until Bud calls out, "But you're wrong, preacher you are not!"

Paul asks, "I am not what?"

"Immovable!"

9

> *June 9, 1963*
>
> *Dear Dr. Barron,*
> *Just a quick note to tell you how much we appreciate your ministry. It is so refreshing to see our church get back to its spiritual roots. Your sermons based on the Bible are just what the doctor ordered. It seems all that racial nonsense may be loosing its grip on our city, especially here in Redmont. Thank you for your amazing insight to the needs of our congregation.*
>
> *Two thankful believers,*
>
> *Beatrice and Harvey Land*

The secretary's chilly reception warns Paul Peterson not to expect his meeting with his newly elected Bishop to be pleasant. He takes a seat and tries to engage in small talk, but her short detached responses conjure up the image of the prophet Daniel standing before the gate to the lions' den. She jumps at the sound of the buzzer. "That's for you Reverend Peterson. Bishop Grand will see you now," she drones, briefly peering over her glasses before she resumes typing. The instant Paul crosses the threshold of the Bishop's office the typing ceases.

Bishop Grand remains seated at a broad polished desk framed by the window's green silk drapes. He appears much taller than his five-and-a-half-foot frame as he sits high in his chair bolstered by a thick cushion. He looks up briefly and flips his hand as a signal for Paul to have a seat opposite the desk. The Bishop normally makes himself comfortable in one of the upholstered chairs in the conversation corner, but today he distances himself behind the large mahogany desk. So Paul pulls up a captain's chair and sits on the edge.

"Tell me, Brother Peterson, how are things going at your church?" the Bishop opens with his standard line, but his rigid voice is drained of all sincerity.

"I guess you've already heard, sir."

"All the way down in Florida, Paul. That's why I cut my vacation short." Paul wonders: *Since the local newspapers and television stations ignored the attempted kneel-ins and the national media has not mentioned any church by name, someone must have informed him about the St. Francis incident, someone who was there.* "But, in all fairness, I like to hear my pastor's side of the story."

The Bishop's office suddenly loses its color and warmth leaving an atmosphere devoid of compassion. Fully aware that his version of Sunday's unfortunate accident might fall on deaf ears, Paul proceeds anyway, stopping short of the confrontation with the men of the church on Monday night.

"And what else?" the Bishop asks appearing to trap Paul in a half-truth. Before Paul can respond, Bishop Grand changes the subject, realizing that he might be forced to reveal who had placed the clandestine call to him at the beach. "Never mind, that's not why I called you in today," a strong breath of hypocrisy spews across the desk.

"Oh?" Paul slides back in his chair, not the least bit relieved.

"You heard about Brother Overstreet's unfortunate accident New Year's Eve?" Paul nods and asks for an update on his condition. "I'm afraid he didn't make it. The Lord received his soul two days ago."

"Oh, I'm so sorry to hear that. What about Louise? I heard she was in the car with him."

"His wife's barely clinging to life in a Gulfport hospital, so we need to get a prayer chain going for her in the district."

"I'll be glad to do that right away," Paul offers and pushes his chair back preparing to leave.

"Hold on, that'll be taken care of. I've talked with the District Superintendent and we've decided that you're the best man to replace Oscar." Paul's back stiffens as if seared by a live wire.

"Now? Go to Hope? But what about...?"

"The decision's final. You'll announce it to your congregation this Sunday and move into the Hope parsonage the following Wednesday."

"That's awfully sudden, Bishop. What about St. Francis, my replacement? What about Louise's belongings? We might need more time."

"Those are my decisions to make, Paul. You've got some packing to do. Now go ahead, and don't worry about your moving expenses, we'll take care of that. If you want to call Lorna and prepare her, feel free to use the phone in the outer office."

Paul doesn't want to break the news to his wife with the Bishop's receptionist listening, so he leaves. He ponders this abrupt turn in his career on the drive home: *Aside from the short notice, the change appears to be a left-handed promotion. Hope Methodist's membership is increasing about the same as St. Francis' congregation. I don't recall exactly, but I think the salary and benefits are somewhat better than my present level. Maybe I should express appreciation to the Bishop—he's looking out for my welfare.*

"When do we move and where?" Lorna asks as Paul enters the kitchen. From where she stands with arms braced against her chest there's barely enough room for Paul to open the door from the carport.

"How did you find out?"

"Don't you know the women of the church operate faster than F.T.D? Now, answer my question. How long do we have to pack, a month, two months or 'til conference?"

"None of the above, the Bishop's sending a moving van over a week from today."

"Holy macaroon! That soon? There's no way I can get this house cleaned and everything packed by then!" Lorna stomps her foot and storms out of the room. She comes right back. "And I suppose the Barron's will move in here the same day."

"The Barrons? The Bishop didn't tell me..."

"Yes, Ollie and Betty Barron, the two most fastidious people in North Alabama. She'll find every dust bunny in this old house and spread the word about my lousy housekeeping all over the conference. Oh, I'm going to be sick, Paul, sick, sick, sick."

"The Bishop's sending us to Hope. It'll be a good move," Paul says pulling his wife into his arms. "In addition, he's paying our moving expenses."

Lorna draws back. "That's a switch. The big boss must want us out of here pronto. What about poor old Dr. Overstreet and Louise, is he retiring all of a sudden?"

"I'm afraid so, Hon, the hard way. He didn't recover from his accident and Louise is barely alive in a hospital somewhere in Mississippi."

"O my God, Paul! I thought they just had a minor fender bender. What can we do?"

"Bishop Grand told me his staff is handling everything. It's out of our hands." For one pensive moment Paul presses Lorna closer to his chest. "You know, Hon, somehow I believe Oscar's death is what brought the Bishop back from Florida, not the race thing."

"Don't bet your tithe on it, Reverend Peterson. My source tells me that a member of our church phoned the Bishop Tuesday morning to tell him about your ultimatum to the ushers."

"I can't imagine who would go behind my back like that."

"Oh yes you can. Think. Who's the most powerful member of St. Francis? Who takes the Bishop out to The Club for dinner every now and then?"

"But, H. R. Wood was not even at the meeting Monday night. How could he..."

"That's the way he operates, pulling strings in the background. If you think J. B. Colley at Coal City had a monopoly on controlling church affairs, he was just a lightweight compared to H. R. Wood. That man wants you out of his pulpit so badly, he made it happen overnight."

"Drat! Why didn't I see that coming?"

"Because you're an incurable optimist. H. R. Wood has you dangling on the end of his watch chain, that's how he controls everybody. His approach to being the church boss differs from J. B.'s. H. R. has invested a lot of money in his church—the organ, the prayer chapel—his name is plastered everywhere."

"O. K., O. K., you made your point, but answer one question, where did you get all this insight into the motives of church people?" Paul asks, easing Lorna back to look her in the eye.

"Living with a preacher whose idol is Dietrich Bonhoeffer rubs off on a body after twenty-five years." She breaks away and flips her hand in the air. "But packing up to move every few years is not a *benefit* of the ministry I relish."

Paul meets with Chad Willis before choir practice that evening and breaks the news. "I'd rather you not announce my departure to the entire choir. Leak it to three or four key members after practice."

"So, you want the word to spread along the grapevine, huh?" Chad replies.

"I'm sure the lines are already buzzing with plenty of other versions of the Bishop's action. I just want to be sure the innocent folks in the church won't feel left out this Sunday."

"And I thought you detested church politics, Paul," Chad quips.

"True, my musical friend, but not politic; being prudent in perilous times is part of my calling."

Paul rises early the next morning deprived of sleep but craving coffee. Leaving Lorna in bed, he goes over to the church kitchen, puts a small amount of water in the coffee urn and watches each burp gradually turn the glass tube deep brown. When it's done, he warms his cold cup with hot water from the faucet before filling it with coffee. Instead of heading to the warmth of his office, Paul goes upstairs to the front of the chilly sanctuary and sits on the only pew covered with a long velvet cushion. The steam rising from the coffee mixes with his breath's vapor as he warms his hands around the hot cup. He reflects on the rapid changes of the past few days. *Why has the Bishop sidestepped the opportunity to make a stand against segregation? Is his restraint political, or because he has been a bishop less than a year? Perhaps St. Francis is not the venue he chooses for condemning the Klan and white citizens' councils as he does in private. And Katy has a genuine concern, but her attempt to reach out to the Carver students is so naïve. She deserves the support of the leader of her denomination just as much as I do, perhaps even more.*

Paul's reflective mood is shattered by the rattling of the front door to the sanctuary. He downs the last sip of tepid coffee and looks at his watch. *Not even seven yet, who wants to come and pray at this hour? Nevertheless, the church should not deny entry to anyone, regardless of...*Paul finds himself thinking back on his ultimatum to the men of the church three days ago. He makes his way up the aisle as the wintry morning sun projects slender shards of light through the tops of the windows. He approaches the darkened narthex but the noise has stopped.

"Hell-ooo, who's there?" Paul's pastoral voice chimes. No response. "Hell-ooo," he repeats. Hearing no answer, he twists the deadbolt knurl and opens the door a crack. Seeing no one, he opens it wider. He decides it must be the wind, but the air is calm. He releases his grip and allows the door to close. *That's odd,* he thinks as he re-enters the sanctuary through the swinging doors. He hears another doorknob shaking, this time it's the door behind the pulpit dais, the one he had entered from the basement. The door opens and a figure emerges.

"Morning, Brother Paul," the man doffs his tan sports cap and steps into a solitary shaft of sunlight, his flaming shock of hair announcing the presence of only one person.

"Ollie! What on earth..." Paul cannot say what he's thinking. *You couldn't wait, could you? What an opportunist! A raptor in clerical vest and collar already here to pick over my remains!* Paul looks at his watch as if to question his fellow pastor's premature visit.

"Oh, I know it's a mite early, my friend, but I was just on my way to my doctoral seminar and thought maybe you'd join me for a cup of coffee."

He just has to rub it in about the doctorate.

"Lorna said you'd be over here at the church."

He woke up Lorna! I wonder if he also brought his wife to inspect the parsonage.

"I told Lorna that Betty would like to come over later this morning and discuss the logistics of the move. Is that all right with you?"

Paul delves deep into his reservoir of patience and takes a silent oath to remain civil. "I've just had coffee, Ollie, and there's a little more left…"

"My, what a wonderful old church," Ollie proclaims, "Mind if I look around a bit. I've always admired St. Francis from a distance, but I've never entered this marvelous sanctuary." Ollie moves around pointing out the carved wood features, the windows with pink cherubs set in stained green glass and the organ pipes that scale the high wall of the choir loft. He performs his own guided tour, cataloging each detail in his mind as he describes it aloud. Gripping both sides of the pulpit, he lifts his square chin high and fantasizes preaching his first sermon from that spot.

Paul heads to the door, "Look around all you want, Ollie. I have a lot of packing to do. Just let yourself out when you've finished."

"Oh no, I'm done here. Are you going to your office?" Ollie jumps off the dais to follow Paul.

"I have a good deal to do, Ollie, so I'd appreciate if we could postpone this orientation until another time."

"Well, I just happened to be in the neighborhood, so I thought…"

Paul leads Ollie to the parking lot between the church and the parsonage. "And please convey our regrets to Betty also. We're too busy to entertain her at the parsonage today, perhaps next week."

Paul opens the door of Ollie's new Thunderbird to facilitate a speedy departure. Ollie stuffs his wieldy red locks under his cap and warns, "I'm afraid it's too late. She's probably left Mimosa already, heading this direction."

"That will afford me the pleasure of inviting her back at another time." Paul punctuates his statement with a slam of the car door, "Excuse me, Brother, my hand must've slipped."

~~~

Oliver Barron waits impatiently in his new lavender academic gown with three velvet stripes on each sleeve—in spite of the fact his Doctor of Ministry degree has not been officially conferred. He remains out of sight until H. R. Wood addresses the congregation immediately following the opening hymn then proceeds to give his new pastor a glorious introduction. Prior to the service, Mr. Wood had suggested to a choir member, "Wouldn't it be rather nice to have the choir stand as Reverend Barron makes his entrance?" But he had neglected to mention it to Chad Willis.

Right on cue, Ollie opens the anteroom door and struts across the dais with all the pomp of a royal coronation. The designated choir member starts to rise to her feet, but fearing no one will follow, she remains seated. Realizing that no standing tribute is imminent, H. R. nods his head towards the woman several times, but she gazes at the ceiling, disregarding his cues. Ollie approaches the pulpit trying to ignore the unsettling snickers from choir members amused at the comical red-headed figure outlandishly attired in purple. It's not the dignified reception Ollie had envisioned. "His robe clashes with those orange sideburns," a soprano whispers aloud.

"Shh," Chad cautions, putting a finger to his lips and thinking, *This guy would be perfect for the role of the priest in the opera Tosca, leading the processional at the close of the first act.*

The reactions of the congregation vacillate between fascination and ridicule as they strive to remain respectful. Collecting all the charm he possesses, Ollie thanks the beaming H. R. Wood for his most gracious introduction and then announces a theme for his ministry that resonates deep in the hearts of his parishioners, "My greatest goal, dear friends, is to place my humble ministry in your hands that together we may take up the yoke of Christ and return this great church to its spiritual roots."

Oliver Barron's leadership skills are no greater than those of Paul Peterson, but his flamboyancy adds an alluring gloss that captivates his listeners. A short four weeks after his introduction, Ollie is skillfully using the pulpit to divert the congregation's attention from the festering cankers of civil strife that plague the downtown neighborhoods, safe distances from their booming Redmont suburb. Oliver takes his lead from the daily newspapers, believing that protests and demonstrations represent only temporary bumps in the road of progress for the city. H. R. Wood feeds Oliver the idea that local black folks don't want integration, convincing him that trouble is stirred up by outsiders who take up collections and leave town with the money. He reminds Ollie repeatedly that even the slightest hint that a Negro family might buy a house in Redmont would devastate real estate values.

～～～

After Easter, Bishop Grand directs the Birmingham District Superintendent to assemble his ministers at St. Francis for an important message.

Following an opening prayer by the District Superintendent, Bishop Grand positions his portly body behind the pulpit, fingers his double chin, and addresses the rapt clergy. "My brothers of the cloth," his plantation drawl curls aristocratically about the words that slide slowly off his tongue pleasantly softening the hard leathery voice, "we live in precarious times, which is nothing new to bearers of the cross." Heads nod and muffled "amen's" bubble from the assembly. "Some of you have requested, yea demanded that the Episcopacy issue a public statement in support of the efforts to integrate certain facilities in this great city. I have called this meeting to address the issue and to clarify the position of my office, which shall become the official policy of the Conference, more specifically, this District." A young pastor rises to speak, but an older pastor seated behind him pulls on his coat to curtail the interruption. Dejected, he sinks back into the pew.

The Bishop continues, "The Methodist Church, as you are all aware, supports justice for all mankind. Our church is clearly working to relieve suffering and injustice all over the globe. Let there be no doubt about that. While all who sit in this sanctuary may agree with our purpose, some may disagree with our methods. There are those among you who would take to the streets and join the protesters or pursue other spurious actions that would place your congregations in jeopardy," he says looking straight at Paul Peterson on the front pew. Bishop Grand then shifts his attention to Oliver Barron seated on the other end of the same pew. "However, I am pleased to acknowledge that most of you are going about the business of serving the spiritual needs of your parishioners instead of participating in the temporary social upheaval that plagues our city."

The Bishop's words reverberate throughout the cavernous sanctuary as he recites several accomplishments initiated by the Methodist Board of Missions and the National Council of Churches. Having laid the groundwork for his main point, he removes his spectacles and leans forward on the pulpit, buttressing himself for the conclusion—with expectation that the monumental pronouncement will rattle the organ pipes that tower behind him.

"What I am about to share with you at this time is so sensitive that it must remain within the walls of this sanctuary. Do not divulge this information to another soul, not even your lovely wives." The pastors fall breathlessly silent. "Your Bishop has not been sitting in a Sycamore tree like Zacchaeus waiting to be called to action." He waits for the twitters of laughter to cease. "I come before you today to bring you up to date on some significant behind the scenes progress in race relations that should soon put an end to the ongoing violence and destruction in Birmingham. First, a group of interdenominational clergy, including your Bishop, just completed a letter addressed to the Southern Christian Leadership Conference which outlines a faith-based rationale for discontinuing public demonstrations in favor of more reasonable and peaceful negotiations. We have conferred with the city's Negro leaders and they concur with our points. Secondly, this same group of spiritual leaders met with major downtown businessmen who have agreed to abolish separate lunch counters, dressing rooms, and restrooms in their stores." Spontaneous applause bursts forth from several of the preachers while others pat their hands politely. The Bishop responds with a smile. "And lastly, the Director of Public Safety has agreed to remove his State troopers from the city streets before Mother's Day." The applause is led by Ollie Barron who jumps to his feet in enthusiastic support of the Bishop's position.

When the applause subsides, everyone sits down—except Paul Peterson. Bishop Grand pauses a moment, hoping Paul will follow suit. But Paul persists, "What does this mean for our congregations, Bishop Grand? They are asking questions."

"You haven't allowed me to finish, Brother Paul. Now, with your permission, I'll continue." Paul settles back into the pew cushion and watches Ollie Barron lift his chin and grin like a child who has just seen his older brother get a spanking. "First of all, I expect none of you to invite trouble into your church. God's sanctuary is no place for violence and placing your congregation in harm's way. Your strength as a spiritual leader lies in the ability of each of you to do as I have done, working quietly and effectively behind the scenes, to promote peace and understanding. I shall not look kindly upon any one of you who uses your pulpit to lead your congregation into the cauldrons of conflict." This last statement affirms for Paul the real reason he had been ousted from St. Francis' pulpit.

The young associate minister who had risen to challenge the Bishop's opening statement jumps to his feet again. "With all due respect, Bishop Grand, you have told us what not to do, but we need clear instructions as to what we should do."

Clearly incensed by such unmitigated impertinence, the Bishop glances first at the district superintendent and then at the associate's senior minister before addressing the question. "Perhaps, you could shed a bit more light on your concern, my son. Where have I not been clear?"

"Thank you, sir. Two specific scenarios come to mind. Last Sunday, the pastor of First Baptist Church openly welcomed some black students to the worship service. The Easter service went on without any confrontations. Should I follow his example the next time a black person appears at the front door of my church? Secondly, our Sunday School Superintendent has refused to order Methodist literature because of an illustration in the one of the children's books."

Bishop Grand looks puzzled. "What illustration?"

A pastor on the back row fumbles in his briefcase and holds up an opened fifth grade lesson book. "This picture, Bishop, the one where a black girl is holding hands with two white girls." Reactions from the others affirm that the picture has caused problems in their churches also. The Bishop motions the pastor to bring the book to him. He studies it for a moment and shakes his head. Instead of responding to the young man's concerns, the Bishop asks if he has conferred with his senior pastor about the problems.

"Yes sir."

"And what was his advice, may I ask?"

"He said that I should ask you, sir." A surge of laughter spills over the pews and down the aisle to the dais, rendering the Bishop's ample jowls a rich red hue.

The senior pastor, determined to defend his position, rises alongside his associate, but the Bishop motions him to sit down, "Never mind, Dr. Ross, no explanation is necessary. I shall take these questions under advisement and respond in good time." Several other ministers try to call for an immediate discussion of the issues, but the Bishop ignores them. "Please rise for the benediction and remember that a peaceful initiative to promote racial harmony is close at hand and you are to do nothing to invoke discord among your parishioners at this time."

"There's nothing like good solid leadership from the captain of our ship, is there?" Paul Peterson expresses his disappointment to a fellow pastor as they leave the meeting.

"I have a feeling that no matter what instructions the Bishop might render, you will follow your own conscience, Brother Paul," his colleague casts a discerning grin.

Paul winks.

10

> June 20, 1963
>
> Dear Rev. Barron:
> Have you seen my Angeline? She's not at college anymore. She didn't come home yet. I thought she might be coming to your new church. If you see her, let her know that I want her to come back home.
>
> Marie Shook

At the close of the District Meeting, Oliver Barron glides weightlessly out the doors of St. Francis fawning over the Bishop, "Excellent meeting, Bishop Grand, excellent indeed," the words dripping with honey slide easily from his lips.

"The Lord was with us today. I certainly appreciate you hosting our little gathering. You're a good man, Dr. Barron. Your service will not go unrewarded. Please give your lovely wife my best."

Ollie's elation increases with each step until he nearly bursts the stitches of his saintly vestments. The Bishop's affirmation stirs bitter-sweet memories Ollie has tried to forget. His thoughts flash back six months to the lowest point of his ministry, *Bishop Grand called me when he heard about the tragic accident that took my four-year-old daughter's life. He delivered a touching eulogy, but it was what he said after the interment that gave me hope. "Oliver, if there's anything I can do for you, don't hesitate to ask." Without thinking, I blurted out "Please, can you get me out of Mimosa before I begin to hate the place that took my child's life. I can't stand it here any longer!" I was surprised at the Bishop's response to my intemperate outburst. "I'll see what I can do; I'll see what I can do."* And the Bishop stood by that promise, he sent me here to St. Francis.

Shaking his memories, Ollie waves to the departing Bishop. He hurries to the parsonage with another mission on his mind that requires a change of clothes. "Betty, I'm meeting my seminar for lunch, so don't fix anything for me," he brushes a kiss across her cheek as she sets the table.

"Those boys still rag you about wearing a collar, huh? But you should at least wear a tie with that dress shirt," she advises as he bounds out the door. He snaps his fingers and returns for a tie. "Romping with the Bishop's gotten you all flustered, hasn't it?" Ollie blows her a final kiss and hurries off.

Ollie's eagerness for his afternoon venture easily overshadows the Bishop's visit. He has less than an hour to drive halfway to Mimosa, conceal his Thunderbird behind a row of stores at Sargent's Crossroads and steal away to the motel.

Turning right at the crossroads, Ollie parks the convertible under a large tree and presses the button to close the top. Opening a gym bag he keeps on the back seat, he extracts a sweat jacket and pulls it over his head hiding his wavy red hair under the hood. Exchanging his polished leather oxfords for Keds, he gets out and locks the car. His routine is practiced and methodical—scanning the area before heading to the motel.

Ollie's steps are deliberate as he winds his way past the overflowing trash cans and back doors of the shops. He can already feel the warm curves of her body, smell the inviting scent of her hair, and gaze into her bottomless brown eyes that demand domination. Circling around to the front of the motel Ollie hesitates before entering the tiny office, to ensure no witnesses are in sight. After penning a false name on the register, he pays cash for the day rate, grabs the key and scurries through the passageway to the row of rooms at the rear.

A heavy mixture of stale cigarette smoke and disinfectant assaults Ollie's nostrils as he pushes the door open. He leaves it slightly ajar to air out the drab cubicle and to mark the room for

Angie. Then Ollie presses the button on the window unit. It groans like an old man and rattles the window before settling down to a whiny roar. He sits in the semi-darkness and parts the plastic curtains to watch for her.

Angie rarely keeps Ollie waiting more than a few minutes. Since that brief moment of intimacy in Ollie's office when she was a troubled sixteen-year-old, the two have developed a close relationship. Although Ollie enjoyed the prolonged hugs and caresses behind closed doors, he did strive to maintain a modicum of propriety with the hot-wired teenager. While Angie was attending college in Birmingham, she had expressed a desire to see Ollie often to continue her counseling sessions. At first, they would meet halfway at Sargent's Crossroads and talk for hours in his car. When the weather turned cold, Angie suggested he rent a room at the nearby motel. Reluctantly, Ollie agreed after she convinced him they needed more privacy to talk. "We've become so close, we need to be able to talk without nosy church folks getting the wrong idea," she explained.

With only one chair in the room, Angie would sit on the bed with Ollie in the chair, but after a couple of counseling session she began to stretch out on the bed to more freely express her feelings. Massaging her back in a healing gesture, Ollie continued to resist Angie's seductive writhing on the bed. It happened to be shortly after the death of his child that they consummated their affection for each other.

Ollie had blamed the indiscretion on his inability to cope with his grief. He apologized, but Angie rebuffed his apology, promising not to let it go that far again. "Don't blame yourself Brother Ollie, it was bound to happen. We are so close." She was careful not to be the first to utter the "love" word in their discussions even though they had gone this far. Returning to Mimosa following their ultimate union, Ollie tried to sort out his sinful obsession with an eighteen-year-old college freshman. *It's just too risky. I have to exert better control. She made love like a pro. Where did she learn? Of course, those young daughters of coal miners are known to be promiscuous. Perhaps I was not the first. What if she's carrying a disease? How did she know about that truckers' motel?* Ollie had pledged to break off the affair if he could find a way to do it without shattering her ego, without driving her to confess her sins to another preacher. When he was away from Angie, his moral resolve strengthened, but as their "counseling" sessions continued his strength invariably crumbled in her presence.

Ollie, deep in thought, doesn't hear Angie's footsteps on the gravel path leading to the motel door. She knocks gently then opens the door springing Ollie to his feet. He braces for a warm welcoming hug, but she lingers near the door. As the outside light outlines her figure he notices her hair has lost its bounce and clings to her head. Her fresh young lips, now dry and drawn, show no trace of her favorite bright red lipstick. "Hi," she mumbles, closing the door behind her.

"Is something wrong, Angie?" Ollie hesitants to approach her. She drifts toward the bed, tosses her jacket aside, sits on the edge, and draws her knees up beneath her chin. He pulls the drapes together and switches on a light.

"Don't," she says, shielding her eyes, "I look a mess." He flips the light switch down and stares as she curls in a fetal position on the bed. "I shouldn't have come today."

"You look fine to me, Angie," Ollie takes a step toward the bed. "We all have these days." He kneels and places a hand on her knee, adjusting his eyes to the dim light. She turns away and rolls her eyes from side to side to avoid his persistent gaze. Her eyes are shallow, no longer beaming with the excitement his presence usually stimulates.

"We're in trouble," she whispers.

He jerks his hand away from her knee as if he'd touched poison oak and sits back on his heels. "Trouble?" Ollie frantically shuffles through several possibilities under the heading of trouble: *She's contracted a venereal disease. She's told someone about* us—*a roommate, a counselor, her mother. Somebody from Mimosa or St. Francis has seen us together. She's about to crush my ministry into a useless dust heap.*

"I told my roommate and she said I should talk to you."

Oh God, I knew it! Now everybody will find out about us. My career... "You mean you told her about us?" he dares to ask.

Angie becomes more animated. "Oh no, she has no idea. She just knows you're my pastor...or was. She said that I should tell you that I'm pregnant."

Ollie jerks his head back and rises to his feet. "Pregnant? Are you sure?"

"I've missed two periods, but I haven't told anyone whose baby it is."

Ollie stiffens and asks without thinking, "Do I know him?"

"Damn it, Ollie, damn it, damn it!" She had never called him by his first name nor spoken so harshly to him. Her words cut to the core of his ego and crimp his breathing for an instant. He paces back and forth on the worn carpet, repeatedly running his fingers through his hair. Angie wipes tears that meander silently down her cheeks and gathers her jacket close to her chest, embracing it. "I knew I shouldn't have come," she cries, reacting to Ollie's intemperate remark. "I really didn't want to do this." She slips off the bed, heads for the door, and disappears. He runs after her leaving his hooded sweatshirt on the bed.

"Come back to the room and let's talk," he pleads as she opens her car door. "We'll work out something."

Angie climbs behind the steering wheel and slides the key into the ignition. "I'm all out of talk, Ollie, just plumb run out."

He holds the door open. "Look, Angie, I know you're upset and confused."

She sniffs and looks him in the eye. "I'm not the one who's confused." Switching on the ignition, she says, "Please let go of my car door."

"All right, all right, you go on back to the dorm and calm down. Call me tomorrow at eleven. I'll be in my office at St.

Francis. You're absolutely right, Angie, we're in this together and I'm sorry I acted like a jackass. I was totally in shock."

Angie pulls a tissue from the box in the passenger seat to dry her eyes. Then, she nods to Ollie and puts the gear in reverse. Ollie watches as she backs across the gravel and wheels her car onto the road.

~~~

"Did you have a good luncheon, dear?" Betty asks as Ollie ambles numbly through the kitchen.

"It was O. K.," he drones, preoccupied with thoughts of his pregnant angel.

"So, how were the boys today? Did y'all take turns calling each other 'doctor'?" The strange tone of Betty's voice snaps Ollie out of his daze. "Oh, what were you saying, dear, I had my mind on something else?"

"Oh nothing, just curious, Burt Sanders called trying to locate you, seems he didn't know about the seminar meeting today."

Think fast, Ollie Barron! "Er...he didn't know about it because...I had the date wrong. It's next week."

"Then, where have you been all this time?" Betty's lips twist, a sure sign of spinning a web of entrapment.

"Just doing my job, you know, those pastoral things," he offers tentatively.

"Like what?"

"Making hospital calls."

"Who's sick?"

"Look Betty, if you have a problem with the work I'm doing, maybe I should get a job at Wood Real Estate." She drops the inquisition, but makes a mental note of his defensive posture for future reference. "I have a sermon to write, so I'll be in my office the rest of the afternoon." He borrows some time to think about her question. Unwilling to leave his wife in a suspicious quandary, he says, "For your information, I made the rounds to see if any of our members had been admitted this week. Nobody's sick and nobody's scheduled for surgery. Now with your permission I'll head to the church."

Mrs. Green hands Ollie several pink while-you-were-out notes as he hurries by her desk. "Nothing urgent, Brother Oliver, except Reverend Sanders called three times, long distance I think."

"Yes, I know, he called the parsonage. Please hold my calls, I'll be working on my sermon."

"Yes sir." She has already learned that her pastor uses that excuse for privacy, no matter what he's doing behind the closed door. The illuminated button on her telephone confirms her assumption that other business has taken precedence over writing a sermon.

"Dr. Warren, this is Reverend Oliver Barron...Yes, I'm just fine...No, I have no complaints...Yes, I told your nurse the matter is urgent, but it concerns a church member who needs immediate attention...No, not our church, she's from my former parish...Yes, I understand, but rather than discuss the situation over the phone, I wonder if you would have some time to meet with me, perhaps after office hours...That sounds fine, at your office or mine...Good, I'll meet you at the hospital cafeteria around seven."

"Reverend Sanders please, Dr. Oliver Barron calling...Burt, Ollie, I understand you've been trying to reach me. What's going on?...Oh, you know my mind's not what it used to be...Yes, I realized too late that we're getting together next week...I know...Betty's fine...I just left her at the parsonage...I know...ever since we lost little Amy, she's been tracking me like a coon dog...no, I didn't mean it that way, she's just afraid something's going to happen to me...She'll get over it...Yes, the meeting with Bishop Grand went fine...No, nothing new that should concern your church in Anniston...The literature problem? Barely mentioned it, but I expect he'll be in touch with the publishing house very soon. Yeah, thanks for calling...you too."

Ollie lays the other messages aside and tries to get Angie off his mind. He pulls a book of sermons by Charles Allen off the shelf and selects one he can tweak to sound original.

Angie drives until the roadside motel disappears entirely from her rear view mirror. She pulls off the highway at a gas station and backs her '56 Bel Air to a spot beside the service bay partially hidden from the road. Hank Williams' nasal voice whines from the radio, *I'm so lonesome I could cry since my baby said goodbye,* as she waits and watches every car headed toward Birmingham. The 50,000-watt station serves as a pacifier in her time of stress, puts her in touch with Mimosa memories. The simple country strains, tunes she cut her teeth on, offer her some comfort but seem so far removed from her now sophisticated bel canto voice. By the time the song ends, Ollie Barron's T-Bird zooms past the gas station. She cranks her car and heads the opposite direction with *Blue Eyes Crying in the Rain* pining from the speaker.

She wonders: W*here can I go to shed my shame? There's an abandoned quarry out this way somewhere. Daddy took us there on a picnic once, but the water was so cold he couldn't swim in it even on that hot July day. He tried to teach me how to skim stones across the surface of the deep blue lake and told me stories about thieves that dumped stolen cars there. If I only can remember how to get there, a perfect place to drown my troubles.*

Rounding a bend, she notices a weathered barn, its faded Sinclair sign on the side barely visible. It marks the narrow road, overgrown with weeds, leading to the quarry. She negotiates potholes and broken asphalt to a spot near the lake. Clumps of daffodils bobble their yellow heads where the crumbling caretaker's shack is now a pile of gray siding. The placid water trapped in a large hole is surrounded by mounds of quarry tailings held together by jack pines and budding gum trees.

She drives close to the bank and stares at the reflection of the afternoon sun quivering on the surface of the dark blue water. Ollie's words keep echoing in her mind, *we're in this together...we'll work out something."* She turns off the ignition and hesitates before stepping out of the car. The cool April breeze winds her uncombed hair around her face as she wavers towards the water. At the water's edge, she looks down and pictures that graveyard of stolen vehicles on the bottom, rusting and filling with sludge. *I could get back in the car and drive it straight off the edge. Nobody would ever find me. Mama would never know that her little angel had repeated her life-shattering mistake. Ollie would never have to worry about his sorry-ass reputation. I can solve everybody's problems with one quick push on the gas pedal. The water's so deep I would drown before the car hits the bottom. Dammit, why am I crying?* Her eyes fill with tears, Angie returns to the car for a tissue. She reaches for it and erupts in giggles as though she has been playing a joke on herself. *Why am I wiping off these tears, so my face will be dry when I hit the water?* Her giggles swell into full body-shaking laughter. *Maybe I ought to put on some makeup and comb my hair to boot. No need going to meet the devil looking like a tramp.*

She cranks the car and races the motor, still laughing and talking to herself. But instead of lurching forward into the frigid water, she jerks the gear into reverse and careens backwards to a screeching halt just inches from a tree. *No, no, Reverend Ollie Barron, we are not in this together. I got myself into this mess and I'll get myself out of it.* Angie takes off down the quarry road talking to herself, ignoring what the rough road might do to her tires. Filtering through the crackling static, a familiar tune struggles to be heard on the radio, so she turns up the volume and begins to sing along, w*hen my blue moon turns to gold again.*

The next day in the dorm begins the same as every other has for the past month. Angie eats a Mars candy bar, throws up twice, and then stretches out across her bed instead of going to class. But today her routine changes. As soon as her roommate leaves for class, she rushes to the shower down the hall and begins putting herself together. As she prepares to meet Oliver Barron, her plan unfolds in her mind: *No sir, a telephone conversation will not do Red Barron. I want to see the expression on your face when I toss you out of my life for good.*

Around ten-thirty, she parks across the street from St. Francis, wraps a scarf around her head and puts on sunglasses. Being unfamiliar with the layout of the church, she observes carefully to determine which door leads to Ollie's office. His Thunderbird is parked in the driveway between the church and the adjacent parsonage. Feeling a little queasy, she fishes a packet of crackers from her purse and nibbles, trying not to disturb her newly applied lipstick.

At one minute before eleven, Angie leaves her car and walks across the street to the side door that faces the parsonage. As she enters the hallway, Chad Willis emerges from the kitchen balancing a full cup of coffee in one hand and a stack of music in the other.

"Oops, excuse me Miss, I almost spilled coffee on you." He pauses to let her pass.

"Which way to Bro...the Pastor's office?" she asks without looking up.

"Through that door," he points across the hall.

Angie grips the doorknob and inhales deeply before turning it. Mrs. Green greets her from behind the desk. "Good morning, may I help you?"

"I...I would like to see the pastor please," she tries to appear nonchalant.

"Is he expecting you?"

"Not exactly."

"I'm sorry, but he left strict instructions not to be disturbed for the time being."

"Oh."

"He's expecting an important telephone call. If you'd like to have a seat, I'll let him know you're here as soon as he's finished with his call, Miss...Miss..."

Knowing he will not finish, Angie dashes out without leaving her name and resumes surveillance from her car.

A few minutes before noon, Ollie Barron relinquishes his vigil and comes out of seclusion. "Are you sure there were no calls for me, Mrs. Green?"

"I'm afraid not, Brother Barron. It's been pretty quiet out here." The Pastor thumbs through the opened mail she has deposited in a wire basket on the corner of the desk. "Oh, there was a young lady—about an hour ago, but she left when I told her...

"Young lady? What did she look like?" Ollie drops the mail in the basket.

"Like a movie star, if you ask me, with those dark glasses."

"What color hair did she have?"

"I couldn't tell. She had it all done up with a scarf and tied on top sort of like Dorothy Lamour in those old movies. Don't know how tall she was either because she was wearing high heels."

"What did she want?" Ollie asks as he looks toward the door.

"She didn't say, she seemed awfully nervous, kept fiddling with a pendant on a neck chain."

"Pendant?"

"It looked expensive, it was an angel."

"An angel?"

Before the secretary answers, Ollie steps into the hallway perplexed, *why would Angie dare come by the church looking for me? She knows we can't talk about her situation here. Maybe she went upstairs to the sanctuary, perhaps to pray.*

"Brother Ollie," Mrs. Green calls as she joins him in the hallway. "If it's all right with you, I need to go on to lunch. It's my circle day and we're meeting in the parsonage."

"That's fine," he mumbles, distracted. He decides he'll wander through the building searching for her, until Mrs. Green calls to him from just outside the entrance. "Brother Ollie, come here!"

"Yes?" he says responding to the urgency of her request. As he goes to meet her she steps inside the door.

"That young lady is sitting in a car across the street."

"Are you sure?"

"I can tell by that purple scarf wrapped around her head. Shall I go over and tell her that you can see her now?"

Ollie pauses to think, "No, you go on to your circle meeting. I'm going to make some hospital calls. I'll just speak with her on my way out." He returns to the office to get his coat and his briefcase containing the information that Dr. Warren gave him. He tries to think of a place to talk with Angie, away from the church.

"Hi, Brother Ollie," Angie's voice startles him as he is about to leave his inner office.

"Oh, Angie! I thought you were going to call," Ollie whispers.

"I just drove over to…say goodbye in person, that's all."

Angie turns to leave slowly, knowing that he'll find an excuse to stop her. "Goodbye? Where…? Why…? But we still have a little problem to solve." Ollie steps around her and closes the door. "Come in my office for a minute, I have something to tell you."

"Say it right here, then I'll get on with my life."

Ollie snaps open his briefcase and retrieves the envelope. "O. K., I'll make this quick. I have a friend, a doctor, who's agreed to help you…us out. You need to follow his instructions carefully. I wrote them down," he hands the envelope to Angie. "My friend knows a doctor in Bessemer who's very good in situations like yours…ours. You should call and make an appointment as soon as possible. It's extremely important that you describe your symptoms, word for word as I have written them when you see him."

"But, I won't need to see a doctor for a while yet. Besides, I don't have any money right now."

Ollie continues, "The money is in the envelope. It's the least I can do for you." Angie opens the envelope and peeks at several bills folded inside a sheet of paper. The tough expression that she had rehearsed to convince Ollie she is capable of solving her own problems begins to crumble. Her eyes moisten and threaten her carefully applied mascara. The urge to cast the envelope at his feet and run is abated by the lingering affection still simmering beneath the surface. She wants to hug him despite the chasm that has opened between them. Her emotions remain suspended until he speaks again.

"I want you to know that I'll be here if you need me...after...you take care of the problem," he offers in a pious, hollow tone.

Angie's mood quickens. "Problem? What do you mean, problem?"

"You'll understand after you read those instructions, Angie." She starts to unfold the paper, but Ollie insists that she wait and read them later. "I have some important calls to make right now. I think it's best if you leave before my secretary returns, she's extremely meddlesome."

Angie regrets not leaving earlier, before he stole her chance to break off this clandestine love affair on her own terms. Her energy spent, and on the verge of tears, Angie has no choice but to go.

"O. K., I'm going. I'll get out of your way, preacher. I'd hate to see you get in trouble for talking to a little tramp." She spins around and bumps into Chad Willis as he opens the door. "Excuse me," without looking up she bolts down the hall.

Chad watches Ollie close his briefcase and pick up his coat. "Another gypsy looking for a handout?" he quips.

Ollie rushes past his nosy choir director and says, "Yep, you got that right, Chad, just another little angel with broken wings."

11

> *July 14, 1963*
>
> *Dear Momma,*
> *I just want you to know that I didn't fall off the edge of the earth. I had to drop out of college because I got really, really sick and missed too many classes. When I got well, a band offered me a job singing, so I took it. Right now, I'm in New Orleans, but by the time you get this I don't know where I'll be. Don't worry, I'm fine.*
>
> *Love and kisses,*
>
> *Angie*

Angie throws the envelope on the passenger seat of her Chevy and peels rubber leaving St. Francis Methodist in her wake. She's determined not to read Brother Ollie's note until she has time to sort through particulars of the awkward conversation in his office. His words play over and over in her mind like a scratched record *I'll be here if you need me, after you take care of the problem, after you take care of the problem, after you take care...*

Katy is spread across her bed studying for senior exams when Angie bursts through the door and heads straight for the built-in chest on her side of the room. Katy glances at her watch, "Did your English class get out early?" she asks, with her nose still in the book. Angie yanks open the top drawer of the chest and takes out a miniature bottle of scotch, a fraternity party souvenir. Sensing something's wrong, Katy rolls over on the bed to check on her roommate. "No, Angie, not here. You'll get kicked out of school for sure," Katy warns as Angie unscrews the top and pours the contents in a coffee mug.

"Are you gonna report me?" she snaps and tosses the empty bottle into the metal trash can.

Katy pushes herself up on the bed. "You know better than that, but if you get caught drinking in our room, I'll be in trouble, too." Angie lifts the cup to her lips and swallows more than just a sip of the scotch. The virgin throat only familiar with the foamy essence of beer rejects the whiskey's fiery assault. She coughs and chokes almost spilling the remainder of the booze. Katy jumps off the bed and pats her roommate on the back. "There now, put that poison down and tell me what's driving you to strong drink." Angie gladly relinquishes the cup and Katy leads her to the bed.

Although she does not condone Angie's naïve dalliance with sex, Katy offers the tolerance and understanding of a squeaky-clean older sister. Angie has led her roommate to believe that the object of her affection is a university student in another town. Now Angie's desperate to tell her best friend the whole story, to scream to the world that Ollie Barron is a jerk, to relieve the anguish raging deep within her. It's been only one day, but she is already sick and exhausted from carrying this heavy burden of anger. But she stops herself—too embarrassed to admit having an affair with a married man, too afraid no one will take her word over that of a respected man of God—and her better judgment surfaces. *I can't tell the whole truth, but just enough to get Katy's advice.*

She proceeds to paint the picture of her crisis with broad brush strokes. "Thanks for being here, Katy, I just don't know what to do."

"Did you go talk with Reverend Barron?"

Angie shifts her eyes from side to side, searching for an opalescent response, intending to shed only a glimmer of light on her dilemma, "No…not yet."

"Did you go see a doctor like I told you to?"

Another question to parry, "No…but I…I have a name."

"You know, Angie, you may not even be pregnant. I've heard of women who missed a couple of periods who weren't pregnant."

"I'm not stupid. I've puked every morning for two weeks and I know that's what pregnant women do." Angie begins to weep again. Katy hands her a box of tissues. "Thanks."

"O. K., then we must get you to the doctor. Let's go call him right now and make an appointment. What's his name?" As Angie goes to the drawer to get the envelope Ollie had given her, Katy asks, "You're not going to drink any more whiskey, are you?"

"Hell no, I'm just getting the doctor's name from this piece of paper." Suspecting that Ollie may have signed his name, Angie meticulously unfolds the note and scans the handwritten lines before handing it to Katy. "That son-of-a-bitch!" she screams when the words on the paper trigger her gnawing resentment of Ollie's rejection.

"Angie!"

"So that's what he meant by handling the problem. Son-of-a-bitch!" she drawls slowly and deliberately to emphasize her description of the man she once idolized.

Bewildered by the uncharacteristic outcry, Katy approaches with an intended hug. But Angie retracts, waving the paper above her head, perusing it again to verify it does not reveal the writer's identity. Then she thrusts the note at her astonished roommate.

Katy reads the note. "Who gave you this?" she asks. Angie rolls her eyes from side to side. "You know, when you do your eyes like that, I suspect you're conjuring up something short of the truth. You don't have to tell me if you don't want to."

"I want to tell you, I just don't want to mention a name, that's all."

"All right, have it your way."

"I went to see the baby's father..."

"To talk about getting married?"

"Uh, yeah, that's it. And the bastard, oh I shouldn't use that word, the son-of-a-bitch told me to take care of the problem myself. He even suggested the baby isn't his. After we argued, I got mad and left."

"But where did this note come from?"

Again Angie has to think fast. She shuts her eyes fearing Katy will see the deception and asks dozens more questions. "Oh, I left out that part. He's washing his hands of the whole deal, sending me to a doctor he knows. He thinks he's bought me off with a few hundred dollars of blood money. What will I do with the baby when it comes?"

"It's not that simple," Katy peruses the hand-written note again.

"I know, there are some instructions here that I don't understand, but I'm sure the doctor will know...like, I need to have a D&C, whatever that is."

"You don't know?"

"No, I guess it's some kind of exam to tell if I'm pregnant or not...but, I'm not to use that word." Angie takes the note to read it more carefully. "Probably, because the doctor..."

"Wait a minute, Angie," Katy interrupts. "You really don't know what he's asking you to do?" Angie looks puzzled. "My mother had a D&C last year. It's not a diagnosis; it's a procedure, like an operation."

"An operation, but I don't know...?"

"It's when the doctor scrapes the womb lining. Mother was in the hospital for a couple of days."

Angie stares at the note again. "That sounds like...like..."

"Exactly, an abortion."

"Abortion! Damn him! Damn him!" Tears fill her eyes, released from a new reservoir of rage within her. "That's what he meant by taking care of the problem. I can't do it, I can't do it," she cries. Katy draws her close and waits for the emotional storm to subside.

"Let's sit down and discuss it before you make a decision, Angie," Katy pulls the two desk chairs close together. Katie has exhausted her entire repertoire of advice for helping her distraught friend. Her handful of psychology courses are insufficient to offer the professional counseling Angie needs now. She tries one last approach. "Let's calm down and review the situation, Angie. First, abortion is illegal in Alabama. That's why you should not admit being pregnant. Once the doctor completes the D&C, he'll know the truth, but he probably wouldn't tell you about it or even note it on the record. So that's one option."

"You think I should do it?" Angie sniffs.

"Not necessarily, but I am saying that you need to talk to somebody more qualified to help, maybe Dr. Barron since you know him so well."

"No! I could never tell him," Angie protests. Realizing that her strong reaction might give away her secret, she explains, "He's too close to my mother."

"Then, what about your mother, she..."

"Absolutely not! She's the last person I would want to know about this. If she hadn't gotten married right before I was born, I'd be just another Walker County bastard. It would kill her to find out that I have made the same mistake, especially since I'm not going to get married."

"Then, maybe my dad would know a contact for you. I think he's had to deal with this before." Angie's greatest fear grips her insides. She must end this discussion before she slips and reveals the name of the man who planted the seed growing in her belly.

"I think I'm O. K. now, Katy," she says, rubbing the remaining tears from her cheeks. "I know what I have to do. Thanks for being here for me."

"You're going for the D&C?" Without answering, Angie opens the top drawer and takes the money out of the envelope. She folds the bills around the note and stuffs them into her jacket pocket. Then she drags a matched set of luggage from under her bed.

"What are you doing?"

Angie stuffs her clothes into the luggage, ignoring her roommate's persistent questions. "Don't know why I'm taking these with me, the shape I'm in," she quips as she dumps cosmetics into a smaller case. "Here, I don't have room for these," she hands Katy two large cans of hair spray.

"When will you be back? You know finals start in two weeks," Katy's inquiry about Angie's plans meets with silence. "I might as well be talking to the door for heaven's sake." Angie cocks her head and gazes at the cans of hair spray, then looks at Katy. No words are necessary.

Katy gets the message, "You're leaving for good aren't you, not coming back? What about classes, voice lessons, your choir job, and…"

Angie snaps the luggage shut and wedges the makeup case under one arm. She grasps the handles, drags the two heavy pieces off her bed and makes her way to the door. "I've already missed too many classes, my voice teacher has given up on me and I haven't been to choir practice for a month. Take my books and sell them at the bookstore; I haven't cracked a single one of them."

"What'll I do with the money? Will you let me know where to send it? What about your sheets and towels, your favorite pillow, and your Raggedy Ann?" Katy walks around the room pointing out things Angie is leaving behind.

"You keep it all."

"I can't let you do this, Angie. You're not thinking straight right now. Come and sit down and let's finish talking about it."

"I'm gone, but I do appreciate your trying to help. I'll be in touch."

"Let me carry your pillow and Raggedy Ann to the car for you. You wouldn't last a week without your favorite bedfellows. What's more, I'll pack the rest of your stuff in some boxes and keep them until I hear from you again. And that includes the money for your books," Katy says as she fishes the empty scotch bottle from the trashcan. Then she grabs a pillow and Raggedy Ann and follows her fleeing roommate down the hall.

Angie points the car south to the Bessemer Super Highway, and then turns west. It seems to take forever to drive away from Birmingham, every traffic signal turning red, but she needs the time to think. She passes the Bessemer city limits sign and turns into a Texaco station to check the address on Ollie's note before heading downtown. The numbered streets laid out in squares make it easy to locate the doctor's office. Angie hesitates at a sign in front of a church building next door to the clinic: *Think before you sink.* She parks across the street from the squat brick building partially hidden behind a wall of painted designer concrete blocks that form a pattern of X's and O's resembling tic-tac-toe. Angie ponders the situation: *It's not big enough for a hospital and the doctor's name is barely visible above the street number painted on the block wall. I don't like the looks of this place.* Nothing fits Angie's concept of a medical building where professionals can help solve her problem, so she throws the gearshift into low and speeds away from the abortionist's laboratory.

Back on Highway 11, she stops at a burger and shake drive-in to placate her rumbling stomach. Rather than choose curb service, Angie goes inside so she can use the bathroom. Sitting in a booth munching on the hamburger, she ponders returning to the abortion clinic. *That will solve my problem once and for all. I remember another music major that dropped out of college after one quarter to return to New Orleans to sing in her brother's band. That's it, New Orleans, a perfect place to take my problem, not Bessemer, or Birmingham, or Mimosa. All I need to do is find my way to New Orleans.*

Angie approaches a truck driver in the parking lot, "Mister, can you tell me which road to take to New Orleans?"

"That's easy, just get on number 11 and keep going 'til you see the biggest lake in the South," he laughs, "then turn right. Just don't go too far unless you wanna go shrimping."

Angie checks her money supply and the gasoline gauge before beginning her journey. Tooling down Highway 11, she sings along with every country tune that Pinestraw Davis plays on station WWOK until the station fades to a crackle. Then she dials up other disc jockeys whose selections suggest that her troubled life won't get any easier. Angie's predicament is the stuff country music is made of.

As she approaches Laurel, Mississippi the big red ball dips below the western horizon, relief to her tired eyes. Angie realizes daylight is about to fade quickly and she's only half way there. Not wanting to drive all night, Angie stops to rest at a tourist court outside of town. The indignant older man at the desk snorts, "We don't rent rooms to unescorted ladies, don't run that kind of business." The image of his lurid sneer follows her down Highway 11 and through town. Not wishing to be mistaken for a lady of the evening, Angie drives a few miles further to a roadside picnic area, parks behind one of the concrete tables and tries to catch some sleep before moving on.

Truckers getting an early start wake her before dawn. She crawls out of the car to relieve the kinks in her joints and approaches an antique water fountain. "Hey there, good looking, what-cha got cooking," a male voice chimes through the misty air. A man about her age emerges from the shadows a few feet away zipping up his fly after seeking relief behind a tree. A red bandana headband not quite controlling his wiry hair, alerts Angie to possible danger. She walks vigorously toward her car, but he catches up with her. "Hey, where ya goin' sweet baby?" He races ahead and places his dirty hand over the door so she can't open it. "You out here on the road all by yo' lonesome? What a shame," he smirks. His pungent body odor overpowers her and draws her stomach tight. Whether from fright or her morning ritual, Angie throws up in his arrogant hippie face, causing him to curse and back off. Raucous laughter breaks out near the tree he had used as a urinal. Three more unwashed campers hoot and holler as he recoils in disgust, trying to remove his vomit-drenched shirt.

"I reckon if you're so ugly you cause her to puke, then you'd better leave her alone," the taller of the trio shouts. "Clean up puke-head and let's roll." The four men retreat to a rainbow colored Volkswagen bus just beyond the row of picnic tables. Angie returns to the water fountain, shaken but triumphant, to wash her face, then hits the road for New Orleans.

On the outskirts of the big city, Angie finds a pay phone to call her former partner in music theory class. Her unusual last name should be easy to find, but Angie opens the phone book and faces a half page of Thibideauxs listed. She searches her memory to recall Vickie's father's name or street address. Sliding her finger down the worn page, Angie almost gives up hope until she reaches the last name on the list, Victoria Thibideaux. "That's her," gasps Angie. "She's got her own phone."

The phone burrs in Angie's ear at least a dozen times before a sleepy voice drawls, "Who the hell's ringing my damn phone this time of day?" Angie's watch indicates noon.

"Vicki, is that you?" Angie asks, barely recognizing her friend's husky voice.

"Sure the hell is, who'd you think would answer...wait a minute...is this Angie?"

"Sure the hell is!"

"Well, excuse my bad manners, honey, where are you?"

"Almost in New Orleans."

"Here...in town? Can you come by and say hello?"

Following Vicki's directions, she finds the apartment easily, an old brick walkup with two balconies, one for each of the two upper levels. The strong stench of urine in the stairwell immediately marks the building as a refuge for winos. She knocks on the third floor apartment door; Vicki had warned the bell's out of order. Her friend greets her warmly, pulls her inside and locks the door. "You probably notice this is not quite the elite section of town. Did you lock your car?"

"No, lock's broke."

"Anything valuable in it?"

"Only my luggage."

"Hell, let's haul ass and bring it in before somebody lifts it." Vickie throws on a chenille robe and leads Angie down the squalid stairwell. Two men in ragged coats too heavy for the warm humid day are already stalking her car. "Nice car," one of the men comments with a sly grin as he draws his gloved finger across the hood.

"I've called the cops, bozo, so just wait right there 'til they get here," Vicki yells. The men, not sure if they should call her bluff, disappear around the corner. "Is everything there?"

Angie opens the driver's side door and looks inside. "My two bags are in the back seat. Damn, my makeup case is gone."

"Consider your ass lucky," Vicki says, offering no sympathy. "Let's get these bags upstairs and visit a while."

Vicki offers her guest one of the two beers in the refrigerator, but Angie declines and asks for a glass of water instead. "You don't drink this crappy tap water unless it's boiled, honey."

Angie finds herself studying her former classmate. *I can't believe how much she's changed in four months—a few pounds heavier, streaked hair and language that would put my own daddy to shame.*

"Let me move this crap off the couch so you can sit down. I know you're wondering what a nice lady like me is doing in a goddamn place like this," Vickie snickers. "It's simple, I moved out of my parents' house to make it big in the Bourbon Street music scene. I'm not there yet but I'm making enough to pay the rent." Vicki walks to the window to keep a vigil on Angie's car, then glances at her watch. "Time for me to shower and doll up for tonight's gig."

"I'm sorry I've kept you so long. I'd better get out of here." Angie reaches for her bags.

"Wait a sec, hon, have you got a place to crash tonight?" Angie shakes her head. "What an asshole I am. You've come all this way and have no place to lay your weary head. I should know better. I go to work around five-thirty and don't get in until about two in the morning, so why don't you sleep in my bed and I'll sack out on the couch."

Angie protests, but Vicki insists. "The only problem is we have to do something with your car. If you leave it on the street, it'll wind up stripped and in the canal. I'll think of something while I shower. It's my most productive time of day," Vicki laughs.

Emerging from the shower, Vicki suggests that Angie drive her to work and park her car in a nearby garage over night for a buck or two. "Tomorrow we'll pay my parents a visit, leave your car and catch the bus back to the Latin Quarter."

The next day the two women take the long drive across town to deposit the car. Angie takes the opportunity to confess her plight to Vicki. "Shit, I knew something was screwy, with you leaving school all of a sudden like this," she says. "You just plan on staying in my little hellhole, 'til you decide what you gonna do with the little bas...the baby."

By the time they return to Vicki's apartment, Angie has completed the rest of the story except the name of the man responsible for her pregnancy. "I hope you won't be shocked when I tell you that he's a minister, a married one at that," Angie says.

"Shocked? Hell, if you'd been down here it would've been a priest. There are all kinds of little Jesuit bastards romping through the bayous," Vicki laughs. Angie cringes and walks over and looks out the window to hide the tears that trickle down her cheeks. "I'm sorry honey, I didn't mean to be so flip. I reckon living in America's cesspool has turned me to shit."

"That's all right. I just don't know what I'm going to do. Maybe I should go on back to Bessemer and let the doctor clean me out. I just don't know..."

Vicki becomes unusually pensive as she studies Angie's abdomen. She lights a cigarette and decides to do some confessing of her own. "Look, Angie, I want to tell you something. I didn't leave school last December to sing in my brother's band. Hell, I don't even have a brother. I got knocked up by a shit-face married man, too."

"I didn't know…"

"Yeah, but I brought it on myself."

"Oh?"

"I got a wild hair and went to my voice lesson without a bra under my sheer yellow blouse. When I took off my jacket, his eyes about popped out of their sockets and a few minutes later something did pop out of his pants. I knew then why he always locked the door during voice lessons."

"O my gosh, you mean Mr. …?"

"Uh uh, remember, we're not mentioning any names, you'll just have to use your imagination."

"Did you tell him you were pregnant?"

"Didn't tell anybody. I just took my finals and hauled ass back home before the holidays."

"What did your parents say when you told them why you came home?" Angie imagines how her own parents would react to her condition.

"They just thought I was home for Christmas. Dad fussed a little about spending so much money on tuition, so I took a job waiting tables."

"So, what happened to the baby?"

"Down the toilet," Vicki shrugs. Noticing the shock on Angie's face, she recants, "I got lucky, had a miscarriage. It was on New Year's Day while Mom and Dad were watching the Rose Parade on television. I woke up feeling sick, went to the bathroom and St. Agony took over from there."

"St. Agony?"

"Yeah, the patron saint of pain and suffering. Well, enough of this. I might start feeling sorry for myself again. We need to deal with your situation right now." Vicki checks her watch. "We've got two hours before I go to work. Do you want me to show you around the Quarter?"

"That'll be nice," Angie said, "but first, why did you move out of your parents' place to this...?"

"This roaches paradise? That's a long story. It involves a guy who turned out to be a jerk, a fuss with my dad, a singing job that fizzled and a mixture of guilt and pride. It'll make a good novel one day when I get back to college and learn how to write."

A few days later, Angie finds a part-time job serving pizza at a sidewalk café. She offers to pay her share of the rent, but Vicki insists she save her money to pay the hospital bill when the baby comes. The combination of fear and indecision carries Angie past the window of opportunity to abort, leaving her only one option.

As summer approaches, the tourist season attracts more musicians to the jazz Mecca of the world. A foursome of string players from Nashville stops by for pizza one afternoon. Angie serves their order and inquires about the instrument cases at their feet. "Oh, we're just down here trying to bring a little country music to the bayou," quips the fiddle player. "But, we don't have a steady gig, yet."

"Which one is the singer?" Angie asks.

"We can't decide," replies the guy balancing his banjo case upright with one hand. "Our songbird's folks wouldn't let her come with us, so we just take turns hollering out the words while we play."

"That doesn't sound so hot," Angie said. "Y'all need to have somebody to sell the songs, somebody that doesn't have to think about playing the right chords and the hot licks." The guys nod in agreement and finish off their second pizza. "Do y'all know any Hank Williams?"

"Like what, *Jambalaya, Kowaliga, Hey, Good Looking?* You name it, we can play it."

"And I can sing it," announces Angie. She looks around at the empty tables, "Y'all get tuned up while I bus these tables, and I'll show you how Hank Williams should sound."

Within a few minutes the guys kick off a chorus of *Cripple Creek* to warm up, except for the bass guitar player. He can't find an electrical outlet for his amp. They play anyway. Angie joins them on the next number and within a few minutes a crowd gathers around the sidewalk café. A policeman stops by and keeps the street clear so cars can pass. The café owner likes her singing; it's drawing in more customers at a time when business is usually slow. But he needs her to serve pizzas.

After an hour and a half of providing entertainment for the pizza customers and wandering tourists, the guys put away their instruments and prepare to leave. "Wait a minute," the owner calls out, "beer for everybody." He sets two pitchers of beer on a table inside and asks Angie to get some mugs out of the cooler. "What would you boys say to playing here every afternoon for beer and pizza, you know for a couple hours?"

The players look at each other pondering whether to accept or reject the non-paying gig. The fiddle player finally speaks up, "It won't work without the girl. She's what the people hang around to hear."

"But, who'll wait on the customers? I'm the cook and she's the only server this time of day," moans the owner.

"That's the deal, we play, she sings," chants the banjo player.

"Hey, wait a minute," Angie wants to add her two cents to the negotiations. "I love singing, but who's going to pay me for those two hours?" Reluctantly, the owner agrees to keep her on the payroll and hire someone else to wait tables.

The fiddle player ambles over to where Angie is cleaning off a table. "The boys and I think you're just fantastic. What would you think about joining up with us when we find a regular gig?"

"Well, I'm flattered," she says, looking at the other three who stand like Kowaliga, waiting for a sign from their leader. "But, I'm expecting a baby in five months. I wouldn't be much good to y'all after that."

The fiddler confers with his partners, then motions her to join them. "Look, we're only here for the summer. Then we'll head back to college. Surely you can last that long." They seal the deal. The guys crowd around Angie for a group hug.

"Hey, we don't even know your name," the banjo player says.

"And I don't know yours either."

"This here's Mark, that's Andy, Steve's the guitar picker and my name's Roy," says the fiddle player, "like in Roy Acuff. We call our band *The Farmers' Market*."

"I'm Angie, Angie Shook."

"Hmm, no offense, Angie, but can we change your last name to something more glamorous, you know, a stage name?" Angie fakes a little pout. "I have an idea," he says. "What's your maiden name?" Instead of answering his question, Angie begins to finger the angel medallion hanging on the chain around her neck, she looks down at it, and turns it around to face her.

"I should've told you boys my stage name — Crystal Angel."

12

> *September 30, 1963*
>
> *Dear Preacher Peterson,*
> *A friendly warning—beware of taking sides with outside agitators and communists coming to destroy our Christian way of life. The next explosion might be closer than you think.*
>
> *A friend*

The head usher pushes through the gathering choir members and whispers in Paul Peterson's ear. Paul gasps and, without hesitation, walks briskly down the aisle before the processional can begin. A hush falls over the congregation as their pastor steps up to the pulpit and raises a hand for the organist to stop the prelude. After wiping away his tears, he braces himself behind the pulpit and labors to clear his throat. After a couple of aborted attempts to speak, he recovers and begins, "My brothers and sisters, a few moments ago I received word..." he pauses with a deep sigh, praying for a steady voice to continue..."that an explosion destroyed a Baptist church in downtown Birmingham just fifteen minutes ago." The Hope congregation releases a chorus of moans and utterances of disbelief." Paul waits—not only for the bustling chatter to subside but to compose his next words. Wiping his eyes again, he clears his throat, "We don't know the details, but the radio reports the possibility of many casualties." Then, mustering up his most solemn and reverent tone, he adds, "My dear friends, we should all bow our heads and pray for our Negro brothers and sisters who entered their church to worship..."

"No!" A thunderous voice from the rear shatters the somber atmosphere. "No! You said it was a Baptist church, preacher, not a nigra church." Paul stares wide-eyed at the man whose outburst is rendering Hope's sanctuary a devilish conundrum.

The man stumbles his way past others sitting on the same pew. "I'm not gonna stay and listen to any prayers for nigra troublemakers," he says as he elbows his way through choir members huddled in the narthex and leaves the building. Paul begins his prayer and by the time he pronounces "amen," a dozen more men have left the church with their wives tagging along.

Across town at St. Francis Methodist, Ollie Barron receives word of the bombing about the same time as his fellow pastor at Hope Methodist and ponders whether to announce it from the pulpit. His service, scheduled to begin thirty minutes later than Paul's, affords Ollie time to confer with H. R. Wood. He finds H. R. in the Sunday school office counting the Sunday school collection. Pulling him into the hallway, Ollie whispers, "Harry Poole just heard on his car radio that a downtown church was blown apart about fifteen minutes ago." H. R. hands the money to the Sunday school Superintendent and hurries out to his car with Ollie at his heels. He switches on the ignition to activate the radio and they listen to a breathless reporter. "Sounds like some people got killed this time," Ollie says. "I can hardly make out what he's saying because of the sirens and screams. It sounds tragic, but I suppose I should go ahead and start the service, it's almost eleven o'clock. Are you going to stay by the radio?"

H. R. nods and turns up the volume. As Ollie heads back towards the church, H. R. calls to him, "Preacher, don't mention this to the congregation."

His directive startles Ollie. "But, don't you think they should know, in case there's trouble?"

The real estate magnate grabs the door of his Lincoln and pulls his large frame out of the driver's seat. He motions for Ollie to come closer. "Just remember you're a preacher, not a news reporter. This is not our problem, so let's keep it out of our worship service." By the time the prelude begins, word of the bombing had spread among the worshippers faster than a virus in the nursery. Ollie enters the sanctuary and takes his place on the dais. During the opening hymn, Chad whispers to him, "Did you hear about the bombing downtown?"

Ollie looks straight ahead at the congregation without changing his expression and replies, "It's not our problem, so lets just sing the hymn."

At Hope Methodist Paul Peterson leaves the service so distraught he cancels dinner plans with his daughter and her fiancé. In spite of the cancellation, Katy and Lee go ahead to the parsonage to watch the news reports on television. "This is so depressing," Katy agonizes from the hassock as she munches carrot sticks and celery. "Lee, I want you to take me down there. Surely, there's something I can do to help." Her stunned fiancé quietly chokes down his last bite of sandwich.

Lorna objects, "You two just stay put. Look at those bloody firemen. If they're not welcome, imagine what those angry black folks will do to fresh white meat."

"Momma!"

"Your mother's right, baby, this is as close to the action as you should get for a while," Paul asserts.

"Sounds to me like you got pretty close yourself in church today," Katy counters.

"You should've been here, Katy, you would have been proud of your dad," Lorna says. "Afterwards, I didn't know whether to shout 'hallelujah' or rush over here and start packing."

"Oh, it wasn't that bad, honey, just a few hotheads that always overreact. They'll calm down when they realize that innocent children were caught in the crossfire between radicals on both sides. Cooler heads will prevail after this."

"Come on, Dad, you're beginning to sound like Bishop Grand in his letter to Martin Luther King. Some compare him to Lord Chamberlain when he appeased Hitler. And you know what—London got bombed anyway."

"The Bishop was only one of a dozen clergy who signed that letter, and it was addressed to the Southern Christian Leadership Conference, not Dr. King."

"I know, Dad, but it was King's answer written from the Birmingham Jail that made Bishop Grand and his ilk seem more like Philistines than Prophets."

Paul decides to keep a low profile for a few days to allow time for healing and reflection in the aftermath of the horrendous bombing. There are no obvious repercussions following the spontaneous walkout by a handful of members on September 15. He sees it as a move toward reconciliation when the wife of a dissident accompanies Lorna, Katy and him to the funeral service for three of the bombing victims. As all four walk to the distant cemetery alongside a rabbi and an Episcopal priest, Paul is concerned, but not altogether surprised by the absence of Bishop Grand.

~~~

The church bombing in Birmingham makes only a blip on Angie Shook's radar screen, a mere drop that dissipates in the heat of her own predicament. The guys of the Farmers Market Band return to Belmont College in Nashville after Labor Day leaving her jobless. The tourist season closes with a deadening thud like a curtain falls on the final act of a boisterous musical, suspending her career as New Orleans' answer to Patsy Cline.

Angie's disappointment is short-lived. She's only a few weeks from delivery and needs to find a cheap hospital. As she thumbs through the Yellow Pages this morning, her droopy-eyed roommate shuffles into the tiny kitchen. "I sure could use some coffee."

"It's on the hot plate, still warm I guess," Angie mumbles.

"What're you doing, doll?" Vicki massages her eyes, hoping to get them open.

"Looking for a hospital, is there a free one around here?"

"You mean it's time for the baby to say 'hello you piss-ant world'?"

"Just about, but I hear they come anytime in the last couple of months. I'm ready to get it over with," Angie flips the pages.

"I know we haven't said much about what you're going do after the baby comes, but..."

"I really appreciate your not being too nosy. I guess I've just blocked it out of my mind...don't want to think about the future. One thing I notice is you don't have a nursery here," Angie giggles. "It seems I've been psyching up all along for not keeping the baby."

"Good choice, if you ask me. In that case, I know just the place. You won't find it in that phone book. You'll have to let your legs do the work, you know, go in person."

"Where?"

"I don't know."

"You don't know? Are you jerking me around, Vickie? That's no way to treat a woman with child."

"No, no," said Vicki, setting her cup on the table. "I mean, they keep the place hidden behind a big stone wall somewhere out near the lake. A cheerleader I knew in high school had her baby there. But, she wouldn't tell anybody where she went."

"Why, was she afraid?"

"I dunno, but it's a very private deal. She had to sign some kind of secret paper, probably threatening her with a million years in purgatory if she squeals. I'll go with you to talk to the priest at my church. Better pack a bag. He'll probably want me to leave you there and let him handle it."

Two days later, Angie finds herself a passenger in a van being driven by a nun with another sister riding shotgun. After a long silent drive along Lake Pontchartrain, the van turns off on a side road through a canopy of giant oaks bearded with Spanish moss. The van stops at a tall wrought iron gate. One nun gets out, unlocks the gate and secures it again after their vehicle passes through. As the van crunches slowly along the crushed shell driveway, a tiny foot kicks against Angie's abdomen, foreshadowing its own birthday. The van parks in front of a large two-story plantation-style home with tall dingy columns lined across the front. The nun takes Angie's luggage and leads her up the stairs to a broad old veranda where gentleman growers once gathered to smoke cigars and sip bourbon.

Inside the painted-over brick house, black-robed figures glide back and forth casting quick furtive glances at their new tenant. An older nun appears behind a large desk and startles Angie with the quick ring of a brass hand bell that summons a sister. She approaches Angie with a painted smile, expressing nothing.

"I'm Sister Margaret, please come with me and let's get the paperwork out of the way as quickly as possible and then get you to a room. I know you must be exhausted, in your condition," her words oozing with self-righteous condemnation. Angie grits her teeth and follows the sister to a table behind the desk. "Please have a seat and read over these documents before you sign them." Angie flips through several pages of convoluted legal terms not knowing what they imply, doesn't care. Sister Margaret looks away, pretending she doesn't observe Angie's casual perusal of the contract.

Angie's thoughts skip to the future as she tries to avoid thinking about the present. She takes the pen and absently writes *Lily Angeline.* Unintentionally signing her birth name triggers a flood of remorse. *I wish my momma were here. I just want to get this over with, get out of here, and leave it all behind. But Momma, would you want me to leave my baby behind? No...no, I'm not going to cry. There's no other choice, I have to do it this way.* She shoves the papers across the table and follows Sister Margaret to her room.

By the time labor begins several days later, Angie comes to understand that she is nothing more than an anonymous donor of an unwanted baby who will become a commodity at the disposal of the orphanage next door. The nuns rush her downtown to a large Catholic hospital. She remembers being admitted and being given an injection—but really nothing else until she awakens to a nurse calling her, but not by her name. "Time to wake up, Miss." Angie opens her eyes and tries to ask about her baby, but the nuns are busy, too detached to answer her questions.

Later that afternoon, a doctor stops by and instructs the nurse to prepare the patient for dismissal the following day. The nurse asks, "Miss, is there someone I can call to meet you at the church to assist you?"

Angie gives her Vicki's number. "She may not answer if you call after five. She works at night.

The nurse replies, "It's Columbus Day. Everything's closed."

The next day before noon, Angie signs her release from the hospital. She endures the painful ride in the van back to Vicki's church. A wheelchair awaits her arrival under the portico. One nun wheels her into the church office while the other carries her bag. They steal away quietly as they had come.

Vicki's mother is waiting for Angie. "You remember me don't you, darling?" Mrs. Thibideaux coos with her sugar cane laced accent. "Bless your heart, I'm awfully sorry you're not well." She orders an older black man in a white service coat to take Angie's bag. "Take it to my car, Jerald."

During the ride to her house, Mrs. Thibideaux goes on and on about her brother's recent bout with appendicitis. Angie is puzzled momentarily, then realizes Vicki must have told her mother she'd an appendectomy instead of a baby.

Angie recovers in the luxury of the Thibideaux's home by dining on rich food and lounging around the pool. Two weeks later, Vicki rescues her roommate from this leisurely opulence before she becomes infected. "You going back to Alabama," Vicki asks as the bus bumps along the highway back to town, "or do you plan to hang out in Cajun Hell a while longer?"

"There's nothing for me back home and my scholarship is probably down the tube by now."

"The snowbirds start migrating in for the holidays pretty soon. If you feel up to working, I talked to a guy last night about you; he's looking for a singer."

~~~

Christmas 1963 approaches as Birmingham is still reeling from the aftershocks of the bombing of Sixteenth Street Baptist Church and President Kennedy's assassination. Pastors push themselves to the limit searching for ways to lead their flocks out of the darkness and onto paths of righteousness, toward the Babe of Bethlehem. Paul Peterson has the idea that music might provide the spark that can light the path for that spiritual pilgrimage.

"My people are so wiped out that it will take a miracle to get them in the Christmas spirit this year," Paul admits to Chad Willis. "I'm calling to ask if you have any suggestions that might lift them out of their depression...Yes, Chad, I asked our choir director, but he is preoccupied with his own Christmas program at Simpson High. I even offered to devote one Advent morning service to special music...He thinks it's too late to begin rehearsing...Well, thanks anyway, Chad. I know your choir will enjoy doing the Boar's Head Festival again this year...What, you're not doing it?...It doesn't fit Dr. Barron's plan for spiritual renewal?...Oh, I'm sorry...Yes, I know...maybe next year...Yes, you have a wonderful holiday, too...Goodbye."

"Knock, knock, may I come in?" the cheerful holiday voice sings out as Paul hangs up the phone. "Marge is away from her desk, I hope I'm not intruding."

"Not at all, Marilyn, I need someone to brighten up my day. Come on in." The Children's Director peeks around Paul's office door before entering. "What can I do for you?"

"I really hate to bother you with this, but I'm putting together the literature order for next quarter," her smile fades.

"And..."

"Sunday school teachers are requesting lessons from Rapture Press instead of the Methodist Publishing House."

"Do you mean that fundamentalist pulp trash disguised as Bible lessons? Heavens, I'm not ready to throw down the gauntlet before adult Sunday school classes. I've yet to find an antidote for hardening of the categories, so, what else?"

With a grimace, she places the order form on his desk. "It's not the adult classes I'm concerned about, these requests are from the children's teachers."

"Damn!" he blurts. "Excuse my French, Marilyn, but damn."

"My sentiments exactly, Brother, no apology necessary."

"It's about those illustrations, isn't it?"

"One in particular, it shows the children holding hands and playing together—black, white and Asian.

"I think I know what's behind this, but I may be wrong."

"No, I think you're right, sir. It's the racial thing. From the time that drawing appeared in a Sunday school book, teachers have been uneasy. Somebody's been stirring up trouble behind my back and I don't know who's doing it."

"Don't send in that order. I want to meet with the children's division teachers this Sunday…Let's think how we can work this out to make sure they all show up."

Marilyn twists her lips and then suggests a plan. "This Sunday the children are supposed to bring their offerings for the Children's Home. I'll meet with all the classes together to collect their envelopes and…and, maybe tell them a story during Sunday school time."

"No, I want you at the meeting. Who can we enlist to tell the story?"

"What about Katy? She's good with the children."

"Then you'll have to ask her, present it as a favor to you. She's all up in the air planning her wedding right now. And one other thing, don't tell the teachers about the meeting. Just surprise them Sunday morning. We'll meet in the fifth grade classroom."

When Marilyn convenes the meeting a teacher announces, "It's a Communist plot. It's common knowledge that Martin Luther King is a card-carrying Communist who's trying to destroy our way of life here in the South. Look!" she displays an enlarged copy of the infamous picture of mixed race children. "Here's proof."

Paul Peterson bites his tongue, but sticks to his promise to allow the dozen women seated around him to have their say. Their body language indicates that the intemperate comments are comforting to some, but unsettling to others. "And what's more," the spokeswoman continues, "the Methodist Church is being sucked in by the World Council of Churches, which sends money to support the demonstrations in Birmingham." Three teachers nod in agreement. Then silence envelopes the room like a shroud as Paul stands to address the teachers.

"And what about the rest of you, do you agree with Agnes' point?" Most eyes are glued to the floor. "Edith?" Paul persists. "Kathryn?" he waits. "Sadie?" When it becomes apparent that nobody will speak, Paul inhales and prepares to counter Agnes' argument. To his surprise, a white haired woman raises her hand.

"Yes, Kathleen?" Paul recognizes her.

She remains seated and turns to face the empty space between Paul and the teachers seated behind her. Resting her dark rimmed glasses against her white pleated blouse, she fiddles with the chain that holds them as she speaks softly. "My husband helped to build this educational building and he was Chairman of the Trustees when the new sanctuary was built in '55. Before he died last year, I made two promises to him. One was to see that he was buried in the Hope cemetery and the other was to make sure that no Negroes, except he used an expression I cannot repeat, that no Negroes would ever cross the threshold of our church."

Four of the teachers nod and whisper "yes."

Kathleen glances at the women and frowns. "I have been teaching sixth graders in my church for over thirty years, since my own Joshua misbehaved prompting the teacher to quit." A muffled laughter breaks the tension in the room. "Many of those children I taught are now upstanding members of this church, one of them joined the army and never returned—my Joshua. I must admit that when Agnes' husband told me about the Communist connection with the Methodist Church, I agreed with her reasons for wanting to change Sunday school literature."

Agnes' confederates nod their heads, eye each other and inch forward on their chairs.

"But," she says, followed by an intense hush, "to paraphrase last Sunday's scripture reading, I'm afraid that I have been attracted to waterless springs and mists driven by a storm of racial strife." She turns to face Paul. "I suppose you called this meeting, Brother Paul, to prompt us to face our own fears and prejudice. I must admit, it worked, at least with me." Paul resists an overwhelming urge to affirm her statement. "However, a tempest rages within my heart and it shows no sign of letting up. I loved my husband dearly and I love my church. So, which do I choose? Do I honor my departed husband's wishes or bend to the will of the Methodist Church? I regret that I cannot tear my soul asunder and remain loyal to both. Therefore, I regretfully tender my resignation as sixth grade teacher. It remains to be seen if I should also give up my membership in Hope Methodist."

Kathleen has drawn an indelible line between Paul and his Sunday school teachers. The complex reality, the depth, the encompassing breadth of the situation has caught Paul as completely unaware as would an abrupt descent of the Archangel Gabriel. He extends his hands upward in a gesture of surrender. "I suppose there is little more to say. Marilyn, will you please conclude the meeting while I finish preparing for the worship service?"

Paul ducks out and ambles thoughtfully along the atrium. *Those Sunday school teachers represent only the steam rising from the caldron. Before addressing the simmering conflict any further, I must present a carefully prepared defense of the Methodist Church's principles to the core leadership here at Hope.*

After the service concludes, Paul sends Lorna to eat out with Katy and Lee so he can retreat to his study to contemplate his next move. He lays his Bible and Hymnal on the desk beside Bonhoeffer's *Letters and Papers from Prison,* leafs through the book and reflects on his situation.

Yes, Bonhoeffer was right about how some people practice their religion. Here at Hope racial exclusion has become the center of religious practice for some members. These short-sighted individuals have extracted a simple illustration from a children's Sunday school book and blown the issues surrounding it out of proportion. They have removed Christ from the center of their faith and replace Him with a picture they transformed into an icon. Simply, within their belief system, their focus on this issue has made it more important than the Christ's message. What can I do to rebuff the rising tide of segregationist propaganda and prevent a major division of the congregation? I pray that God will guide me.

Paul closes Bonhoeffer's book and whether by fate or fortune opens the Hymnal to number 263. He reads the first stanza:

How appropriate, thank you, God. James Russell Lowell's words could not have come at a better time.

> Once to every man and nation
> Comes the moment to decide,
> In the strife of truth with falsehood,
> For the good or evil side...

There's no better opportunity than the present to take a firm stand against the bigotry that's spreading like cancer disguised as patriotism and loyalty. Ah, the upcoming Board meeting, that's the setting, the moment to decide...However, the last time I made a stand for truth...well, this third stanza says it all:

> By the light of burning martyrs,
> Christ, thy bleeding feet we track,
> Toiling up new Calvaries ever
> With the cross that turns not back...

I shudder to think what the Bishop will do if the Board rebels against my mandate to follow Methodist principles.

~~~

During the board meeting, Paul cannot keep his feet still, acting out a subconscious wish to run away from the men he is to confront in a few minutes. His mind wanders: *Only a year ago at*

St. Francis I mounted the scaffold of truth only to have a trusted leader slip a noose over the clerical stole that draped my neck. Paul grips his knees and, overlooking his poor record of predicting the actions of his parishioners, tries to look calm and casual as he counts the number of men he might depend on for support. *If only the Bishop had come forward and given his pastors some positive moral guidance instead of seeking backroom political solutions to the blatant racial injustices that gnaw away at the foundations of local churches.* Paul is certain of his position but he longs for a measure of confidence that should have come from the conference leadership—the Bishop, the District Superintendent, or even one or two distinguished pastors of lighthouse churches. He assumes the local leadership surrounding him will not tolerate racial prejudice within the walls of Hope Methodist. But will they remain silent as their pastor writes that ultimatum clearly on the virtual wall of hope?

"Brother Paul," the chairman beckons his pastor to the lectern, "We're ready for your report."

Paul prays silently for his message to come clear and strong as he faces his board members. "My dear friends, for a year I have had the privilege of concluding these meetings with a pastor's report, each one filled with optimism and hope for the future of this great church. We have experienced phenomenal growth in membership, finances and programs, even in the throes of conflicts and trials that have tested the very fabric of our faith. None of us in this room is guilty of inviting the turmoil that rages in our city. We have not lit a fuse to explode a bomb at a church or in any person's home. We have not attacked innocent people with baseball bats, bicycle chains or pistols. You and I did not cause the race riots in Birmingham."

A unified chorus of "amens" affirms Paul's introductory statements. "Yet, in our innocence we face a serious challenge." Paul picks up a Bible and raises it above his head. "The source of our faith, our wellspring of God's spirit, is under attack and we must take action to resist this evil intrusion. If we fail to take action, Hope will lose its identity as a Methodist Church and you will forfeit your right to be called Christians. As pastor of this church, I would like to clarify two issues that threaten to divide our congregation. First, in the matter of Sunday school literature, all of Hope's educational leaders will use only materials published by the Methodist Church in their classes, including youth counselors, leaders of Bible studies, etc." Agitated mumbles roll across the room. "Secondly, the doors of this church will remain open to all who wish to enter regardless of race or creed." The buzz in the room escalates to a rumble.

A man in the back of the room rises to speak over the noise. "Preacher, are you telling us that we can't have lessons from the Bible in Sunday school?"

Paul wonders: *Is this crisis precisely what Bonhoeffer meant by God grasping a pastor at the center of life rather than on the edges. Once again, I am being challenged by a man clinging to the edge of religiosity.* Paul prays silently for the courage of his faith and places the Bible on the lectern. All eyes focus, unyielding, on their pastor.

"No."

"Then what are you saying?" the man persists.

"Everyone who teaches within the walls of Hope will use materials published by the Methodist Church. It's that simple, Henry."

"And what if we don't?" Henry asks, turning his head from side to side looking for support. A few nod, but most have blank expressions.

"Then, I suppose you will have to find some other place to meet." Paul's response and staunch demeanor leave no question that he means business, although his heart is racing miles ahead of his mind.

Henry jumps to his feet, his nostrils flaring like a bull about to charge. "This is *our* church, preacher, not yours and we will teach whatever we want to in *our* Sunday school classes. What's more, as long as I'm an usher, I'll block anyone who comes to disrupt our worship services." A few men say "yes," but the growing tension in the room dampens their enthusiasm. Most of them have never experienced a minister taking a firm stand against the wishes of the board. The confrontation mortifies most of those in the room.

Paul stiffens and refuses to withdraw his gaze from Henry's agitated brow. "This is not your church, it belongs to God and the Methodist Church holds the deed. The property has been placed in the hands of duly elected trustees who may serve only as long as they follow the guidelines set forth in this book." He lifts a book gripped in his other hand. "The *Discipline of the Methodist Church* authorizes the pastor to provide guidance in spiritual matters and this issue, my fellow Christians, is a spiritual matter. Therefore, while I am pastor of Hope Methodist, no one shall be denied access to any gatherings in Jesus' name and those who seek to grow in their faith will be taught according to the Holy Bible and with literature approved by our denomination." Paul lowers the *Discipline* and waits for a response. Henry finally takes his seat, but grouses under his breath to the men near him.

The Chairman of the Board rises to adjourn the meeting, but a white haired gentleman on the front row stands and faces the assembly. "Mr. Chairman, if you will allow me a point of personal privilege, I would like to respond to our distinguished pastor's remarks." In spite of a stroke-induced lisp, Charles Hawthorn commands the group's full attention. Paul grips both sides of the lectern. This church pioneer, along with his sister, Kathleen, wields enormous influence. Paul senses his future at Hope teetering precariously as Charles begins. "As you all know, my momma and poppa helped to charter this church nearly seven decades ago. You've heard this a dozen times, but I was the first baby baptized in that log chapel that used to stand right about here before this building was erected. All three of my girls were raised in this church and now some of my grandchildren are in Sunday school and the youth department. Now, I didn't tell y'all that piece of history to justify what I'm about to say. But as Chairman of the

Board of Trustees, I feel obligated to respond to what our distinguished pastor has just reported, since he mentioned the trustees. As one who has invested his entire life helping to build this great church, I do not wish to stand by and watch it crumble over a disagreement. After all...we're not Baptists, are we?" Laughter breaks the tension in the room and everybody loosens up, except Paul who isn't sure where Mr. Hawthorn is headed with his remarks. "Many of you in this room send your children and, like me, your grandchildren to Sunday school to learn to live better lives, and to behave themselves. The lessons take hold with some, and with others, well, I don't know." Again some titters of laughter rise from the group. "The Sunday school that I went to in the old log chapel was not the same when my girls came along. And what's more, my grandchildren come here to a Sunday school different from that of their mothers. Everything's changed over the years, the buildings, the teachers, the clothes, the Sunday school books. Even the Bible is different. Now I'm not saying everything has changed for the better, but changes came along anyway. I for one do not regret that I now ride to church in an air-conditioned car instead of an old wagon pulled by a team of mules. That's one change for the better."

Then Mr. Hawthorn turns sideways to face Paul whose knuckles are now white from gripping the lectern so tightly. "So, what I'm trying to say, Brother Paul, is this—as a trustee I stand behind you one hundred per cent." Paul smiles and utters a weak "thank you" as Hawthorn concludes. "I may stand alone in this, but I respect your decision to help our church live up to its name, Hope Methodist." A smattering of polite applause rises from the group, but as the message sinks in, all but four men stand and pound out a thunderous ovation. Unknowingly, Hawthorn emerges as the Gideon Paul needs to liberate Hope's flock from their doubts.

~~~

The day after Easter, Paul picks up the telephone to place a rare call to St. Francis Methodist. "This is Dr. Barron speaking,"

Ollie projects his oval voice into the mouthpiece after being buzzed by Mrs. Green.

"And this is the Right Reverend M. Paul Peterson speaking," Paul answers with all the sarcasm he can muster.

"Oh, hello, Paul, I thought maybe you were the Bishop calling to congratulate me on my Easter sermon." Paul knows Ollie is blowing smoke, that it is Mrs. Green's custom to announce the names of all callers.

"Bishop Grand came to your service yesterday?" Paul asks, egging him on.

"Where else would he go?" Ollie revels in his response, sparing no mercy.

"Well, that's not why I called. I understand that you and Chad Willis are, how shall I put it, not singing in harmony right now."

"Between you and me and the lamppost, Chad has difficulty harmonizing with anyone. He's been that way since we were roommates in college," Ollie huffs.

"I'm surprised to hear you say that. You know he worked with me at Coal City while attending college," Paul counters, catching Ollie off guard. He had forgotten about that connection.

"So Chad asked you to patch things up between us, did he?" Ollie suggests, a note of defensiveness resounds in his response.

"No, he did not. Actually, I got my information from another source. What I was wondering is, if you would object to my approaching Chad about coming here to work with me."

"Mm...that's a bit surprising considering the circumstances at your church," Ollie says with a smirk.

"Circumstances, what do you mean?"

"I have sources, also. My sources tell me that most of your members left to build their own church just a few blocks from Hope. Won't that affect your budget? Are you sure you can afford a full-time music director?"

Paul is amazed at how the rumor has evolved, the number of dissident families now multitudes rather than the actual dozen. He instantly realizes that his nemesis is cleverly picking him for exact details of the rumored turmoil at Hope. "God will provide," Paul utters the euphemism for which there is no comeback. "What's your answer, Doctor Barron, yes or no.

"Yes...I mean no," Ollie says. "I have no objection to your approaching Chad if he's that unhappy here. As a matter of fact, I've spoken to a couple of likely prospects for his position anyway."

"Yes, I know," says Paul.

"You know? That's impossible? Our discussions were held in the strictest confidence."

"Haven't you learned anything, Ollie? There's very little a pastor does that doesn't get back to his congregation," Paul says, trying to rattle his pious colleague's cage, "so you'd better watch your step, Dr. Barron, someone knows your every move."

Paul chuckles and hangs up the phone not realizing how deep an incision his mischievous remark has cut. Ollie sits and stares at the phone, suddenly curious about what has become of Angie Shook.

13

> *March 3, 1964*
>
> *Dear Rev. Peterson:*
>
> *I misplaced Katy's address, so please tell her I'll be happy to be in her wedding, even sing if she wants me to.*
>
> *Sincerely,*
>
> *Angie Shook*

"Angie, hon, I can't stand watching you mope around like this forever. Pull yourself together. You've had time to get over that baby thing." Vickie tries to draw her friend out of her post-natal doldrums.

"I guess you're right, you go on to work and I'll get cleaned up and look for a job." Angie exorcises the demons that have possessed her for the past month by re-inventing Crystal Angel—a new and improved model. She takes a gig with a '50's style dance band for the holiday season at Live Oak Country Club. To compensate for low pay, the aging band leader drives her back and forth every night except Mondays. *No wonder the band can't keep singers*, Angie thinks, *not enough money in this job to keep the gas lights burning.*

After New Year's Eve, the band takes a break, leaving Angie idle again. Not wanting to drift back into depression sitting alone in the apartment every day, she hooks up with an itinerate rock-a-billy group that has drifted into New Orleans hoping to land an engagement for Mardi Gras season. The *La Paree* Club books the band for weekends and also hires Angie to wait tables on weeknights. Angie's thoughts turn to Mimosa. It doesn't take long for the glittery image of cabaret singing to lose its sparkle. Even with Mardi Gras in full swing, Angie's Mimosa memories crowd out the revelry that surrounds her. The yearning to reconnect, to restore the parental bonds she had so abruptly severed overwhelms her. Angie resolves to find a way to return to her home.

~~~

Birmingham's racial unrest threatens to derail Katy Peterson's preparations for a spring wedding, sending her mother into a tailspin. "Paul, you need to talk with Katy about keeping her priorities straight," Lorna complains to her husband. "She has to realize that she can't single-handedly rectify Birmingham's social sins."

"How can we complain, Lorna? We have taught Katy, since she uttered her first words, to follow her conscience."

"I know, but can't we figure some way to distract her until after the wedding? Then she becomes Leland's responsibility." Paul laughs and agrees to talk to their daughter.

As they strip the ornaments from the Christmas tree, Paul makes Katy an offer. "Your mother and I thought it would be a good idea for you to take a few days off and go to the beach, or Lake Junaluska. What do you think?"

"In the dead of winter? No way, Dad. Besides, I have too much on my plate.

"I understand, my dear, but you need some R & R, away from here, just a few days to refresh your…"

"I don't want to be away from Lee right now. We have a wedding to plan."

"Perhaps you and Leland could," Paul glances at Lorna pleading for support, "could persuade Art and Lisa to go somewhere with you…"

"And talk about the wedding ceremony," Lorna adds.

"Dad, Mom! I can't ask Lee to pay my way. After all, we're not married yet."

Paul stuffs the angel from the top of the tree in a box. "Your mother and I will help, sort of a pre-wedding gift."

After much persuasion, Katy gives in and accepts train tickets to New Orleans during Mardi gras. Art and Lisa happily volunteer to join her and Leland in their "wild" excursion to the Big Easy.

Their last night in New Orleans, the foursome seeks refuge from the parades and frenzied revelers, ready to enjoy dinner and dancing off the beaten track. The concierge at their hotel recommends a small café with good food, a live band and a dance floor. A short cab ride later, they stand in the crowded foyer of *La Paree* Café waiting for a table as the band competes with the loud chatter. Suddenly, the chatter is reduced to a hushed buzz as a female steps on stage and takes the microphone. "Listen to that voice," Lee whispers to Katy.

"Sounds vaguely familiar," muses Katy as she elbows her way to the bar trying to get a peek at the singer.

"Yeah, a lot like Patsy Cline," Art says.

"Overhearing their remarks, a bar patron volunteers, "She's a whole lot better'n that band she's with." The hostess signals their table is ready. They zigzag through the crowd and smoke to a table with a red and white-checkered vinyl cover, where each orders a beer. When Katy finally gains a clear view of the singer, she tugs excitedly on Lee's coat sleeve.

"What is it, honey?"

"That's Angie up there, my college roommate! She's cut her hair short, but I recognize her angelic face, that voice, and nobody has dimples like hers."

When the band finishes the set, Katy sends Lee over to the tiny stage wedged into a corner to retrieve her former roommate. Katy watches across the room as Angie smiles and declines the invitation from a strange man. She stands and waves at Angie as Lee points to their table. Angie's face lights up and she plows through the maze of tightly packed tables to embrace her friend.

"Kate-e-e-e," she squeals, throwing both arms around her. "I can't believe it, I can't believe it."

"Just look at you, Angie, you're all..."

Angie puts her finger to Katy's lips. "No, no, I'm Crystal now, Crystal Angel. Didn't you see my name on the marquee outside?"

"I want you to meet Lisa and Art. They're going to be in my wedding."

"Wedding! What fun, I mean, that's wonderful," Angie exclaims. Lee finds his way back to the table. "Honey, this is my...my dear friend, Ang..."

"Crystal Angel," Angie extends her hand, "Pleased to meet you. So, what's the deal? When's the big day?"

"Third weekend in May," replies Katy, displaying her left hand for Angie to admire the diamond. "And I've been asking everyone, trying to locate you."

"And here I am, on my way to stardom, right here in the jazz capital of L. A., you know...Lower America."

"I want you to be a bridesmaid in our wedding."

Angie's spirits skyrocket as Katy has unwittingly provided the excuse Angie needs to return to Alabama. *Three months away, just enough time to save the money for a one-way trip to Birmingham.*

"Angie, I mean Crystal, what do you say?" Katy waits as Angie turns pensive.

"Well, I don't know, you've thrown me for a loop. So-ooo, you're getting married instead of becoming a missionary," Angie cuts her eyes at Leland. "Good move!"

"Not instead of, in addition to. There's enough mission work to be done right there in Birmingham, as you probably know..." Katy's voice trails off as her attention wanders to Angie's deflated abdomen. Fleeting silence and mutual glances suggest that pregnancy is not an acceptable topic at this time. "We need to get together and talk when you're not working," Katy says, breaking the tension.

"Yeah, I need to start my next set before I get fired. I get off around 2:00 a.m. Where'll you be?"

Katy glances at Lee. "In bed, asleep. You know me, I turn into a pumpkin at midnight. Why don't we have breakfast together, say around eight?"

Angie laughs, "Be serious, honey chile, canaries aren't early birds, we don't rise for breakfast 'til after noon."

"Darn, we'll be on the Southern Flyer headed back to Birmingham by then. Tell you what, give me your phone number and I'll call you…when would be a good time?"

Angie tears a sheet from the back of a waiter's pad and writes down her number. "Call me any afternoon around two, that's right after I've had my coffee."

"O. K., Ang…I mean Crystal, just remember to keep the third weekend in May free for the wedding."

The day after Fat Tuesday, a religious pall descends over New Orleans as the mood shifts overnight from revelry to reflection. *La Paree* hires a jazz trio to replace Angie's group, so she and the boys hit the road, playing weekend gigs along the Gulf Coast. The prospect of living out of a van with six guys a couple nights a week throws Angie into a tizzy. Vicki shares some of her street smarts in an effort to calm her roommate's anxieties. "To keep those horny bastards from shoving you in the sack, woefully confess that a mysterious infection keeps you from going all the way. And wear those thick god-awful cotton panties to make your point in case they don't believe you. The damn bozos don't know shit about female problems, so they'll buy it every time. They'll be treating you like a buck-toothed sister before you know it."

~~~

Angie hangs on to her weekday job waiting tables a *La Paree* to sweep the cobwebs from her mind between weekend gigs. Then about six weeks before Katy's wedding date, she returns to the apartment late one night and retrieves a letter with a Birmingham postmark. She opens it and a swatch of blue satin material falls at her feet. Unable to see in the dark hallway, Angie rushes upstairs to read the letter:

March 20, 1964

Dearest Angie,

Thanks for taking part in my wedding. Enclosed is a sample of the fabric for the bridesmaid's dress and a pattern. If you can't find someone to make the dress, let me know by next week. Send me your measurements and I'll have it made for you. It was soooo good seeing you again.
See ya on the 16th at the rehearsal,
Love,
Katy Peterson

The next day Angie inquires among the waitresses about a seamstress. After the dinner rush, the dishwasher beckons Angie to the kitchen. "Y'all looking for somebody to sew a dress?" asks the young black woman as she wipes her hands on a towel. Before Angie can respond, the woman insists, "Lemme see yo' pattern." Angie retrieves her purse from the office and hands the envelope to the dishwasher. As they look over the pattern, a piercing shriek from the dining room diverts their attention. They look up to see the bartender bolt through the kitchen door shouting for the manager.

"Rob, Rob, where's Rob?"

The manager rushes from his office. "What's wrong, what's the matter?"

"Some dame just passed out. She walked in the door and…" the bartender's words are lost in the commotion as he follows the manager back to the dining room.

Angie takes advantage of the confusion in the dining room to discuss her bridesmaid's dress with the dishwasher. "I can do it in three days from the time you bring me the material."

Angie agrees and wanders back to her station in time to see paramedics carrying a loaded stretcher out the front door. "Anybody we know?" she asks the tearful hostess.

"No, but I thought she'd died," she sniffs. "She just walks in and stands there looking around like she's lost or looking for somebody. I pick up a menu and asked if I can help her. She says, 'Y'all got a singer working here?' and then she crumples to the floor. I screamed to high heaven…just lost it…she looked dead."

"Is she?" Angie whispers.

"Don't know. I ran to the toilet and threw up."

~~~

The paramedics roll their patient into the emergency room and sign her over to the resident in charge. After a quick check of the unconscious woman's vital signs, the doctor directs a nurse to put her in a stall and start an I. V. An attendant enters the stall with a clipboard and tries without success to arouse the comatose patient. He opens a cloth bag attached to the gurney and locates a wallet, carefully examining some currency, a picture of a little curly haired blond and a high school picture of a brunette cutie. The only clue to her identity is a Trailways bus ticket to Mimosa, Alabama and a motel key embossed with #115. He takes the key to the desk and calls the motel.

"I'm sorry, sir, I'm not allowed to give out information about registered guests," snaps the voice at the other end.

"Your guest is lying in our emergency room and I need to know who she is, miss," the hospital attendant insists.

"Then, you should ask her, sir."

"The lady is unconscious. If you can't tell me who is registered in room 115, then I'll have to turn the matter over to the police."

"Just a moment, sir…Yes, the lady registered in room 115 is a Marie Shook…Yes, there is an address…Yes, also a phone number, but it's long distance."

Tucker heads for New Orleans and drives all night arriving at the hospital in the wee hours of the morning. He bundles his exhausted wife in his jacket and makes the return trip to Mimosa. Tucker, shaken by Marie's pale and drawn body, tries to make her comfortable, but he is unaware that her physical and emotional reservoirs are drained and her will to live disappeared with Angie.

~~~

Angie bubbles over with anticipation as she hands the dishwasher at *La Paree* forty dollars to make her bridesmaid dress. Her escape from New Orleans back to Birmingham is within her grasp. Three days later, the dishwasher comes to work with an excuse in place of the promised dress. "Miss Angie, I got down to puttin' in the hem and my sewing machine broke down."

"What am I going to do? Just bring me the dress and I'll finish it myself," Angie fires back at her.

"Jist gimme fifteen mo' dollars to git the machine fixed and you'll git it by Friday, I swear."

Angie retrieves the money from her purse and goes ahead to finish her shift. At closing time she goes to the cabinet to gather her things and discovers something is missing.

"Son-of-a-bitch!" she screams, throwing her empty purse on the floor. "Somebody snatched all my money."

Back at the apartment, Angie slams the door and unloads her anger on Vickie. "I'm really pissed off. I trusted that bitch and she screwed me royally. Nobody knows where she lives and the police told me I may as well kiss that two hundred dollars goodbye. How will I make Katy's wedding now, no dress, no gas money, not even money for a gift?"

Vicki patiently listens to her roommate's woeful tale and falls asleep on the couch. Angie pulls a blanket over her and starts a letter to Katy that she does not finish.

Angie, depressed and hopeless, drifts into the lifestyle she has come to detest—stumbling through each day like one of those recovering drug addicts on the streets of New Orleans. She collects her tip money and crawls into bed before daybreak, hoping the angel of death will pay her a visit before she wakes up. But her angel of hope, Vicki, returns from work and snaps Angie back into reality with another lifeline. She waves a business card in Angie's face. "Read this."

"What is it?"

"No, no look on the back. It's the guy's phone number. He wants you to call him this morning. He's looking for a singer to work on the biggest cruise ship in the Gulf. It's your big chance Crystal Angel. God, he loves that name."

"Why don't you take it?"

"Look, hon, I've got a job, besides I get seasick," Vicki laughs.

Angie auditions with the band leader aboard the Bahama Breeze Cruise Ship. "Go home and pack your bag, doll. I'll have your contract ready when you return. It'll be for the summer, but if the passengers like you, we'll work out a deal for six more months."

Angie hurries back to the apartment to pack and leave Vicki a note. While writing the note, she remembers to finish the letter to Katy.

~~~

Paul Peterson walks Katy to the altar of their church and places her hand in Lee's. Then, he steps up on the dais and announces, "On behalf of the bride's mother, I have just presented my daughter Katherine's hand to Leland Major that they may be united in holy matrimony." Laughter bubbles among the guests, who had tried to envision how their pastor would handle both roles in the wedding. Paul Peterson looks over the packed sanctuary, admiring the dignity and beauty of the Hope Methodist sanctuary, quite different from some of his previous churches. The St. Francis sanctuary would have been more elegant, but Hope's new building provides an ideal venue for launching a new generation. His heart is warmed by the presence of the women on the back pew, dissidents who had left the church in disagreement with Paul's stance on integration.

Ollie and Betty Barron are not at the wedding. At first, Paul thinks Ollie is miffed over Chad Willis' decision to leave St. Francis to become the Minister of Music at Hope. But, an announcement in St. Francis' newsletter the following week corrects his misconception:

Dr. and Mrs. T. Oliver Barron
are pleased to announce the addition of
Angela Olive Barron
to their family
on
May 17, 1964

The day after Lorna receives the announcement, she drives to Pizitz Department Store and selects a tiny pale pink Feltman day gown with a row of tucks across the front. She has it beautifully gift-wrapped in pink and white and then heads to her former parsonage at St. Francis Methodist. Betty Barron opens the front door. "My goodness, Lorna, what a pleasant surprise!"

"Speaking of surprises, I had no idea you were pregnant," Lorna laughs.

"Well, nowadays we recover from childbirth pretty quickly," Betty giggles and steps back to welcome her guest. Lorna is bewildered at the sight of the frizzy headed baby leaning forward in a walker, wobbly legs flouncing in opposite directions. "Come in and meet our newest addition."

"My goodness, now I know I should have called."

"No, no that's all right. I'm glad you came."

"I mean, I had no idea the baby was half grown," Lorna exclaims. "She must be six or seven months old. And I brought her a newborn size. Well, I won't even let you unwrap it, I'll exchange it for a larger size."

"Don't worry about that, Lorna, come meet our Angela. Ollie prefers to call her Olive, named after him of course, but I'm afraid kids will tease her about being Popeye's girl friend."

"Where did you get those cute little dimples? Hello, precious." Lorna kneels and stretches out her arms.

"Aren't we fortunate? The orphanage had two to choose from, a boy and a girl. Ollie wanted a boy, but he couldn't resist those penetrating bright eyes and winsome giggle."

"I had no idea you were considering adoption. Where did she come from?"

Betty bites her lower lip. "Out of state, but we're not at liberty to disclose any of the details."

"I understand," Lorna says. "I wonder if I could have a hug, precious. I have the feeling you're going to wrap your daddy around your little finger in no time." Lorna hugs Angela Olive, lifts her, and the baby clings to her neck. "This could be addictive," Lorna says, smothering the seven-month old with kisses.

~~~

Several weeks after her wedding, Katy stops by the church office to pick up a letter from the secretary. "Somebody doesn't know you got married. It's addressed to your maiden name. Wonder who that could be."

"Thanks for calling me, Marge, it would have taken Dad weeks to remember to give it to me. Anyhow, most people still call me Katy Peterson and sometimes I catch myself signing my name that way."

"Yeah, I know how that goes," Marge laughs. Noticing the New Orleans postmark, Katy stuffs the letter into her purse and hustles to her car to read it.

> *My Dearest Katy,*
>
> *I am really, really sorry that I missed your wedding. I wanted to be there more than anything in the world. Please, please forgive me. I'll explain when I see you. Your husband seems to be such a nice man.*
>
> *I'll be out of touch for a while, but we'll talk when I return.*
>
> *Angie, a.k.a. Crystal Angel, Songbird of the South*

Katy searches but finds no return address on either side of the envelope or letter. *Mmm, did Angie just forget to include the return address? Or, perhaps she's subconsciously trying to make a clean break from her troubled past.* Katy takes the letter home and places it in one of the two boxes where she has stored the things Angie left in the dorm room over a year ago. She picks up the envelope bulging with forty one-dollar bills, proceeds from the sale of Angie's textbooks. *I never noticed this before. The black ink marks over the return address have faded to brown. Now I can barely make out the print underneath—St. Francis Methodist Church. That's strange, Angie must have picked up the envelope at Dr. Barron's church the day she left. Did someone at St. Francis give Angie that money for an abortion?* Katy places the two envelopes in the box. *I wonder if I will ever hear from the New Orleans songbird again.*

14

> *September 6, 1964*
>
> *Dear Momma,*
> *I know it's been ages since you heard from me. I have been a really, really bad girl, but I promise to make it up to you when I see you. I have finally landed a singing job. It's with Les Gilbert's band. He gave me a contract to sing on a cruise ship. I won't have to wait tables at all, just sing. When I get back in six months, I'm coming home to see you and daddy, if he's talking to me again. I'll see y'all then.*
>
> *Love,*
>
> *Angie*

Tucker Shook is not one to act on impulse. Although he won't admit to believing in God, he suspects there is some kind of mystical force that manipulates people's lives, a force over which they have little or no control. And he is sure the energy from that force will make Angeline miss her mother and call home. Six months pass with no call from Angeline, punching holes in Tucker's shallow theology. Tucker considers it time to give destiny a nudge by trying to locate his daughter. He makes feeble attempts to reconstruct in his mind those one-sided conversations with Marie and arguments between her and Angeline to which he had barely paid attention. As Angeline was struggling to gain release from her momma's virtual apron strings, Marie had often turned to Tucker, but only to complain. Now he is full of remorse for not having listened more closely. One particular situation has gnawed at his innards since Marie's death.

It started with Angeline's last year in high school. Her job at Pizza Palace, rehearsals, voice lessons, and church choir kept her away from the house nearly every night. When his daughter would return to the house, no matter how late, Marie would start in on her about her lack of interest in the family. The one-sided inquiries would escalate into screaming fits that would chase Tucker out of the house until the storm subsided. One night, following a catfight he left and returned home late to find Marie on the front porch rocking and crying. "It's a mite cool out here, Marie, better go on in the house," he said. She launched a barrage of complaints about Angeline's lack of respect and appreciation for her mother. Tucker remembers retreating into the house, but something Marie said stuck in his mind.

"That preacher's turnin' my girl against me, I know. People are talkin'. She loves him more'n she loves her own momma."

~~~

Tucker calls two Birmingham phone numbers he finds among Marie's things—Methodist College and St. Francis Methodist Church. The College offers no help since Angeline left no forwarding address. The secretary at the church suggests he might reach Dr. Barron at the parsonage.

"It's for you, Honey, it's a man calling long distance," Betty shouts from the kitchen as she tries to wrest the birthday cake from its bakery box without disturbing the decorations.

"Ask him to call back after the party," Ollie replies.

She relays the message into the mouthpiece and hesitates. "He says it's very important…won't wait."

"You go ahead, Brother Ollie, I'll watch the kids," offers a parent who brought her child to help celebrate Angela Olive's first birthday.

"Dr. Barron here, how may I be of service? Watch out, Dear, the cake's slipping," Ollie becomes momentarily distracted. "Oh, pardon me, now what can I do for you?" He listens briefly before being distracted again. "Betty, the matches are in that top drawer." Then, back to the phone call. "Pardon me again; I don't believe I caught your name...Oh..." Ollie presses a finger in his other ear to block out the festive chatter from the dining room as Betty presents the cake. "Do I know you? Mr. ah...say your name again." Ollie pulls the phone into the laundry room as far as the cord will reach and speaks in hushed tones. "No sir, I have not seen your daughter. Yes, I'm very sorry about Mrs. Shook, but I'm afraid I can't be of any help to you. Now, if you will excuse me, I must go...No, I don't think coming here will be very fruitful, because...Yes, I understand...Again, my deepest condolences on your loss, goodbye."

Ollie presses the button to sever the connection and stands motionless holding the receiver in his hand. Betty looks in from the dining room, "Are you off the phone, Ollie...Ollie? Come on, I'm lighting the candle."

After the guests leave, Betty lifts her daughter and seats her on the counter next to the kitchen sink to clean the pink icing from her hair, hands and face. "Do you have to go take care of some emergency?" She watches Ollie stuffing pink and green paper plates and napkins into the garbage bag. "I'll do that after I get Angela Olive cleaned up."

"No, why?"

"The phone call, that man sounded desperate."

"Not really...not really," he mutters opening the door to take out the trash.

When he returns, Betty sets the birthday girl on the floor to play with her new toys. "The call was from Mimosa, anybody we know?" She gives him that look reserved for times when he becomes evasive for no obvious reason.

"It's confidential, so let it go at that."

"O. K. *Father O'Barron*," Betty sallies with a mock Irish accent, "You don't do confessionals in your family kitchen. You're supposed to let Mimosa's pastor handle his own flock's emergencies. Now, if you've dragged something over from Mimosa that's going to affect your mood as much as that phone call, then I suggest you cut it loose, and quick!" Before he can think of a logical comeback to Betty's perceptive jab, she picks up Angela Olive and zips out of the kitchen.

～～～

Tucker Shook drops the phone into its cradle and leans back in the cane bottom chair, staring at the space heater's orange glow across the room. "Dammit, dammit, dammit," he shouts to the empty room and shifts his gaze to an eight-by-ten picture of Marie posing like a model in front of his then-new pickup truck. "For a goddamn preacher, he ain't worth a shit, Honey," he talks to the picture. "He don't know me from Abraham's goat, but he owes it to ya' to help find Angeline." He coughs and heaves several times, then leans over and spits into a coffee can on the floor. The two decades he has worked underground has clogged his airway with coal dust. The company doctor basted Tucker's symptoms with gallons of codeine-laced cough syrup until a union probe discovers most veteran diggers are suffering from silicosis. He had just been placed on disability when the call came from New Orleans about Marie.

Tucker picks up the metal frame and focuses his blurry eyes on Marie's picture. "I should've paid more 'tention to y'all's troubles, Baby, but I promise I'm gonna find our girl. I jist gotta connect with the right people." Tucker's pledge to his deceased wife triggers a flood of regrets. He wishes he had gone to church, at least once so he would know somebody to contact about Angeline. He should have helped Marie search for their daughter instead of assuring her that Angeline would just show up one day when she ran out of money. Marie's ravings over the past two years had numbed Tucker's memory beyond recall.

Tucker sets the frame back on the table and opens a drawer. The contents of Marie's purse fill the narrow drawer like pieces of a jigsaw puzzle. She had meticulously written dates and places of Angie's singing engagements on small strips of notepaper. Tucker begins to thumb through the notes as he has done many times since Marie died. Arranging the posthumous reminders of his negligence in chronological order, Tucker tries to piece together the last few years. He reads what Marie wrote on Angeline's letter from New Orleans. *See what bus goes to N. O.* Tucker is still mystified by two notes that read *Sargent's Crossroads* with separate dates scribbled underneath. He has already been there looking for clues, but found only a country church, two gas stations, a strip of small stores and a motel. Sargent's Crossroads lies between Mimosa and Birmingham, so Tucker reasons that Marie may have met Angeline there after she was at college. But, Angeline had the car. Frustrated, he puts the notes back in the drawer and shoves it closed. He gets up to turn off the gas heater and catches a glimpse of his image in the mirror over the mantle. *I look like a damn hippie. Better get rid of this beard an' git cleaned up 'fore I leave the house. I reckon it's high time I straighten up an' pay the Methodist Church a visit.*

    Tucker parks his truck across the street from Mimosa First Methodist in front of the drug store. A cup of coffee will buy him some time to think of a way to approach the preacher about Angeline's whereabouts. He takes his coffee mug over to the same table where Angie had sat watching Ollie Barron drive up in his T-Bird over five years ago. Tucker gazes trance-like across the main street at the brick church. Its white arched doors glowing in the afternoon sun were designed to invite people inside, but for Tucker they might as well be the gates of hell. He has been to church only twice in his life, to marry Marie and to say goodbye to her, neither time by choice. In Tucker's world, Number Ten mine was his sanctuary, the union was the congregation and his favorite anthem was Tennessee Ernie Ford's *Sixteen Tons*. He knows that going to church serves no purpose except to alienate hard-working husbands from their womenfolk and give jobs to wimpy preachers. Tucker descended to hell every time the tram lowered him into the mine, so whatever punishment he might face after death would be no worse than digging coal.

A coughing spell bends Tucker over. He tries to silence it with a slug of warm coffee. Spinning a dime across the counter, he bounds outside and crosses the street to avoid embarrassment. The big white church doors are locked, an omen to forget the whole search and go home. As he trudges back down the concrete steps, he spots a small arrow shaped sign in the grass pointing to the office around the corner. Tucker shuffles along the sidewalk to the office door and goes inside. Mrs. Green glowers from behind her typewriter. "Yes?"

Fighting the urge to bolt through the door, Tucker stifles back the urge to cough and asks, "Is the preacher here?"

She looks at her watch, then at him again. "He's gone for the day. Would you care to leave a message?"

"Naw, I just want to talk to him about my girl. I'll come back another time," Tucker turns to leave.

"Your girl, ah, you mean Angie? You're Mr. Shook, aren't you?"

Tucker is taken aback. "Uh, Angeline, do you know…?"

Mrs. Green rises from her desk and approaches the counter between them, softening her manner. "I remember you from the funeral…so sad…Mrs. Shook was so young and such a devoted mother. I was surprised that Angie was not at the funeral. Was she…?"

"Angeline didn't know 'bout her momma, still don't."

"Oh, I'm so sorry," eyebrows raised in an inquiring manner, she stares at Tucker.

"That's what I wanna talk to the preacher about. I'm tryin' to find Angeline."

"Well, he wouldn't know much, she went off to college before he came to this church. Maybe you could ask Dr. Barron. He's now in Birmingham at…"

"Yeah, I know. I've already talked to him. He ain't seen her a'tall."

Mrs. Green bites her lower lip and shakes her head. "My, that's strange, Dr. Barron and Angie were very close. She used to come by and...well, they spent a lot of time together."

"Uh huh," he grumbles in a deep voice to indicate he understands exactly what she means.

"He helped her get a scholarship to Methodist College, but I'm sure you know that."

"Umm huh."

"I'm sure she must have been at his church in Birmingham, maybe even in his choir. She had such a lovely voice."

"Umm huh," Tucker utters the same expression he often used with Marie, not to keep her talking but to close down the one-sided conversation. But this time he hangs on to the church secretary's every word, trying to fit this new information into the puzzle of his girl's disappearance.

Suddenly Mrs. Green stops talking about Dr. Barron and Angie. She checks her watch. "It's four-thirty, Mr. Shook. I have to get to the post office before it closes. I hope you find Angie...Angeline very soon."

Tucker lets the office door close behind him knowing he needs to have a straight face-to-face talk with Mimosa's former preacher despite the denial over the phone.

He drives straight home to sit over the vaporizer and loosen the crud in his bronchial tubes. The next afternoon, Tucker sits in his rocker and basks in the warm October sun until long shadows cloak the front porch. Just as Tucker starts indoors to escape the chilly afternoon, the postman wheels up to the mailbox on his bicycle.

"Howdy, Tuck, mighty fine weather for the big game today."

"Game? Oh, you mean Bama."

"Don't you know Bear's kicking that Big Orange butt over at Legion Field?" the sweating postman asks as he pulls a letter and a flyer from his bag. "Hey, Tuck, it looks like somebody don't know 'bout yo' wife yet," he says. "It's addressed to Mrs. Tucker with a New Orleans postmark."

Tucker snatches the letter from the startled postman, letting the flyer fall to the ground. He examines both sides of the envelope addressed to Marie and retreats inside the house. Shaking his head, the postman picks up the flyer, sticks it in the mailbox, and pedals back to the main road.

Tucker breaks open the plain white envelope and reads Angie's letter. He counts the months on his fingers. "Goddamit, she ain't comin' home 'til spring. Angeline, baby, where are ya'?" he wails, bringing on a siege of coughing.

Tucker recovers, settles at the kitchen table and reads the letter over and over. He examines the envelope for any missed clues, an overlooked return address. Then focusing on the photo of Marie, his emotional dam breaks, flooding his insides beneath a wave of self-pity and blame. "She don't even know ya' ain't here. She don't even know ya' died lookin' for her. She's gonna be floatin' on a goddam boat not knowin' how bad I feel...an' not knowin' that ya' ain't feelin' nothin' no more. Dammit, Marie, why'd ya' die 'fore I did. It ain't fair. Ya' left me behind to suffer ya' dyin' an' mine too. Women handle funerals an' such better'n men do. I ain't got nobody to turn to, nobody to help me like that goddamn preacher fella. What did he ever do for ya' an' Angeline? He didn't put goddamn food on the table. He didn't build ya' a goddamn house. He didn't haul ass to Louisiana an' take care o' ya' till ya'...till ya'..." Then, Tucker falls to his knees and breaks down crying. "Sorry, Marie, I'm real sorry, didn't mean to cuss like that, but it ain't Sunday yet, an' my little girl ain't here to..." Then, he curls up on the floor sobbing, releasing sixteen tons of shameless remorse.

~~~

Six months later Angie calls home as she promised in her letter. "Daddy, it's Crystal, I mean Angie. What are you doing home? Are you on strike or something? Let me talk to Momma, I'm calling long distance and don't have much change."

Silence.

"Daddy, Daddy, can you hear me? I said..."

"Yeah, I hear. Uh..ya' momma's gone...she ain't here."

"When will she be back?" Angie asks. Tucker struggles to recover from the shock of hearing his daughter's voice again, but a muted sobbing is all he can manage. "Daddy, where is she, I need to talk to her, quick."

"When ya' comin' home?" Tucker manages to utter.

Angie senses something is wrong. "What's going on, Daddy? You sound funny. Are you and Momma all right?" The operator breaks into their conversation demanding more coins for the pay phone. Angie squeezes in the last word, "Bye, Daddy, I'm out of change, I'll call again." She stands on the dock waiting for the ship's porter to unload the trunk load of stuff she bought in various Caribbean ports.

The porter declines Angie's gratuity, "Miss Angel, yo' singin' made me feel so good, I can't take yo' money." Angie thanks him and returns to the telephone booth. A disembarking passenger gives her change for a dollar and she thumbs through the address book in her purse. There should be somebody she can call to find out if her parents are separated, or if her daddy lost his job and her mother has gone to work. Flurries of ominous scenarios clutter Angie's mind, but rather than spend the rest of her change on daytime long distance calls, she dials Vicki's number.

"Who the hell's calling me so early?"

"April fool...no, don't hang up, it's me...Angie. I need a place to hang out for a while, can I come over?"

"What d'ya mean, a while? I thought you were on a slow boat to China." Vicki drawls into the mouthpiece.

"I'll tell you all about it as soon as I park my trunk somewhere and catch a cab to your place."

The reunited friends spend a good deal of time giggling over Angie's adventures and misadventures aboard the cruise ship. "Crap, I've barely got time to shower and dress for work," Vicki exclaims. "Oh, I almost forgot to tell you, my roommate stops by the bar after work. I'll tell him you're here so he won't call the cops to toss you out."

"Him? He?"

"Yeah, but don't worry, he's like one of us girls," Vicki giggles and feigns a limp wrist, "if you know what I mean."

"You're serious, aren't you?"

"Remember when I told you that rooming with a gelding has its advantages? Not only does he split the rent, but he keeps heavy breathing stallions away from the stall."

Angie waits until after six to call someone who might know about her momma and daddy. One by one, she ticks off in her mind names of people she dares not call. *Let's see, Katy won't know about my parents, Ollie Barron is out of the question, Mimosa's new pastor probably doesn't have a clue, the church secretary was never any help and doesn't even know my daddy. My best bet is to call Claude Ray, if he hasn't left Mimosa.* She dials information and writes down Claude's number.

"Mrs. Ray, this is Angie Shook, could I please…"

"Angie! My goodness girl, are you all right? Everybody's been looking all over for you honey, ever since your mother died." Angie collapses onto the sofa as the telephone had suddenly zapped her with a million volts. The voice on the other end sounds garbled, "Angie, Angie, are you still there?" then distant, "Angie, Angie. Claude, it was Angie Shook, but we got disconnected," as it fades away.

15

> *September 3, 1965*
>
> Dear Mr. Willis,
>
>   I was pleased to attend your choir's fall kickoff musical last weekend. It was spectacular. I have lived in the Hope neighborhood over a year but have not yet located a church home. Do you need another tenor? I sang in my college choir and with a community chorus before moving to Birmingham. I won't be able to make every practice because occasionally I will be out of town on business. If you think I could fit in with your group, please drop me a note and one Wednesday night I'll show up.
>
> Best regards,
>
> *Micah Lovette*

Angie's heartbeat quickens when she spots the sign. *Hope Methodist Church—where hope is alive! Rev. Paul Peterson, Pastor.* She turns into the parking lot, admires the stained glass window above the portico, and switches off the engine. *I'm finally back where I belong thanks to my old jalopy and Katy forgiving me for missing her wedding. I'll miss Vicki but not New Orleans. I swear I'll never set foot in that hellhole again.* Angie caresses her crystal angel pendant and loses herself in thoughts of Mimosa. *Well, my little namesake, what will I do with you? Send you back to Mimosa where you came from? God, I want my Momma back...Why didn't Daddy die instead...I wish I could've told Momma about my baby, and that I could've held my baby in my arms just once, just once...O God, Ollie, why do you keep popping up in my mind? Go away you bastard, go away for good...I never should have dropped out of college and lost my scholarship...I have to find a job in Birmingham so I can go back to college...I can hear Vicki now if I were telling her this—"Get off your ass and get a life."*

Angie blots her eyes with a tissue and steps out of her car. She studies the directions on the scrap of paper in her hand and traipses across the pavement to the choir room adjoining the sanctuary. She peeks her head around the door. "Excuse me, is this where the choir meets?"

Chad jumps up from his chair, "Sure is, come on in, Brother Paul and I are just chatting."

"Then you must be Katy's dad," Angie steps forward and extends her hand. "She was my roommate at M. C."

"You're Angie?" She bobs her head vigorously. Paul rushes to grasp her hand. "I'm so glad to finally meet you face to face. What brings you back to..." A sorority rush squeal bursts from Katy as she enters and spots Angie.

"An-geee, An-geee, I wasn't sure you'd really come. I'm so glad to see you," and she breaks into a good sorority sister cry as she embraces her friend. "You look great."

"You look good too, both of you," Angie giggles, pointing to Katy's ballooning waistline.

"Baby's due in two months," Katy beams.

Paul intervenes, "Before you two get all wrapped up in girl talk, you should introduce Angie to Chad."

"Chad, I want you to meet my college roomy, Angie. She's a terrific singer, so I thought we might interest her in joining our choir." As Chad cradles Angie's hand, the soft ivory skin, the graceful fingers, he wonders if her voice is as captivating as her chocolate brown eyes. "Angie, this is the fabulous Chad Willis I told you about, my favorite choir director." Angie's smile broadens as Chad squeezes her hand.

"I see you two girls have a good deal to catch up on, so I'll get back to the parsonage and let you talk." Paul leaves Angie and Katy, two magpies breathlessly revving up to a seamless conversation. Chad putters over to the piano and lets his fingers wander over the keys as if ignoring their animated chatter. He cannot tear his eyes away from this arresting young woman in the shimmering black dress, her body moving in sync with her hands.

Katy signals to Chad over Angie's shoulder, "I hope you won't mind, Angie, I told Chad about your to-die-for voice and he insists on hearing you sing."

Angie, caught off guard, hesitates, "But, I didn't bring any music…I'm not sure."

"I won't take no for an answer. You two work it out while I run and make sure the nursery worker showed up, I'll be back in a sec."

Katy zips out the door, allowing her friend no recourse. Angie moves toward the piano and thumbs through a stack of solo books Chad had placed conveniently on top. "It's been a long time, Mr.…."

"Just call me Chad."

"All right," Angie utters softly, wondering how long Katy will be gone. "Well, to be honest, I haven't had a chance to sing much choir music lately. I've been singing in clubs."

"Night clubs, country clubs, bridge clubs, health clubs?"

Angie pouts coquettishly, "Now you're making fun of me."

"Oh no, no I know what you mean, like supper clubs."

"Actually juke joints, honkytonks, bars and dives would be more like it."

"A church choir director is not supposed to know about those kinds of places," Chad quips with a wicked chuckle. "Where did you perform, around here?"

"Mostly around New Orleans, the Red-Neck Riviera even did a tour on a cruise ship."

"Have you given up that glamorous life style, or just taking a break?"

"If you mean that life of unsteady work, choking on other people's smoke and creepy guys with wandering hands, yes, I've had it up to here with that blend of glamour." Angie shuffles the books and selects one from the stack on the piano. "Actually, my momma passed away a while back. She was buried before I ever knew about it. I guess I'm trying to reclaim old ties, so I decided to come back home."

"So Birmingham's your home?"

"Now 'tis," she replies. "I grew up in Mimosa, know where that is?"

"Isn't that a little town over in the next county?"

"It's smaller than you think once you get to know it. What shall I sing for you, Mr. Willis?"

"Please."

"I mean, Chad." She hands him the book of popular sacred solos.

"How about *He Touched Me?* It's a new one and becoming a favorite in this church." Chad leafs through to find the piece, but Angie picks up a file folder of sheet music. She slips one out and slides it across the piano, suddenly moved to sing something to impress the charming choir director.

"Here, let's go with this one, it has a little more zip!" She straightens her back and places a hand on her abdomen as Chad plays the introduction to Mozart's *Alleluia.* "That's the last number I sang in recital. I hope ol' Wolfgang won't turn over in his grave."

Chad pauses, "Are you sure you want to try this number? It's awfully high. You're voice sounds more *mezzo* or alto than soprano."

"That's probably because most clubs go for a deep sexy voice," she replies with a crooked smile, "I mean rich and full, like whipped cream." Her mind flashes back to Ollie Barron—whispering in her ear, y*our sexy voice makes me almost forget I'm a preacher.* She moves her hand from her diaphragm up and touches the crystal angel pendant hidden beneath her dress.

After Chad repeats the introduction, Angie struggles to sing through her dormant vocal cords, but soon the sharp clear notes take wing, as the turns, the trills, the runs seem to purify the atmosphere. Choir members drifting in for practice huddle just inside the door, mesmerized by Angie's crystal clear voice. Chad is unaware of the gathering group until someone breaks the magic spell tripping over a metal chair. Angie stops singing when the metal strikes the floor—and the choir members break into applause. Angie tucks her chin in a subtle response, demonstrating that she's no stranger to such an ovation.

"Folks, I want you to meet Angie, our new choir member." Following Chad's announcement, an older lady comes over to greet the glowing soprano.

"Come on, honey, let's fit you in a choir robe before you change your mind," the lady takes Angie by the arm. The men stand slack-jawed, watching Angie try on the green robe, wiggling around to be sure it fits. "My name's Evelyn, honey, what's yours?"

"Angel...I mean Angie, Angie Shook."

"As in 'all shook up'?" a guy launches a bad Elvis impression to emphasize his question.

Angie smiles at him, the youngest member of the bass section. He is entranced by this doe-eyed singer with the shimmering black curls that bounce in rhythm with every toss of her head. He is certain her positive response to his quip carries a deeper meaning.

Two young women huddle in a corner and in hushed voices, analyze the impact of the new soprano on the eligible men—Chad Willis, Spencer, the comedic bass, and Howard, a fifty-something tenor who lives with his mother. "Wonder which one she was wiggling her prissy little ass at," one whispers, "couldn't be Howard, he's too old."

"And too horny," whispers the other. "He's forever wanting to come by the house after choir practice, but only if I promise to put the kids to bed first."

"Do you?"

"Ha, they have strict orders to never leave me alone with that weird creep." Their laughter draws unwelcome attention from the group.

A third young woman arrives and joins the gossiping pair. "What are you two up to now?" They gesture toward the new choir member. "Omigod, I hope she's married." The gossipers shake their heads woefully. "We're in trouble, girls, big trouble," the latecomer says, ogling Angie Shook.

Angie's presence in the choir loft during the summer lifts Chad's spirits in more ways than one. Despite his pledge to avoid emotional entanglements with members of the choir, he creates opportunities to steal time alone with his new discovery—extra rehearsals, "chance" meetings at outdoor concerts and jogging at the high school track on Saturdays. It becomes increasingly more difficult to hide his feelings for Angie, undaunted by her pretentions of discouraging his solicitous behavior.

Angie's remarkable talent raises Chad's expectations of producing a major oratorio during Advent. He takes advantage of her technical skills and extensive range to improve both sopranos and altos by moving her from one section to the other during rehearsals. Chad plans a fall kickoff program of secular music from Broadway musicals and movies. He surmises selections from *Oklahoma, Showboat, and Sound of Music* will spill over to their sacred music with the same level of passion and energy as the musicals.

Practicing on stage in the fellowship hall helps Angie to regain her confidence in the choir loft. The coy, cabaret-honed voice she projects in the fall kickoff makes a hit, especially in a duet with Spencer. It appears to the audience as well as members of the cast that the two star performers have blurred the boundary between acting and reality. The drama extends backstage when Chad catches Angie behind the curtain and comments, "Your performance with Spencer, *People Will Say We're in Love,* is," and he punctuates the final words with biting sarcasm, "extremely convincing."

Angie smiles and taps Chad on the nose. "Could I be mistaken, or do I detect a note of jealousy in your compliment?" She blows him a kiss and whispers, "Maybe you can't tell the difference between who I'm singing with and who I'm singing to." Chad continues through the remaining numbers of the program pumped up, but perplexed.

People flock around the performers after the finale showering them with generous accolades. As the crowd disperses, a man sidles up to Chad and pulls him over to the side for a chat. "I'm Maynard Poe and I'd like a word with you about that girl." He tips his head in Angie's direction.

Chad follows the stranger to a back corner of the fellowship hall. "Mr. Poe, I have to help break down the set. I hope this won't take long."

"It won't. I thought you ought to know about that girl with the sexy voice. Her name's not Angie. Her real name is Angel Crystal, or Crystal Angel, but she's no angel. She's been around. She's a call girl from New Orleans. I know that for a fact."

Chad's eyes widen. "Really? Are you sure?"

"I spend most of my time calling on customers along the coast and I've seen her at work in those dives in the French Quarter. Oh, she's a singer all right, but there's not enough money in singing to keep a pretty little thing like her out of the red light district." The man casts a furtive look around the room and adds, "It's no sweat off my back, son, but between you and me, you should be more careful picking who sings in church."

Chad doesn't want to believe this traveling salesman whose stock and trade could be bawdy stories and fantasies. Still, this complete stranger has cast a pall of suspicion over Chad's image of Angie.

"Marge, do we have anybody named Poe on the church roll?" Chad asks the church secretary the next day.

"Nope, not to my knowledge, but I'll scan the Rolodex to be sure."

"That's strange," Chad muses as Marge flips through the cards. "Somebody with that name showed up last night at the kickoff and introduced himself to me. I figured he was a member I had not yet seen."

"Not here either," Marge said. Chad is relieved that Mr. Poe will not be around to contaminate others with his slanderous venom and lies about his beloved Angie. Now Chad can concern himself with preparing a spectacular Christmas music program, Handel's *Messiah*.

At the first choir practice of the fall season, Chad lays the groundwork for the oratorio. "We had a fantastic kickoff last week and I want to thank all of you for your enthusiastic support. You are an immensely talented and dedicated group." Spencer stands and surveys the room left and right in the style of an Indian scout. "What are you doing?" Chad doesn't hide being peeved at the untoward disruption.

"Oh, I'm searching for the group you just described. Seems they've not arrived yet. Should I go look in the sanctuary?" The group laughs at Spencer's predictable attempt to keep the rehearsal on a lighter plane. These outbursts of his that steal time from practice have become more frequent since Angie's arrival.

Unable to ignore the antics, yet not wishing to antagonize his bass soloist, Chad spins Spencer's comments to his advantage, "Thank you for making my next point, Spencer. You folks don't realize just how good a choir you've become. Next week, choir practice will begin fifteen minutes earlier." Chad hesitates to allow the mumbling to die down. "You ask 'why?' I'll tell you. We need the extra time to bump up our skills for performing Handel's *Messiah* the second Sunday in Advent...," he pauses while the mumbling grows louder, but more positive, "...at the morning service!" A cheer rings out.

"The morning service?" Evelyn asks. "Does the preacher know about this?"

"Yes, it's all arranged. And I plan to hire a full orchestra." A second round of cheers fills the room.

Despite their apprehension about the long, demanding hours that will be required, each choir member leaves practice in high spirits, charged with a new personal image as a singer.

Chad is elated with his decision to challenge the choir to extend themselves beyond the status quo, that is, until the next rehearsal. He receives word that two members feel inadequate to sing Handel, so they have dropped out until after Christmas. Their sudden departure sharpens Chad's awareness of the tenuous threads that bind a volunteer group of singers to the director. He recalls Paul Peterson's caveat from several years ago: *Choir singers bring more than their singing voices to church twice a week—their egos. As long as they feel safe and comfortable with your demands, they will stay with you. But if you push them too far beyond their capabilities, their trust in the director diminishes and the threads that bond the choir and its director begin to unravel. It's a delicate balance to strengthen those ties without breaking them.*

Fearing the defection of two members might spread panic among the others, Chad is encouraged by the emergence of a silver lining. A seasoned tenor and his alto wife attracted to Hope after attending the fall musical and learning of plans to perform the *Messiah,* have joined the choir. And a former bass soloist tells Chad, "the members of the new church we joined have splintered worse than a lightening-struck cottonwood and I intend to bring my family back to Hope Methodist."

Chad is all set to start working on the *Messiah* when, in early October another rift threatens to rip apart the choir's fragile fabric—Maynard Poe's pernicious portrayal of Angie reaches some choir members and feeds their voracious appetites for gossip. A trio of busy-bodies, Ester, Irma and Ann, set about to shatter Chad's image of his new *prima donna.* They march toward the choir room armed with pointed questions to confront Angie about her past in front of Chad and the choir. As they enter the room they find Katy and Angie huddled at the piano with Chad. "Perfect," Irma whispers to the Ann and Ester. She tugs at Chad's sleeve and whispers as loudly as possible, "Can we interrupt you for a moment? We have a few questions to ask Angie."

"We're expecting some folks momentarily," Chad replies, "They are coming to go over some wedding plans. Can it wait 'til after practice?" Irma is about to insist when a woman and her daughter enter the door behind her.

"Excuse us, please," the older woman rushes past Irma and her two cohorts to greet Angie. The thwarted trio watch as Angie leads the wedding planner and bride-to-be out the door to meet with the organist in the sanctuary. Chad hits a chord on the piano and begins warming up his singers, "On la, la, la."

The organist finishes her business with the wedding and returns to the choir room without Angie. Irma, anxious to spread the dirt about Angie, whispers to Ann, "Where's Angie?"

"I don't know, but we can't do this without her in the room. If she doesn't come in before practice is over, we'll wait until Sunday." Ann relays the word to Ester.

Chad directs the final run-through of Sunday's anthem in the choir room instead of the sanctuary. He dismisses the group with a brief prayer and slips away to his office, closes the door and dials the phone.

"I knew it was you," Angie says, picking up the phone. "Is practice over?"

"You didn't come back to the choir room," Chad says. "Are you sick…got a test…what happened?"

"Whoa, whoa, Mr. Willis, hold your horses, I'll explain."

"O. K., I was a bit worried."

"Nothing to worry about, nothing at all. I guess I have too many things on my mind right now."

"Things?"

"Yeah…on second thought, I need to think through these uh…things before we talk about them." Her voice begins to quiver.

"Uh oh, sounds serious…I mean…are we…?

"Now don't start fretting, my prince, I have enough on my mind without having to worry about you. Listen, I have a test tomorrow...need to study now. Let's meet for lunch after my class at the Spinning Wheel, a little past one. Love ya, bye."

Peaceful slumber eludes Chad this night as the good and the bad chase through his mind. He tries not to imagine the worst, but dour scenarios dominate his thoughts. *She did say "my prince." And for the first time she signed off by with "love ya." But she's worried about something out of my range. Maybe she's having trouble balancing her job at the Dance Club with choir and school. Maybe she's considering singing in a large church choir for pay and can't find the words to tell me. The twelve-year gap in our ages has tripped her fuse. We aren't even a "thing" yet and she wants to end it. I know I kidded her about being so much younger than I but she always countered with, "Look, you may be a little older model but I've got a whole lot more miles, so that makes us even."*

The next day, Chad drives downtown, still mulling over Angie's mysterious quandary. *I bet Angie wants to move back to New Orleans and she's going to ask me to go with her. No, she's decided to take Roger's offer at Cedarwood Independent Church. He's been after her for weeks to come sing in his choir.*

Chad drives around the block trying to park near the Spinning Wheel. Angie spots him from the malt shop window and runs out to wave him down. She jumps in the car and pecks him on the cheek, "Wipe that scowl off your face, my prince. Whatever it is you're worried about, that's not the problem, so drive on."

Chad emits a nervous laugh, "O. K. Where to?"

"Let's go to a drive-in where we can talk, it's too crowded here," she throws her books in the back seat. "And by the way, hello good looking and give me a real kiss so I can be sure it's you." The touch of her lips is not only reassuring, it's euphoric.

"You're a real sweetie, Angel-eyes, like no other."

Chad drives over Red Mountain past the Vulcan statue and down to Argo's Drive-in. Angie rattles on about the questions on her psychology exam, "One question had no correct answers and the professor said for us to choose the closest one—closest to what? Does he think we're playing horseshoes?" Chad waits for an opening to inquire about her skipping out last night, but her patter about the exam is seamless.

"Let's grab a couple of burgers and go to your place so we can eat in peace," Angie suggests as he pulls into one of the drive-in bays. "I'm so tired of people I could puke." Chad speaks into the squawking intercom. Angie continues ranting about the test, often repeating herself. Chad hands her the drinks and sack of food, diminishing her chatter. She sips the Coke and nibbles on hot fries as Chad drives to his apartment.

"Here we are at *Mouldy View*," Chad jests as they enter the nearly empty Mountain View parking lot. "This time of day is perfect, I can park at my front door."

Angie follows Chad and plops the sack on the kitchen counter. She rushes to the bedroom and separates the drapes. Chad observes her puzzling behavior, not knowing what to expect next. *Why has she invited herself to my apartment? Could Maynard Poe's story of her promiscuous past be true? Does she suddenly need to satisfy her sexual appetite?*

"Oh, I just love this view. I've always wondered what downtown would look like from up here. Oh, the color of the trees is like an oil painting in motion," she exclaims in one breath as if all her problems have suddenly vanished. She places both knees on the loveseat next to the window and stretches over the back to get a better view. Before Chad has time to react, she springs backwards and exclaims, "Let's eat, I'm starved."

Chad follows her to the kitchen, amused at the prank his mind has played on him. *Obviously, sex is not on her agenda today.* She takes a couple of plates from the cabinet. "I swore off eating out of paper bags after being on the road so long," she plunks the plates on the table. "Did I tell you about living out of a Volkswagen bus, eating cold grill cheeses and singing in every bayou bar from Panama City to Houston?" With a shake of his head, Chad dismisses Maynard Poe's accusations altogether. "Well, I'll save that horror story for our kids," she giggles.

"Our kids?" Chad chokes on his mouthful of burger.

Angie takes a sip of Coke. "I'm sorry, my prince, I know I've talked up a blue streak since you picked me up and haven't said a damn thing about last night. And here you've almost finished lunch and you have to get back to work." Sadness dulls the sparkle in her eyes. "You don't realize, it's really hard for me to do this," she says, wiping fresh tears from her cheeks with a napkin.

"No, no. I'm not due back any certain time. You go ahead, take your time. I'll listen."

"I've thought and thought about this and haven't found the right words to say to you. So-o-o-o, I guess I'll charge forward like an old billy goat." She swallows hard. "About last night—I'm not coming back."

Chad's winces in pain, "You mean to choir or church?"

"Both. And please don't interrupt or I may never get it all out. It's not your fault, don't get me wrong. My lurid past has caught up with me and some of the so-called ladies in the choir are about to smear my reputation all across your hide."

"You mean those single…" Angie places her fingers over his lips. "I'm sorry. I'll be quiet." Once again, Maynard Poe's warning flashes through his mind.

"I learned long ago to let nasty cuts slide off my shoulders, but last week they went too far. One of them called and got really ugly. She wouldn't give her name, but I know damn well who she is. Apparently, she saw us together somewhere, she didn't say where, but she said that you are about to be fired because of me."

"What? But we haven't even…!" Angie touches his lips a second time.

"The bitch told me there's a rule about staff going out with church members and the preacher's been told to fire you if you don't stop seeing me." Rage chokes Chad, but he fumes quietly over the lie about church policy. Angie continues, "I know how this upsets you, but listen. My way has always been to handle problems alone, not depend on anyone else to help. I try to take stuff in stride and run with it. That's why last night I just came to decline the wedding gig and skipped choir practice. I knew things were about to explode and I didn't want you to be caught in the position of having to defend me. I'll never go back to that church not even to sing at that bitch's funeral."

Chad is beside himself, wanting to jump on his high horse and defend his maiden in distress. But, drawing on all his reserve, he refrains. Angie fiddles with her straw and sips the watery soda. "I haven't come to the real reason I made this decision. There's more to the story, a secret that no one else knows except two ex-roommates and they would die before telling anyone." She takes another sip. "Do you realize how hard this is?" Angie's tears flow again. "It's because I've only been close to one other man in my life and he turned out to be a sorry bastard." Chad straightens up in his chair, and remains silent. "Oh, don't worry, I got over that. I don't know who's to blame. I swore off men forever, but you changed that when you became my prince charming. That's why I'm dropping out of the choir. As long as I'm around, those jealous bitches will collect their gripes, even make up some, and dump 'em all over you at choir practice every week."

Angie bawls as if releasing a lifetime of dammed up frustration. Chad reaches over and tilts her chin upward. He sees the pain that still dwells in those deep brown eyes, magnified by the tears, pain that she has yet to release. "I'm not done. There's more...the hardest part is yet to come," she sniffs, and backs away from Chad as though he might become contaminated by the next revelation.

"The fact is I've fallen in love with you, Chad, in spite of all I did to prevent it, but it happened. I've tried to convince myself that you deserve better, but no dice." Angie reaches for a dish towel to catch the new flood of tears. "What I said earlier about having kids, well I wasn't kidding. Someday, when you get used to crazy ol' me, and the garbage I drag around from my past, you and I might be able to think about a family. But first, there's something else you should know about me. When I tell you, I won't blame you if you kick me out of your life forever." Angie drops her head. "I had a baby." She jumps up from her chair and rushes back to the bedroom window, as if to leave the bitter confession in Chad's hands. Staring at the city below, she hears the floor creak behind her and continues. "He was a charming older man like you, but married. I became infatuated with him when I was just a kid still in high school, but nothing came of it. When I went to college, we fell in love, at least I did, and the next think I knew I was pregnant. We argued, he gave me money for an abortion and I never saw him again."

"But, you said that..."

"...that I had a baby. True, but that son-of-a-bitch doesn't know it and never will. I took the money, left town to have the baby, gave it up, went crazy, recovered and now I'm back to start all over. End of story." Angie turns to face Chad. "So, now what do you think of your 'Angel Eyes', Prince Charming?" She waits for his answer, tears streaming down her cheeks.

Chad pulls Angie close and snuggles for a long time before saying anything. "Did you really think your secrets of the past would scare me away? Not in a thousand lifetimes." She squeezes him tighter. "Do you realize what you were saying all the while you wouldn't allow me to interrupt?" She shakes her head. Chad pushes back just enough to look her in the face. "I think I heard a roundabout proposal of marriage."

Angie jumps back and squeals, banging her fist playfully against his chest. "You jackass, if that's all you heard..." Then, she pauses, realizing that Chad is, in his own awkward way, confessing that her past doesn't matter to him. She grabs him again and says, "I hope that doesn't mean I have to buy the ring. I'm not that liberated."

"Wait a minute, smarty pants, I haven't said 'yes' yet."

"Then say it!"

"Yes!"

16

> *November 25, 1965*
> *Dear Brother Paul,*
> *I understand the choir plans to sing the Messiah during the morning service before Christmas. I have nothing against classical music, but substituting it for the sermon is going too far. I beg you to reconsider and not let Chad Willis devote the entire service to music. The Hallelujah chorus would be enough special music for one service.*
>
> *In loving disappointment,*
>
> *Louella DeVann*

Tucker Shook sips cold coffee and shuffles two envelopes on the table before him. Ignoring doctor's orders to avoid coffee and tobacco, Tucker slips a pouch of snuff in his cheek and justifies his habit. *At least I quit smoking.* Beginning his daily ritual, he opens the most painful letter first, the one from Angeline addressed to Marie that had come a year after her death. *Why does she act like I ain't worth nothin'? I never done nothin' to hurt her.*

Tucker's mind wanders back a few months to spring when he expected Angeline to call a second time after her cruise. When the phone rang the voice on the other end was not his daughter's. "Hello, Angeline?"

"No sir, this is Katy, a friend of Angie's. May I speak to her?"

"What in hell made ya' think she'd be here?" Tucker remembers exploding in Katy's ear.

"I'm sorry to bother you, sir. I'm just curious about when I can expect her to arrive here in Birmingham. Perhaps her mother would know?"

Her perfectly innocent inquiry had struck him so hard that he could do nothing but curse. Before he could come to his senses, the petrified Katy had quietly hung up the phone.

"Damn," Tucker condemns himself again for failing to keep the young woman on the phone long enough to ask what she knew about Angeline. Typically, he had allowed rage to trump reason.

"Katy...Katy...Katy..." Suddenly remembering the caller's name, Tucker scrambles to open Marie's private drawer and rummages through the layers of paper scraps, searching for notes with information about Katy. Finding none, Tucker eases back in his rocker to think, takes another pouch of snuff from his overalls, and stuffs it into his other cheek to absorb the pain of desolation.

The rocking and the snuff having temporarily assuaged his despair, Tucker returns to the table and pulls a business letter and some blank forms from the other envelope. *Marie wanted Angeline to have her insurance money. I've searched an' searched but I can't find her to sign this claim. Seems that Katy woman who called expected Angeline's to show up in Birmingham. I've gotta quit settin' here by the phone jist waitin' for her to call. Time's a-wastin'. I gotta go find her. I gotta find Angeline.*

The ensuing weeks Tucker drives to Birmingham as often as his strength allows. His single clue tells him to begin his search at Methodist churches. His first choice, St. Francis is where Ollie Barron preaches. His lingering distrust of that man prompts him to recall his army ranger days and pursue furtive tactics. For several muggy August evenings, he stakes out the side entrance, but sees no sign of Angeline going to choir practice. He must look elsewhere. But the weekly trips between Mimosa and Birmingham have depleted his energy so much that he stays in bed for several days, certain that his exclusive diet of baloney sandwiches and bootleg beer will lead to recovery.

The beer and baloney regime having worked, a renewed Tucker resumes his trek along Highway 78 to Birmingham—this time to First Methodist. An armed guard patrols the church parking lot, so Tucker parks a couple blocks away next to a city park. Getting out of the truck, he catches his reflection in the side mirror. "Damn, I look like that bum sprawled out on a bench," he mutters to himself. "I'll never find my girl lookin' this bad." He gets in the truck and heads back to home to clean up—and try a fresh approach.

The next time Tucker arrives in Birmingham he is clean-shaven, wearing a starched work shirt, and sporting a new haircut. Armed with a fistful of dimes, he goes to the bus station and begins calling Methodist Churches. On the third call, Marge answers, "No, I'm sorry, there's no Angeline in our choir." Tucker thinks for a second and starts to hang up. Then he remembers Katy asking for *Angie* when she called a few weeks ago. "Oh yes, Angie, she's one of our best singers...Yes, her last name is Shook...How may I help you, sir...sir?" He hangs up quickly to avoid alerting his daughter. Now he has a target for his search.

~~~

The weary choir members just can't seem to get it right. "Come on folks, this is the final rehearsal before the orchestra joins us and those sixteenth note melismas still sound like mush. Try separating the notes slightly," Chad Willis suggests, glancing at his watch as the men on the back row have been doing for fifteen minutes.

"We're tired," moans an alto on the front row.

"Maybe if we take it a little slower, Chad," pleads another member of the section.

"All right, I know you're tired. Tell you what, let's take it once more, from the top, at my tempo and then we'll quit, right or wrong. Pitch, please, right on the soprano's entrance. Here we go, and uh." Chad lifts his arm and the sopranos sing:

For un-to us a child is bo-o-o-o-o-o-o-o-o-rn.

A man on the back pew in the shadow of the balcony scans the faces of the choir members intently. He rises in sync with the final note of the organ, moves to the center aisle and melds with the darkness of the vestibule. Pulling his black toboggan down over his ears, he snuggles within the topcoat hanging loosely around his frail frame as he opens the front door of the church and disappears into the night. An alto leans forward to warn Chad. "He was out there lurking on the back row again! How can we concentrate on singing with that weirdo staring at us during every practice?"

"Relax, Evelyn, maybe he's just homeless, looking for a place to keep warm," Chad assures her, concealing his own apprehension.

Spencer peevishly chimes in, "Or maybe he's from the half-way house up the street and has a fetish for Handel."

"Yeah, he's been out there ever since we started on the Christmas music," Evelyn responds wild-eyed, not realizing that Spencer is merely pulling her string.

Chad chuckles as the choir members shuffle out of the choir loft.

"It's not funny, Chad." Evelyn admonishes, a bit of an edge to her voice. "Are we that amusing?"

"Oh no," Chad retracts, "I'm just excited and nervous about dress rehearsal next week. Stand back, I may come apart at the seams any minute now."

"You're not the only one, brother. You'd better pray that our soloists don't come down with sore throats."

"Thanks, dear, for giving me one more thing to worry about." But Chad puts his worries aside and pauses to count his blessings. *This choir is primed for their first major test. When the last chord of "Hallelujah" echoes through the rafters, Handel will be proud to claim this dedicated group of volunteers.*

"By the way, Chad," Evelyn probes as she follows him to the choir room, "what's happened to Angie? Is she planning to do her solo? We especially need her on that last number where we drug our tongues over those runs."

"I know." Chad shrugs off Evelyn's concern about Angie, but she persists.

"She told me *Messiah* is her favorite. Have you called her? You want me to...?"

"Don't worry, Evelyn, she may show up. That's the problem with volunteers—they come, they go, you never know."

"Now don't you get too big for your britches, young man. You'll be waving your arms at empty seats," she says with feigned admonition. "Do you have her phone number?"

"It's unlisted."

"Then, tell me where she lives, I'll drive by on my way home and see what's going on with her."

"No need for that, Evelyn," Chad pivots and faces her as though she has struck a nerve. "It's...it's too late. Her landlady has a curfew. I'll check on her in the morning."

Evelyn peers over her half-moon lenses and twists her mouth indicating she knows there's a reason he's blowing her off. "Humph, just offering to help," she grumbles as she heads to the choir room, curious about his reaction.

"I couldn't help overhearing you two talking about Angie," chimes Irma, "Is something wrong?" The divorcee lingers after choir practice and competes with Ester and Ann for Chad's attention. All three have pursued Chad since he arrived at Hope and immediately became the church's most eligible bachelor. With minimum success, Chad maneuvers to embrace the women as choir members while keeping them at arms length—a practice he had perfected at Coal City with teenagers, but now he's up against sophisticated women.

"I don't understand all this concern about Angie," Ester badgers him. "We've got more altos than sopranos. Besides, Kay can sing the *Good Tidings* solo as well as Angie can."

"Maybe it's not her voice that..." Ann dives into the conversation but stops in mid-sentence before exposing the slanderous characterization of Angie she has promoted. Chad pretends not to hear the churlish chatter, choosing to keep Angie's secret to himself. He straightens up the music scattered across the piano, hoping these coquettes will leave him in peace.

"Are you worried about the *Messiah?* Chad? Chad?" Ann tries to get his attention.

"What?" Chad looks up from a stack of anthems on top of the piano. "Oh, excuse me, my mind's a thousand miles away."

They snicker in unison. Irma assures him, "Don't worry, Chad, we'll pull it off like we always do." The three women, none of whom is willing to be the first to depart and leave Chad with the other two, are behaving like teenagers jockeying for the last word with the captain of the football team. As Chad reaches for the light switch, Ann scampers to hold the door open, an act of courtesy that positions her for a parting word with Chad while the other two retrieve their children from the nursery. Ann figures: *Now that Angie's out of the picture, I can do a full-court press on the man of my dreams.*

Chad walks Ann to her car and waits for Irma, Ester and the nursery worker. "Good night all," Chad calls, eager to escape. But Ann hesitates as the others drive away. "Excuse me, Ann, I promised Paul Peterson I'd drop by the parsonage." Ann drives away, leaving the parking lot empty, except for Chad's red Mustang and a light colored Ford truck parked behind it. Thinking nothing of the other vehicle, Chad crosses the street and taps on the back door of the parsonage.

Paul, with Louella DeVan's complaint in hand, rises from the kitchen table and opens the door. "Have a good practice, Chad?" Paul greets his choir director through the screen.

"Fair, I think we're almost there. You wanted to see me?"

"Yes, briefly," Paul steps outside to confer in private, "I just want to check with you about the problems with the orchestra."

"We're all square, Paul. The union musicians wanted assurance that we would not violate our contact by paying the two amateur wind players. And the Jewish violinist from the symphony insisted the *Messiah* be presented as a secular concert and not a Christian worship service."

"And how'd that work out?"

"I told him that passing the collection plate during the program would be as close to religious as we would get. 'That's all right,' he said, 'We Jews also practice that sacred ritual'."

"Was he afraid I'd preach a sermon?"

"That did come up, but I told him Handel had left no room for homily in his composition," Chad laughs. "Anything else, Paul?"

"Nothing major, but I did receive a little flack about not preaching that Sunday," Paul slips Louella's letter into his pocket, "but don't worry about it. I doubt that anyone except our Jewish brother will fail to recognize the spiritual impact of Mr. Handel's masterpiece about Christ."

"I could not have possibly anticipated the horde of conflicts that would be involved with trying to raising Hope's Christmas celebration to a new level," Chad says, "I understand the altar guild ladies are upset that the orchestra will occupy some of their poinsettia display space around the altar. What's the deal with shifting a few flowerpots for one service?"

"Church members don't handle change very well. You remember that time at Coal City when we were blindsided by the Valentine Day debacle? Don't worry about the altar guild vigilantes. Let Marge handle those gals. Some of them insist on wrapping their religion around their flower arrangements with a satin ribbon." Paul grasps Chad's hand and bids him goodnight. "Carry on my friend and God be with you."

As the pastor closes the door, Chad crosses the street to his car and fumbles in the dark to unlock his car. A raspy voice breaks the eerie silence, and straightens every hair on Chad's head. "What 'cha done with my girl?" Chad spins around to realize the truck is still there, and he can just make out the silhouette of a head protruding from the window. Shaken and unsure whether to jump in his car and take off or risk a mugging by offering a genial response, his keys slip from his jittery fingers and hit the asphalt.

Chad manages to steady his voice enough for a brief response, "Sir?"

The man opens the truck door and steps from the shadows into the faint glow of the distant streetlight. Plunging both hands deep into the pockets of his oversized topcoat, he plants his feet in a menacing pose. "I said, what 'cha done with my girl, mister."

Chad studies the face exposed below the black toboggan stretched across his brow. Without taking his eyes off the stranger, Chad kneels and gropes for his keys. "I'm afraid you have the advantage, sir. Have we met before?"

Before the mysterious phantom can answer headlights from another car sweep across the parking lot and head directly toward them. Chad's fears escalate and his survival instincts jump into high gear. *Here comes his partner in crime to finish off the job.* To Chad's great relief the man inexplicably scrambles to his truck, starts the motor and drives off. Chad shields his eyes from the approaching headlights to identify the intruder's vehicle.

"Ann! What in heaven's name...?" Chad yells as she drives up beside him.

"Who was that? You look like you saw a ghost."

"Oh, nothing really," Chad wipes his moistened brow. "It seems our anonymous music critic is searching for someone. Apparently, he's barking up the wrong steeple." Chad tries to suppress his apprehension. "Why'd you come back?"

"It occurred to me you might need a cup of coffee after that grueling rehearsal, so let me buy you one at Krystal."

"Thanks Ann, but you know I never drink coffee at night."

"You know what I mean. Let me buy you a drink, or will it make you wet the bed?" Ann laughs, halfway expecting him to accept her umpteenth offer after as many refusals.

"I really appreciate your offer, but you know my rule—no socializing with choir members except in groups."

"Then I guess I'll have to quit the choir to be eligible for a date with you," Ann retorts. Immune to her limp threat, he climbs into his Mustang, but Ann signals she has something else to say. He rolls down the window.

"I wonder why that man came this far looking for somebody."

"What do you mean?"

"He's from Walker County. I saw his license plate."

"It's a mystery to me, Ann, but I suppose it's the season for mysteries. Goodnight, see you Sunday." As he leaves the parking lot, he recalls Angie saying she's from a Walker County town. She might know the identity of the mysterious stranger in the tan pickup. But then again, why would she know him? Unless…

~~~

Them headlights scared the shit outta me, screwed up my plan. That fella didn't give me no answer 'bout Angeline. As Tucker turns onto a side road to escape from the church, he wonders why his heart is pounding like a pile driver against his chest. *Hell, I fought the Krauts hand-to-hand in the woods in deep snow. Why should I be afraid of that music fella? I came out of a mine cave-in an' a coal-dust blowout without a scratch an' nearly drowned in a number 10 flood. So why's my heart thumping over this?*

"Goddammit," Tucker screams into the windshield, "still no sign of my girl. She's got to be somewhere around here." His ranting triggers a coughing spell. *Dammit, dammit, this mine crap is choking me to death. What kind of god let's a church drive a wedge between a man an' his wife an' little girl? What kind of preacher steals a man's only family?*

Tucker begins heaving and coughing so hard he has to pull over to recover. *I gotta find somethin' to drink, maybe a cup o' coffee.* When the coughing fit lets up a bit Tucker pulls back onto the highway and locates a gleaming white building with the neon Krispy Kreme sign. He parks in the shadow of the shop, just in case the choir director has called the cops. After watching a few cars drive by, Tucker feels secure enough to brace against the icy wind and go inside. He walks over to the counter and straddles a stool, unaware of a white-capped woman anticipating his order. She draws a steaming mug of coffee from the urn and sets it before him.

"Here y'are, honey, this'll grease your axel. What kind of donut will you have?" Tucker dismisses her with a wave of his hand, wanting to be left alone. Bending over the hot coffee, he inhales the steam to resuscitate his ailing airway.

The letters he pulls from his coat pocket are reminders of why he's sitting in a Birmingham donut shop on a cold winter night like this, against his doctor's orders. Tucker sips the hot coffee and rereads the unsigned claim form from United Mutual Insurance Company. *I wonder how long the insurance company will hold Angeline's money. Marie never told me she had life insurance. I reckon she decided to take care of her baby 'stead of me. But that's fine, I ain't got long to go nohow.*

The donut lady refills his coffee cup and goes about her business, as Tucker wonders why he had not found Angeline at Hope Methodist. *I watched choir practice every week for over a month an' still didn't see her, unless she's changed so much I don't recognize her. Maybe I sat too far back in the church. She jist might've been right there in front of my eyes an' I couldn't see her. My eyes ain't what they used to be, but they ain't so bad I can't find my own girl's face. Maybe she colored her hair back to blond, or red. Did she get fat or skinny? Did somebody tip her off that I came lookin' for her? I thought I could catch the choir director by hisself an' ask about Angeline in a way he'd answer without thinkin', but that didn't work too good. That other car came up an' scared me off, could've been the police.*

Tucker's decision-making apparatus has stripped a gear and the coffee before him is as black as the desperation that shrouds his soul. He senses he has only enough strength left for a limited number of trips to Birmingham before he becomes dependent on others to monitor his slow descent. A plan begins to evolve. *If*

Angeline is still singing with that choir, she'll show up for the big Christmas program. Tucker folds the papers, stuffs them back into his pocket, and flips a dime on the counter. Drawing one last sugar sweet aroma of warm glazed donuts, he pushes the glass door into the frosty air. *The long drive back to Mimosa in the dark might clear my mind enough to figure the rest of my plan for findin' Angeline. I know I'm gittin' close, feel it in my bones.*

17

> *March 6, 1966*
>
> *Dear Katy,*
> *I am writing to let you know that we made it to Selma without any problem. We had to sleep in the car last night because there was no room in the inn (ha, ha). There's talk about re-enacting the march to Montgomery but I doubt if we will go the distance. There's no need to worry about us as we are among friends who pledge to never let such a tragedy happen again. Also, National Guard troops are wall-to-wall here, pretty impressive.*
>
> *Love and kisses,*
>
> *Mom*

The overflow congregation's response to the *Messiah* exceeds the choir members' expectations as demonstrated by an explosion of applause following the final chord of the *Hal-le-lu-jah* chorus. The astounded Chad nods rather timorously as he faces the appreciative audience. He steps off the podium and shakes the first violinist's hand, a gesture he's accustomed to observing at symphony concerts. The lengthy applause subsides, and the congregation stands frozen and awed, expecting something more, perhaps a benediction. But Chad signals the choir to exit after giving the orchestra "thumbs up."

Nobody in the choir seemed to notice Tucker Shook sitting on the back pew. He had cleaned up for church, and left his toboggan and old coat in the truck with the rest of his luggage. As the crowd thins out, he wanders down the aisle holding a clean white handkerchief to his mouth to cover his coughing and to disguise his face, now stubble-free. Chad finishes handing out checks to the orchestra members, unaware the coarse, seasoned coal miner waits nearby.

"Mr. Willis, can I bother ya' for a minute?" The man stands near the side door, face drawn and pale, the frail bony frame swallowed up by the ill-fitting suit. He hopes his more civil approach will disguise his identity. He knows Chad's name from the printed program, but Angeline's name is missing.

"Yes sir, you may. Glad you came to the program," Chad responds cordially.

"I'm tryin' to find my girl. Her name's Angeline an' I hear she's in ya' choir."

"I don't think so, Mr. er..."

"Shook, Tucker Shook."

Chad swallows hard and stares into the man's eyes. *It's the guy in the truck that scared the hell out of me a few days ago.* Chad reaches out to shake hands, giving himself some time to think. "Glad to meet you Mr. Shook. Come on in the choir room and let me unload my arms," he holds up the orchestra score in his other hand. Chad tries to recall the details of his recent conversation with Angie in which she vowed never to speak to her father again. He finds himself in quite a dilemma, determined not to betray Angie's confidence, yet not wanting to lie to Mr. Shook. He's not sure what to say to this desperate father.

Evelyn meets Chad as he enters the choir room. "Don't forget the choir's going over to the Steer House for lunch..."

"I'll be there shortly," Chad hastily cuts her off before she spills the beans about a secret he shared with her earlier. "I've got business with this gentleman first." He points to Tucker who's standing behind the door just out of Evelyn's view.

She leaves the two men alone in the choir room. Chad walks over to the bulletin board and runs his fingers down the list of choir members. "Let me see, Mr. Shook, there was a Miss Shook that sang with us for a short time, here it is, Angie Shook. Would this be the young lady you're looking for?"

Tucker narrows his eyes trying to focus on the name by Chad's finger. "Yep, that could be her, my Angeline." He lifts the handkerchief to dry his eyes. "Can ya' tell me where she'd be 'bout now?"

Chad strokes his chin, trying to keep his words within the realm of truth. "Tell you what, Mr. Shook, let me check with the choir librarian to see if she might have Angie's address or phone number and I'll get back with you. If you'll give me your phone number…"

A rough bout of coughing seizes Tucker. He takes his misery outside. Chad grabs a pen and paper and follows him through the doorway. When the coughing fit subsides, Tucker shakes his head as Chad prepares to write the phone number. "Won't do no good, Mr. Willis. Ya' see, I've got this problem with my lungs an' I'm goin' to the hospital today. Don't know when I'll get out, or if I ever will."

"Which hospital? Maybe she can call you there, that is, if…"

"The V. A. Hospital here."

"Oh, then, I'll try to find Angie and bring her to see you myself, I promise."

"Don't wanna put ya' to no trouble, but I'd be much obliged to ya'." Tucker backtracks through the sanctuary to the parking lot, gets in his pick-up and drives away.

At the Steer House Chad drapes his coat across one of the seats next to Evelyn in the restaurant's private dining room. She removes her coat from an additional chair and winks. "For you-know-who," she whispers. As Chad works the room congratulating choir members, Ann interrogates Evelyn.

"Who're you saving that extra chair for?"

Evelyn coyly draws her lips tight and shrugs her shoulders. "You'll see soon enough."

Everyone has just finished ordering ice tea and sodas when Spencer jumps up and shouts from across the table, "There's Angie!"

Ann shields her mouth and whispers to Irma, "Wonder what the hell she's doing here?"

Spencer tries to squeeze his way around the table toward Angie, but she heads straight for Chad and greets him with a kiss. A deflated Spencer slips back to his chair as Angie smiles and waves at the choir members. Chad raises his hand to quell the flurry of questions and comments from the lively crowd seated around the long table. "You folks remember Angie, she's joining us for lunch." The choir members applaud enthusiastically with the exception of token gestures from the thorny threesome.

"We sure needed you about an hour ago, girl," Marge shouts.

"Me especially," Kay adds, drawing laughter from the crowd.

Chad pumps his hands to calm things down. "Yes, Angie, we really missed you, but in all honesty, this choir handled old man Handel like seasoned professionals. But here comes our lunch so let's eat and visit. Afterwards, I believe some speeches are in order." Groans fill the room. "Whoa…I just made my speech, it'll be Angie's turn next."

While some fiddle with the remnants of red velvet cake, Chad taps a glass with his spoon as Angie stands. "First, let me say I'm sorry to have missed your performance this morning. I'm sure it was outstanding. Chad tells me that next I'm supposed to make an announcement, but…" she grimaces and taps her forehead, "…I seem to have forgotten what it is." She leans over and bends her ear toward Chad who can't contain his laughter. Then he shrugs his shoulders, reaches into his coat pocket and slips a ring on Angie's finger.

"There," she lifts her left hand high to display the sparkling diamond, "I knew it was something important."

Amid shrieks and laughter, the choir members enjoy Angie's little joke, with the exception of Spencer and the treacherous trio with their thinly disguised pouts.

Before the celebration diminishes, someone shouts, "And when is the big day?"

Angie responds, "I'm pleased to announce that Chad and I have agreed to get married—but we have not agreed on a wedding date." The choir members, expecting another joke, smile and wait for the punch line.

After an uneasy pause, Evelyn rises, "Let me be the first to congratulate our fortunate couple."

The choir members swarm Chad and Angie wishing them happiness except Ann who lingers behind to have the last word fraught with faint good will. "Angie, I'm sure you and Chad will be strong enough to overcome the difference in your ages."

After lunch, Chad and Angie spend the afternoon at his apartment discussing plans for their wedding, maybe in late summer. Finally, Chad garners enough nerve to mention his meeting with Tucker Shook. Angie spouts a curt reaction, "You promised to bring me to see him? I can't believe you told him that!" She dashes to the kitchen and fills a water glass. "It seems to me you've got more important matters to deal with than nosing into my affairs...these plants are dying of thirst." Angie frenetically splashes water on his wilted peace plants, with all the fervor of a woman incensed. Moments later, reflecting on the news about her father, she asks, "Did he seem very sick to you?"

"Like walking death."

"You know, all the time I was growing up, Daddy only came to hear me sing once, and then he chickened out. He didn't care whether I chirped like a canary or croaked like a frog. Momma used to beg him to go to church, just to be there for me, but he always refused. He once told Momma that singing canaries were only good for warning about poison gas in the mine. That's when I knew he didn't care about me or my singing. Momma's the one who took me everywhere, 'til I turned sixteen. Then she bought me a beat-up old Chevy and taught me to drive so I wouldn't miss voice lessons, rehearsals and, and..." Angie breaks down and cries, collapsing into Chad's arms. "He didn't even care enough to tell me she died."

Angie remains indomitable about not talking to her estranged father. Chad, intent on keeping his promise to Tucker, doesn't know how to respond; so he vows to continue this discussion later in a renewed atmosphere.

With finals over and Christmas Eve services behind them, Angie and Chad journey to his hometown on Christmas Day. "Chadwick Noah Willis!" his mother exclaims wiping her hands on the gingham apron around her neck, "It's about time you came to see your momma." Chad glances at Angie who is suppressing a giggle upon hearing his whole name for the first time. After introducing Angie to Chad's sister and grandmother, the women guide her into the kitchen to talk about wedding plans while they prepare Christmas dinner.

When the women shoo Angie out of the kitchen so they can clean up after dinner, Chad's mother suggests he show Angie around town. "Be sure to take her by the church where you learned to sing in the choir when you were growing up."

Chad drives through the cotton mill village to a knoll overlooking the community's churches. He parks and shuts of the engine. "Here we are, at the crossroads of Heaven, as my dad used to say."

They get out of the car to view the scenery. Angie raves, "Oh, Chad, how quaint, how perfectly quaint!" Three steeples glisten like tree ornaments in the crisp December sun, stanchions of the community's moral fabric. Angie, cooing in awe, squeezes Chad's hand. "Let's go inside." They get back in the car and drive down to the Methodist Church only to find the doors locked. The Presbyterian Church is locked too, but they find the side door to the largest church, Salem Baptist, is open.

They step into the anteroom from which the choir and pastor make their entrances, then open the door to a cold sanctuary sprinkled with lemony flickers of sun that filter through the west windows. "Oh, don't you just love that rich piney aroma? Those pews must be over a hundred years old." She peeks over the rail behind the pulpit and into the choir loft. "Is this where you learned to sing?"

Chad laughs, "Oh no, we went to the Methodist Church."

"Oh Chad, Let's get married here," Angie pleads, raising her arms and pirouetting down the aisle.

"Here, in a Baptist church?"

"I mean here in the village, it doesn't matter which church."

"But, but..." Chad is dumbfounded, stuck in his tracks.

"Listen, my prince, I just had an interesting conversation with your family. Your grandmother said she'd like to come to the wedding, but she might not be able to travel all the way to Birmingham. And your mother is concerned that either she or your sister will have to stay with her. So we'll have our wedding here and they all can come. Besides, I don't really have a home church to get married in."

"But what about our friends, they'd expect us to..."

"Friends? I don't have enough friends for a bridge game, and who will you invite to the wedding, the choir? You're just hired help. You need to think about your family first."

"What about your family?"

"I don't have any," she snaps.

"Let me tell you a story before we make a decision," Chad says.

"O. K., but let's get back in the car. I'm getting cold."

They settle in the car, Chad cranks the motor and turns up the heater. "Angie, do you remember when I told you about my dad on the way down here?"

"About his passing away while you were in the army, yes."

"I didn't tell you the whole story. When I finished college I only had a couple of weeks at home before I was drafted. One morning at breakfast, Dad and I disagreed over something too trivial to even mention. The argument escalated until I blew up and he hit me across the face with a milk carton. I packed up and left, swearing never to speak to him again. A few months later I received word that Dad was hospitalized with a heart attack. The

Red Cross flew me back from Korea, but I arrived too late. My mother told me Dad had wanted to reconcile our differences, but he was waiting for me to make the first move."

"That's sad, but what does that have to do with our wedding plans?"

Chad pauses, trying to find the appropriate words to make his point. "You see, when I swore never to talk to my dad again until he apologized for striking me, I made a huge mistake. He died before I had a chance to say goodbye."

"I'm sorry," Angie replies with no hint of emotion.

"What I'm trying to say in a roundabout way is that I think you need to talk to your dad before…you know, before it's too late." Angie bristles but says nothing. "You know, it's customary for the bride's father to give her away?"

"You don't understand what I've been trying to explain. My daddy gave me away years ago, the same way I gave my baby away to strangers."

Chad lets her have the last word, and they reach a stalemate in the discussion. He puts the car in gear and faces Angie, "Are we having our first real argument?" She offers a miniscule smile and stares out the window.

On the trip back to Birmingham, Chad brings up the touchy subject again. "What shall I tell your dad?"

"I don't want you to talk to him again. You'll start feeling sorry for him and he'll come between us just like he did Momma and me."

Chad proposes an alternate solution. "What if I ask Paul to check on your dad once in a while? He makes hospital visits anyway."

"O. K. if he wants too, but I don't want him to feel like he has to report to me. Just tell him to do his preacher thing and leave me out of it, O. K.?"

~~~

As the New Year unfolds and churches begin to focus on the upcoming Lenten season, Angie's unyielding attitude towards

Tucker is among the least of Paul's concerns. The Ash Wednesday service rekindles Paul's unflinching passion for ensuring fundamental decency and respect for every person and plunges him further into the rising tide of the struggle for civil rights. He has been drawn in and is inextricably bound by the relentless undertow of his moral convictions, his head held above water by the indelible words of Dietrich Bonhoeffer.

The consequences for Paul's staff are evident as he appears more and more disengaged during their weekly meetings. At today's meeting Marilyn presents her usual rosy report on the children's program. Then Associate Pastor, Edgar, announces the names of hospitalized members, pausing after the last name, "Tucker Shook, Who is that? Is he a member here?"

After an awkward pause, waiting for Paul to respond, Chad steps in and explains that situation, and then outlines his tentative plans for Lenten music. Marge passes around a schedule of church activities for the ensuing week and waits for Paul to conclude the meeting with prayer.

Paul looks up at the expectant gazes of his staff. "Thank you Marge, I know it's my turn. It's just that I…I come before you this morning, as our illustrious President likes to say, *with a heavy heart*." The staff perks up, aware that some sinister spirit has infected his customary convivial demeanor. "My hope for the church and for the world is an engine running on rapidly dissipating fumes. Here it is the second week of Lent and Armageddon looms over us. Already six months have passed since Congress passed the Civil Rights Law and the doors of our white churches continue to remain barriers to our black brothers and sisters. We sit around like Nero, fiddling while the fire rages around us. Who will sound the clarion call for justice if we, the ministers, refuse to take a stand? President Johnson has been bombing North Vietnam for three weeks now and we appear to he headed down the path of nuclear destruction. Help me out folks, what am I going to preach about? My silo of meaningful sermons is depleted. Please don't suggest I pray about it. My whole existence has become a walking prayer for peace, understanding and courage—courage to take action, to lead our church off dead center."

Edgar speaks up, "I wonder what the other preachers are doing. Are they just as discouraged?"

"I've talked to some whose sensitivity and concern range from nil to zero. I think their compassion for the world situation reaches no farther than the back pews of their own churches. One of my colleagues said he's got enough trouble making his budget, let alone thinking about racial problems and war. Another one suggested that I stick to preaching the scriptures and not poke my nose into social issues." Paul wipes his brow with a tissue and sinks back into his chair.

"I have an idea," Edgar leans forward tapping his fingers on the table. "There's a district preachers meeting coming up soon. If you can get on the agenda you could bring your concerns out in the open."

Paul pauses until a long-absent glimmer returns to his eyes, and he perks up in his chair. "That's a good suggestion, Edgar. The Bishop will be there, also. I'll call around and see if we can get a panel discussion going for the meeting. We'd better adjourn before I lose the train of thought. Let's pray."

Paul lines up a quartet of fellow preachers who are willing to contribute their opinions concerning the role of the church in today's society, but when he mails them a letter listing points of concern to be considered, all but one decline and offer their associates to speak in their stead. They are willing to address world hunger, the threat of Communism and the need for more missionaries, but not Paul's suggested topics—race relations and the Vietnam conflict. The possibilities of the panel's impact have been diminished, but Paul proceeds with his plan. He will challenge the pastors to lead the charge toward social justice with all deliberate speed.

The day before the district meeting, he pores over the writings of Ghandi, Bonhoeffer, Schweitzer and, of course, the letters of the Apostle Paul, who had borne the cumbersome yoke of conflict throughout Asia Minor. A gentle knock on the study door intrudes on his reflection. Marge pokes her head in, "I know you don't want to be disturbed, but the pastor of St. Francis is here to see you. He says it's urgent."

Oh no, not the Red Barron. Don't I have enough on my plate without listening to his diatribe? "O. K., Marge," he sighs. *I'll just leave these books open. Maybe Ollie Barron will take the hint and be brief.*

Ollie plows past Marge before she can invite him into Paul's study. "Good morning, Brother, I trust all is well with you and your family," his flush face and furrowed brow contradict the cheerful greeting. Paul shakes hands politely and sits back down, offering his intrusive colleague a seat. Ollie remains standing and makes sure Marge has closed the door before he levels an attack on his colleague. "Are you out of your mind, Paul?" Paul is accustomed to the abrupt manner, the same technique Ollie uses to start his sermons, but this time he is more intense. "Surely you don't intend to turn tomorrow's district meeting into a protest march promoting integration. We're not a bunch of hair-triggered college students. We should be about the Lord's business."

"What on earth are you raving about, Ollie?"

"That panel discussion you've concocted. I hear you're having trouble finding participants. Nobody in their right mind is stupid enough to tamper with that hornets' nest. I hear the District Superintendent and the Bishop are both pretty upset with you." Ollie's fists crunch on Paul's desk, he leans forward, knuckles white. "Take my advice and back off tomorrow. We've got more important business to attend."

Paul struggles to maintain his composure as his blood begins to percolate. "Peace and justice are our business, dear brother. Furthermore, if the Bishop and D. S. have a problem with me, they ought to have the decency to tell me to my face, not send you to do their dirty work." Ollie backs away from the desk, perplexed at Paul's reluctance to even consider his advice. "In the interest of clearing the air, I'll call Philip and the Bishop later, since you come on their behalf. Thanks for the visit, Ollie, goodbye." Paul walks to the door and ushers the amazingly speechless Dr. Barron out of his study. He resumes work on his presentation. *There's no time to call the Bishop and D. S., they'd never admit to using Ollie as a lackey anyway.*

At District Superintendent Jones' invitation, Bishop Grand gives a devotional and opening prayer at the March meeting of his district clergy. "We have an extremely packed agenda today," Reverend Jones announces as the Bishop takes his seat on the dais, "so please keep your comments and reports brief and to the point." Paul Peterson sits patiently through the first two hours, gripping a folded newspaper and watching the clock. With only one hour remaining, he becomes anxious about having enough time for his panel discussion, the last item on the agenda. Finally at ten minutes before noon, Philip Jones announces, "Brother Peterson has organized a panel discussion to conclude today's agenda. While the members of the panel come forward let me remind everyone that lunch will be served at twelve noon sharp in the dining hall next door, and that fried chicken won't keep long."

Paul hurries to the podium. He motions the members of the panel who have risen, to sit back down. "In the interest of time, with Brother Jones' permission, we will forgo today's discussion of the topic listed on your program." Audible sighs of relief fill the room. Ollie Barron's grin and wink at Rev. Jones and the Bishop do not go unnoticed by Paul.

"When I first planned to place a number of vital concerns before my fellow laborers in the vineyards of our faith, I felt we needed to discuss our role in social matters outside the sanctuary walls, like the war in Vietnam and the racial unrest that plagues our state and our nation. But after prayerful consideration, I have changed my mind." Once again, Ollie Barron displays a knowing and assured smile to his superiors, taking credit for Paul's change of heart.

Paul loosens his grip on the newspaper, unfolds it and displays an article hidden on a back page. "This article appeared a year ago, describing the attempted march from Selma to Montgomery by a group of citizens, to affirm their support of the Civil Rights Bill and promote peaceful integration. What happened on Pettus Bridge was enough to challenge every Christian in this country. Last night I witnessed a film of this march on national television, of police and State troopers attacking unarmed marchers. What I saw made me sick. But what made me even sicker was the realization that many of those club-wielding officers were probably sitting in church pews the previous Sunday listening to sermons about the love of Jesus, the justice of Isaiah, the forbearance of Job." Tears fill Paul's eyes and Ollie Barron squirms in his seat, stealing a glance at the Bishop and District Superintendent.

"Please pardon me," Paul wipes his eyes as some look down at their watches. "When one of my staff members suggested that we have a rational discussion about the role of clergy in addressing social issues, I jumped at the chance. I trusted these men of God to be reasonable and thoughtful. Given the facts, they would gladly take up the cross and lead their congregations along the high road. Like Jesus and Paul, yea, even like Dietrich Bonhoeffer, my esteemed colleagues would stand firmly on the bridge between faith and ethics, and rail against the injustices being inflicted on our fellow human beings. But, alas, is it possible I am a victim of wayward thinking? Is it possible that we have shifted our faith from the center of our noble calling to the fringes of political expediency? The bloody fiasco on the Pettus Bridge at Selma last year was not the first incident of injustice perpetuated on our black brethren. The church bombings, the fire hoses and dogs turned loose on school children, the killings intended to halt integration—these should have been calls for action, but here a year later, we remain in our pulpits promoting the illusion that all is well in Birmingham. Brothers, we are not going to solve these problems from the pulpit, we have to shed our lily white robes and fancy stoles and take a stand alongside the peaceful protesters. No, it is not I who suffers from wrong thinking in this room. The time for pious talk has expired. It's time for true ministers of God to lead the way. Personally, I cannot wait for a discussion of pros and cons, nor can I abide a cleverly worded resolution from this group. Instead, I invite you to go with me and stand on Pettus Bridge in Selma to commemorate the anniversary of that march for freedom."

A handful of younger ministers spring to their feet and applaud Paul's challenge. The stern silent stares from the veterans send some of these neophytes melting back into their seats. The Bishop and District Superintendent fumble through their papers in an attempt to distance themselves from Paul's speech.

"One final thought, my brothers," Paul concludes. "Did you ever wonder how many lives could have been saved if the German clergy had followed Dietrich Bonhoeffer's lead in resisting the Nazi onslaught against their own people? It is we who must be the moral leaders of our people, who must derail this runaway train of racism and violence. Some of you are probably thinking, 'Look what happened to Bonhoeffer.' Personally, I would ask no lesser fate than to follow him to the gallows in exchange for an end to the tragic racial strife among our people."

The heavy, almost choking, silence that follows Paul's declaration of intent to take the high road of Christian belief is broken only by a wave of uneasy rustling that moves across the sanctuary. "If you cannot find it in your hearts to accompany me to Selma, please embrace my humble quest with your prayers."

Paul descends the pulpit dais amidst a barely audible sprinkling of "amen's." It is not only the aroma of fried chicken that quickens the exodus from the sanctuary.

18

> April 15, 1966
>
> Dear Bishop Grand:
>
> Pursuant to our previous conversation about the future of St. Francis Methodist Church and its position as a center of faith in the Redmont Community, the Board of Trustees is requesting your permission to begin negotiations with the trustees at Larksdale Methodist Church in consideration for a possible merger between the two churches in the future.
>
> In view of the changing demographics of our neighborhood, the Trustees feel that a unified congregation located in the expanding Larksdale Community will serve the church more efficiently. We look forward to your honoring our request.
>
> Sincerely,
>
> H. R. Wood, Chairman, Board of Trustees
>
> Dr. T. Oliver Barron, Senior Pastor

Light snow bounces off the windshield of Paul's car as he listens to a disc jockey assure drivers not to worry. "It's only a freak spring show shower for Alabama, folks. According to the weather bureau, there's no danger that roads will ice over." He enters the parking deck and slides his clergy card into the slot and the striped cross bar goes up. Minutes later he enters a large room on the fourth floor where Tucker sits on the edge of his hospital bed chatting with three other patients whose privacy curtains are also rolled back.

"How're we doing today, Mr. Shook?" Paul shakes his hand.

"Tucker, Preacher. Remember it's Tucker. Ya' know my buddies, Carl, Ralph an' General Bradley." Paul nods and speaks to each veteran.

"Four-star General Omar Bradley, sir, Fifth Army, European Theatre," the oldest resident states with authority. Paul accedes to his delusion offering a limp salute. "At ease Chaplain, carry on."

Paul has been there often enough to remember not to smile and patronize the war torn veteran or he'd risk getting chewed out. "It's snowin', Preacher, ya' gonna be able to git home?" Tucker directs Paul to the only chair in the room.

"The forecast indicates the ground's too warm for snow to stick," Paul replies. Tucker chats a few minutes about the weather, stock car racing and working conditions in number ten mine. Suddenly, he removes a hospital robe from his bed hook, takes a Gideon Bible off the table and asks Paul to take a walk with him

"You gonna read the Good Book to the preacher?" Ralph quips. Tucker cleverly steps aside to let the preacher leave the room first and as he follows Paul out he gives Ralph the finger behind his back.

As they start down the hall to the day room, Tucker says, "Got somethin' I wanna ask ya', Preacher, if ya' don't mind."

"Angie's doing fine. Remember I've promised that's all I can tell you at this point, but one day…"

"Yeah, I remember, but what I wanna ask ya' is about church."

Paul figures the Bible Tucker has wedged under his arm is a sign he's been thinking about his faith. "Go ahead, I'm sure that's something I can help you with."

Tucker stops and looks Paul in the eyes, dead serious. "I been wonderin', what made that church in Mimosa turn my wife an' kid 'gainst me?" Unable to conceal his shock and curiosity, Paul leads Tucker to a couple of vinyl chairs in the day room and settles in to listen to his concern. "It all started when Marie made Angeline sing in church when she was jist six year old."

Then for a half hour, Paul listens to this un-churched mine worker present an alien perspective of the church—details of a script that might just as well have been created by old Satan himself. He comes down hard on the conspiring preacher and choir director. "They tricked my little girl into singin' for free an' suckered her momma into the deal. On Sundays I wanted to go somewhere for fun, ya' know, like a family, but Marie'd dress Angeline up, put makeup on her an' go off to a singin' at a church somewhere. Now, whatcha call that if it ain't pullin' a family apart?"

"I don't know, Tucker, what did your wife have to say about it?"

"Damn little...Oh, my fault Preacher, that slipped. Marie wan't mor'n a kid herself when we got married. I hate to admit it but Angeline came along jist couple a days after that. It was sorta like they growed up together. It was them 'gainst me more'n I recollect." Paul sees remorse beginning to creep over Tucker. "Dang, Preacher, I know ya' don't wanna hear all this crap."

"So you blame the church for causing this gap between you and Angie?"

"I ain't 'xactly blamin' that buildin' a-settin' on Main Street, but them people what ran it."

"Like...?"

"They was this slick preacher who come along 'n wrapped Angeline an' her mother both 'round his little finger. I never got to meet him, but all I heard was how he drove a baby blue convertible, played a guitar an' sang songs the kids liked." Ollie Barron's image flashes through Paul's mind as he listens. "I been talkin' to people ever since my Marie died. Now I ain't very smart when it comes to church stuff, but things jist don't add up."

"Like what, Tucker?"

"From what people say, that preacher an' Angeline spent a whole lotta time together, 'specially when her an' her momma got sideways with each other. He even got her some money to go to college. I called him last year, tryin' to find Angeline, an' he acted kinda huffy 'cause I asked 'bout her. He told me he ain't seen her since he left Mimosa. I heard what he was sayin', but he acted like somebody that ain't tellin' the truth. Do ya' see what I mean?"

"I understand, but it's common practice for Methodist ministers to sever all ties with their former congregations. It's not meant to offend..."

"But they ain't nothin' common 'bout that preacher!" Tucker is about to work into a rage when a coughing spell intervenes. "Dammit, I don't wanna do this," he wheezes and sucks in enough breath to continue his complaint. "Sometimes I feel like I'm gonna turn wrong side out an' die."

Paul pats him gently on the back. "Is there some reason you're telling me about your troubles with the church?"

"Yeah, but I ain't sure 'xactly what it is," Tucker opens the Bible. "It's too mixed up for a' old coal miner like me to untangle, sorta like one of them soap operas the General likes to watch." He takes several slips of paper from between the pages and offers them to Paul. "It probably don't mean nothin' an' I sure hope it don't, but what d'ya think of this?"

Paul sifts through the papers. "These seem to be dates and places—Mimosa High School, Mimosa Methodist Church, Harken's Methodist, Masonic Hall. What am I supposed to be looking for?"

"Keep on goin'."

"Hmm, Coal City, 1953. That sounds familiar. Christmas Eve at Gallant Heights, 1952 and here's one marked Sargent's Crossroads...and here's another."

"What d'ya figure from all them notes?" Tucker wheezes.

"I don't know exactly, looks like you kept your schedule on these bits of paper...but wait. You said you didn't go to church."

"Them's Marie's. She always wrote down where Angeline went to sing. That was her way of makin' sure she got there. And when she bought my girl a car, she still wrote'em down. Kinda her way o' keepin' up with her, I guess."

"Where is Sargent's Crossroads, Tucker?"

"Halfway b'tween Mimosa an' Birmingham. Funny thing is, ain't nothin' there but a few stores, a motel, and two little churches. Them preachers there told me they ain't never heard of my Angeline, so I been wonderin' what Marie was doin' out in the middle of nowhere all by herself."

"I'm sure she had some reason…"

"Look at them dates. Angeline was in college. When I first saw them notes I didn't think nothin', but me an' my buddies in the room got to talkin' the other day an' Ralph said somethin' that crossed my mind some years back. He said Marie was prob'ly meetin' somebody there."

"So, was that so unusual?"

"Marie didn't have no car. Somebody musta took her to the crossroads an' brought her back."

"Tucker, there must be a reasonable explanation. You mustn't allow your delusional buddies to warp the memory of your wife. There is nothing wrong with *your* mind, my friend." Paul picks up Tucker's Bible and hands it back to him. "It's getting late and I have a couple of other calls to make."

"O. K., Preacher. I don't know what brought on this talkin' streak in me. I 'preciate ya' comin' by. Ya' might even change my mind 'bout preachers, but don't make no bets," he laughs.

Paul follows Tucker back to his room where they find General Bradley glued to *As the World Turns*. Ralph looks up from a comic book. "Tuck, what'd yo' preacher say 'bout that other preacher screwing yo' wife?"

Tucker bellows and flings the Bible at his ward mate, scattering notes all over the floor. "Shut the hell up, Ralph, ya' crazy bastard!" Paul stoops to retrieve the scraps of paper. "That's all right, Brother, I'll clean it up. Ya' gotta go."

Paul gathers his coat and heads out the door. "I'll look in on you next week, Tucker. Give me a call if you need anything before then. You still have my card?"

Tucker nods, "Ain't nothin' I need 'cept for ya' to bring Angeline back with ya' next time." Paul smiles and shakes his head all the way to the elevator.

~~~

Early in 1966, Ollie Baron's ministry at St. Francis begins to fray at the edges like a silk flag on a powerboat. The first threat comes at the breakfast table, the minute he recognizes the face in the photo on the front page of the March twelfth edition of the *Birmingham Post-Herald.* "Oh no, it's Paul Peterson. Look at him standing there arm-in-arm with those men in overalls. He's the only white face in the group."

Betty sets the plate of pancakes in front of Ollie and peers over his shoulder at the paper. "Nice picture of Brother Paul."

"Nice picture? Why, it's the most stupid thing that liberal agitator has ever done since St. Francis showed him the door!" Ollie Barron shuffles the morning paper, agitated beyond control. "Look at that sanctimonious face spread half-way across the page!" Betty retrieves his napkin from the floor and drops it back in his lap.

"Eat your breakfast, dear. I don't understand why you're so angry at Paul for…"

"I'm not angry…I'm…I'm disgusted. He's giving the rest of us a bad name…giving the church a black eye," Ollie scowls as he slams the paper to the floor. He toys with his breakfast—and his subconscious. *Why am I angry indeed? Why do these fools get all the publicity while we who hold our churches together go unnoticed? Where's the justice? I'm not a racist. I'm a pacifist, just trying to keep everybody calm until those demonstrators get tired and go back up north. Blessed are the peacemakers, for they live in quiet desperation.* "Did you know that since no one else volunteered to abandon their churches and join up with that rabble in Selma, he dragged Lorna along with him?"

"Really, is she in the picture?" Betty picks up the paper.

"I don't know, didn't look that closely. But I do know that I'd never let you do such a crazy thing. He's standing on the highway where that woman with the Italian sounding name was shot and killed while driving to Selma for last year's march."

"Mrs. Luizzo?"

"Yeah, something like that. She left her family up north to join that stupid march, and look what happened."

"She'll probably become a martyr, don't you think, Ollie?" Betty wipes two-year old Angela's mouth and releases her from the high chair to go play in her room.

"Ain't no way, if you'll excuse the expression. For that to happen, Governor Wallace would have to go on television and apologize for all the trouble he's causing, then appoint Martin Luther King as his executive assistant and start attending that black church just down the street from the State Capitol. That woman will be remembered as no more than just a deranged housewife who abandoned her family to take care of somebody else's business."

Betty is surprised and shocked at her husband's crude, insensitive characterization of the tragedy. "Is that your hope for Angela Olive, to become just a housewife?"

"She could do no worse. Look at you," he tries to divert the discussion and concentrate on the fit of indignation he'd worked up over Paul Peterson's propulsion into the limelight. But his remark strikes a raw nerve with Betty. She takes her plate to the sink trying to control the simmering animosity within her. "God Almighty, I'll bet the Bishop's hopping mad if he's seen the paper," Ollie continues his rampage. "It wouldn't surprise me if he's not already on the phone arranging to send Paul to the boonies in Jackson County."

The phone rings. Ollie jumps up, "I'll get it...probably the old man himself." He lifts the receiver off the wall by the refrigerator. "Hello...Oh, good morning H. R., how are you?"

Betty leaves Ollie to pander to that real estate magnate. She sits on the floor beside Angela, who's playing with her toys. Picking up *Three Little Pigs,* Betty asks the toddler if she wants to hear a story. Angela crawls into her mother's lap and pops a thumb in her mouth. Betty nuzzles Angela's downy, rust colored hair. *My baby, you need to help me neutralize your daddy's chauvinism before you grow up, or you won't have a snowball's chance in hell to make something of yourself.*

Ollie comes back and kisses them goodbye. "I need to go meet H. R. at his office. He wants to discuss the upcoming meeting of the Zoning Board. There's an issue on the agenda that could affect our church. Call Mrs. Green for me and tell her I won't be in until after lunch."

"Yes, dear," Betty answers with a flip of her hand and a trace of sarcasm that slips under her husband's radar.

~~~

"Y'all come on in my office," the man in the gray suit beckons to the visitors standing in the hallway of the municipal building. He follows them inside and closes the unmarked door to his private office. The man brushes cigar ashes off his coat before taking a seat in the leather chair behind his glass topped mahogany desk scattered with layers of important looking papers. He slips his horn-rimmed glasses on and presses the center against his nose. Touching a pencil point to his legal pad, he asks, "Now let's see who we have here, Mr. Peterson?" Paul turns the palm of his hand toward the man across the desk.

"It's Reverend Peterson," Katy adds.

"And you'd be Mrs. Peterson?" the man checks off another name on the pad.

"No sir, Reverend Peterson's my father and I was just wondering why…"

"We'll get to b'iness in good time Miss Peterson," he interrupts.

"Mrs. Major," Katy corrects him again. "My name is Katy Peterson Major."

The man emits a condescending chuckle, "I see, I see. My secretary must've thought you were in the Salvation Army. She wrote down Major Katy Peterson. Now, I assume you're Grace Baer and not 'bare Grace'," he looks up and chuckles again, "and you would be Jesse Shuman. Now, do I have everybody straight?" Not amused, Paul nods and exchanges glances with Jesse. Grace shifts her weight, still suffering occasional pains from the injuries received during her attempt to accompany black students to a St. Francis service. After that incident she had wanted to give up the mission and return to law school, but her fiancé convinced her to stay and lay a pro bono footing on which she could build a future career practicing law.

Jesse speaks up, "Mr. Farrow, we came here to meet with the Zoning Board. May I ask why we're meeting with you in private?"

"In good time, Shuman, all in good time. For all intents and purposes, I am the Board. It's my policy to meet with people who try to get themselves on the Board's agenda, you know, just to help me understand the nature of your b'iness. You see, boy, I don't like surprises that could embarrass the good citizens on my Board. Now since you wouldn't tell my secretary your concerns, perhaps you'll tell me. Maybe we can work out something without having to put it before the Board, you know, save a little time." Chairman Farrow rears back in his chair and puffs on a cigar, blowing smoke rings towards his visitors. "By the way, Shuman, you're not from around here are you?"

Before Jesse can respond, Paul intervenes, "Mr. Shuman and Miss Baer are law students on leave from Harvard. They're donating their time to help eliminate discrimination in Birmingham."

"And how do you propose to do that, Shuman, have a sit-in, or what?"

Jesse opens his briefcase and removes a legal pad and copies of pages from the City Code. Spreading the papers on the desk, he explains his mission. "Here are sections of Birmingham Real Estate laws that clearly violate the Federal Civil Rights Laws. And here are copies of real estate covenants that prohibit the sale of houses and land to Negroes in certain areas of the city. And here…"

"Hold on there. Where'd you get those copies?" Before Jesse answers, Farrow points to the papers and sputters, "We have laws against larceny too."

Paul rises to Jesse's defense. "Mr. Farrow, I assure you these copies were obtained legally. All we're trying to do is…"

"I know what y'all wanna do, humph…come down heah and upset our God-fearing folks who've done nothing but carry on a decent way of life. Now, I've got a meetin' next door." Farrow crushes his cigar in the ashtray and rises to leave.

Paul says, "Thank you for your time, Mr. Farrow, we'll see you in the Board meeting."

"No sir, that won't be necessary. I'll handle it from here. We already have a full agenda today."

"What?" exclaims Jesse. "But, your secretary…"

"…Gets a little mixed up sometimes, bless her heart. This Board doesn't have jurisdiction over covenants and the City Code. You'll need to take those complaints to the Federal Court. Good luck and…oh, by the way, Preacher, didn't I see your picture in the paper a few days ago?" Paul does not acknowledge Farrow's observation. "Just as I figured, 'nigger lovers'."

"So that's how a local politician's office smells," Jesse remarks to Katy after being ushered out of Farrow's office.

"You mean that stuffy cigar?"

"No, I mean the appalling stench of bigotry."

After months of maneuvering through the political land mines at City Hall, Jesse's quest for fair housing in Birmingham shows little evidence of progress. Although Paul Peterson continues to lend moral support, Katy's time and efforts are limited by caring for her baby girl. Despite their setbacks, Jesse, Paul and Grace maintain the pressure on elected officials and their cohorts. On one of their visits to the Tax Assessor's office, the trio runs into Ollie Barron and H. R. Wood as they are leaving.

"Brother Paul!" Ollie exclaims, "What are you doing here?" He approaches Paul cautiously with one eye on H. R.

Paul offers Ollie a polite restrained handshake and addresses his companion. "Good morning, Mr. Wood, nice to see you again." H. R. shakes Paul's hand, anticipating an answer to Ollie's question.

"And these are my friends, Grace Baer and Jesse Shuman," Paul diverts Ollie's inquiry with introductions.

"I know who they are," H. R. says to Paul, ignoring Jesse's outstretched hand. "Let's be on our way, Brother Barron." With that terse remark, H. R. heads toward the door leaving Ollie to trot along behind his benefactor clicking his heels on the marble floor like a fresh-shod pony.

When Paul returns to his office, Marge waves three yellow slips of paper in the air. "What did you do to that red-headed preacher now, Brother Paul?" she shakes her head and grins.

"Thanks, Marge, I've been expecting these calls." He takes the notes and drops them into the waste can. "No need to call back; he'll beat me to it." Paul smiles and begins a countdown with a finger pointed at Marge's phone, "Ten, nine, eight, seven, six, five, four, three, two, one... zero."

"What're you doing?"

"Using ESP, but..." The phone rings. "Guess my timing's off a second or two."

Marge controls a giggle as she answers, "Hope Methodist, Marge speaking...Oh, hello Reverend Barron...yes, he just walked in...hold on a sec..." She presses the "hold" button. "You are something else, Brother Paul. I don't know what, but you are really something else," she laughs.

Paul barely utters hello when Ollie flies into him like a hawk on a chick. "What in God's name do you think you are doing to the church, Paul?"

"Everything I do is in God's name, Ollie. What specifically do you have in mind?"

"You're consorting with rabble-rousers, for one thing. You surely weren't downtown spreading the Gospel." Paul thumbs through the mail on his desk while Ollie finishes blowing off the steam that has built up since their chance encounter at the courthouse. "Those idiots and their ilk are out to destroy our communities and our churches with their blockbusting campaign. They're taking H. R. Wood to court trying to force him to sell houses to Negroes in Redmont Acres. Now, you know what that will do to his business. One colored family moves in and all the whites will sell and move out. The market collapses and Wood Real Estate goes bankrupt. I think I know why you're doing this, Paul and I don't like it one bit." Ollie stops for a breath and Paul hears labored breathing in the phone. "You're just mad at St. Francis for sending you packing three years ago and now you're out to get even. Well, you're no Joshua and St. Francis is no Jericho, so just back off, my friend, and take care of your own flock."

"Settle down Ollie, sounds like you're about to pop a blood vessel," Paul responds with a modicum of compassion.

"I don't need your pontifical advice, Paul. You better listen to me. I know which way the wind's blowing around here and it's not in your favor. You know that H. R. Wood's got all his money tied up in Redmont Acres and if he goes belly-up, there goes St. Francis."

"Come on, Ollie, I thought you were concerned about the church, not the real estate market." Paul digs deeply to generate empathy for his fellow cleric.

"For Heaven's sake, Paul, are you blind? H. R. *is* the church!" Paul remains mum hoping Ollie's expressions of religiosity will echo in his mind. "O God, you know what I mean. His pledge is paying off the new building. Without his support…well, I…I just don't…Oh, what's the use, you're not hearing a word I'm saying." Ollie reverts to a more penitent approach. "As a personal favor to me, Paul, would you ask your meddling law school do-gooders to go pick on some other neighborhood for a while, at least until June? Just another eight months is all I need. I don't want to be the one to close down St. Francis."

"Close down the church? What do you mean?" Paul is surprised.

"I shouldn't have said anything. You'll have to keep this very confidential. H. R. is talking to Bishop Grand about moving St. Francis out to Larksdale if the neighborhood here turns colored."

"What about the church already at Larksdale?" Paul questions. "That community isn't big enough for two Methodist churches."

"They're considering a merger, not another church."

"What a shame, what a shame," Paul laments. "But I'll leave the backroom politics to you and the Bishop. If you'll excuse me, I have work to do."

Marge notices the light to Paul's line goes off and she knocks on his door. "I declare, Brother Paul, some preachers are hollow as a poplar tree growing on a river's edge." Paul smiles but does not respond to her attempt to siphon information about Ollie Barron's plight.

~~~

"You're supposed to take care of those little details," Ollie Barron yells at Mrs. Green. "Where am I going to find six new candles on Sunday with all the stores closed?" She stands outside her Sunday school classroom waiting patiently until Ollie finishes his tirade. *It's the third time this week you've blown your top Preacher and I don't appreciate the way you take it out on me. You just don't get it Reverend High and Mighty. I don't come to church on Sunday to run errands for you, it's my day off. Maybe I'll find another place to worship.*

"All right, Brother Barron, I'll skip Sunday school and find you some candles," she tucks her Bible under her arm and heads to the office. Finding no fresh candles, Mrs. Green calls the Episcopal Church around the corner and arranges to borrow enough for the Easter service. On her way out, she meets Betty and Angela Olive. "O my gracious, there's my little doll," she exclaims. "Just look at those precious curls."

"Say 'hi' to Mrs. Green, Honey," Betty smiles, unable to hide unabashed pride in her daughter. "We just came by for Ollie. Is he in his office?"

"No, you just missed him, he's in the sanctuary."

"All right, we'll catch up with him, Angela wants to show him her Easter dress."

"Well, I wouldn't hurry if I were you," Mrs. Green shakes her head and clucks her tongue.

"That bad, huh?"

"That man's been wearing his hair coat inside out lately and I don't know what's bothering him. It seems like every little thing sets him off. I can't seem to do anything right anymore. I didn't put new candles out for the service today and he hit the ceiling. The old ones were perfectly good, only been used once."

Betty places her hand on the gray-haired secretary's shoulder. "It's not you, Mrs. Green, I can tell you that."

"Oh?" Mrs. Green looks directly at Betty's eyes.

"And it's not me either," Betty responds to Mrs. Green's gaze.

"Oh, I wasn't implying anything."

Betty glances over her shoulder to be sure no one can overhear. "It seems my husband's been burning his candle at both ends lately, ever since that Negro family moved in Redmont Acres," she whispers.

"My gracious, Betty, it's only one family. It was bound to happen sooner or later."

"I know, it's just that he's afraid of what will happen to the church. Several of our families have already drifted off to another church."

Mrs. Green hunches over and shifts her eyes back and forth. "I'm not supposed to know this, Betty, but," she whispers and looks around, "there's talk of boarding up the church and transferring the members someplace else."

Betty tries to look surprised, although she's already aware of the pending merger with Larksdale Methodist. "That would be a shame," she shakes her head. "I'm sure everything will turn out for the best. Come on Angela, let's go find Daddy. Will I see you in Sunday school, Mrs. Green?"

"A little later, first I have to walk over to the Episcopal Church to borrow some candles. Hopefully they'll be pure white with no charred wicks."

19

> *April 17, 1966*
>
> *Dear Brother Paul,*
> *I am writing to thank you for your support of our efforts to break the neighborhood racial barriers in Birmingham. Despite achieving only token results, Grace and I feel it is time for us to return to law school. Please know that we admire your courage to hold fast to your belief in equal treatment of all races. Perhaps our paths will cross again under better circumstances. Until then, may your good work continue and your faith be rewarded.*
>
> *Peace,*
>
> *Jesse Shuman*
>
> *P.S. I am enclosing a tiny scrap of wood retrieved from Sixteenth Street Baptist Church as a memento of our work together.*
>
> *js*

Angie rushes into Chad's office and plops her history notebook on his desk. "That's it, my prince, I just finished my last exam and I'm done with history—forever!" she cries. She moves around to hug Chad from behind and whispers; "Now I'm ready for something exotic!"

He pulls her head down and smacks her on the cheek. "Here you go." He retrieves a Hershey bar from his desk drawer and hands it to her. "Knock yourself out."

She prances around his desk peeling off the paper as if discovering a priceless ruby. "This will do for a start, but I've got a whole week until spring quarter starts. We need to go somewhere, do something wild, you know, sing a new song in a new land!"

"I hate to tell you this, but you missed Mardi gras. It was a month ago."

"I haven't missed a damn thing in New Orleans," she nibbles gracefully on a tiny chocolate square. "I just want to take you away somewhere and talk about us for a change."

"I'd love to, honey, but its not a good time for me right now. I'm up to my tonsils with *The Seven Last Words* and Easter Sunday's big show. The best I can offer is a day and a half, maybe two, tomorrow and Friday."

"Oh, all right," she puckers up a pout. Then she spots something on Chad's desk that changes her tune. "What's that?" she pushes aside a stack of sheet music that doesn't quite cover an embossed crystal medallion.

"You mean that paperweight?" Angie reaches out to touch the singing angel, but hesitates, suspending her fingers over the familiar etching. "It's my little good luck charm," Chad continues, "but she's usually hiding under all the clutter." Angie releases the top button of her blouse. Slowly lifting the chain around her neck, she fishes out her crystal pendant. Chad continues chatting about taking a couple days off as she stands frozen in place, transfixed by the sight of the paperweight angel.

"What do you think, Angel Eyes?" Chad's question breaks her trance.

Angie mutters, "About what?"

"I asked if you would like to continue our discussion over lunch."

Without answering, she dangles her crystal angel in the air bathing Chad's face in scattered reflections of light as the angel rotates on its chain. "Would you look at that! It's just like mine, only smaller and more elegant." Chad halts the motion with his finger. "Is it new?"

"No, I've had it since high school, but she stays out of sight like yours." Angie retrieves the medallion and drops it back under her blouse.

"For good luck?"

"At first it was my lucky charm, but then it failed me and now I just don't know. What do you think, Prince Charming?"

"With two crystal angels to chase away any pesky demons, how can we go wrong?" Chad embraces his fiancée. "Now, let's grab a sandwich and make our travel plans."

"After you spoiled my appetite with candy?"

Chad laughs. "Oh, I nearly forgot, Katy wants to talk to you. She's subbing in the nursery school today. Go on down and I'll pick you up in a few minutes. She's in room 105."

"O. K., but I'd better finish this first. Wouldn't want to share it with the kids," she giggles, waving the half-eaten candy bar.

Later, when Chad goes to Katy's classroom, he finds the two women conversing in sketchy phrases, as adults are forced to do in a room full of toddlers. Katy sees Chad at the Dutch door, "We're getting ready to go to lunch...*careful with those scissors*...why don't you two eat with us...*look out, Perry, blocks are to play with*...so we can talk." Chad shakes his head as Katy now scuffles to rescue a child from Perry's assault with blocks.

"What's for lunch?" Angie asks.

"Corn Dogs, I think," Katy replies, gripping Perry's hands.

"No thanks, I swore off those ptomaine torpedoes, fish sticks and rubbery Jell-O in the third grade," Angie laughs. "I'll call you tonight."

Paul Peterson runs into Chad and Angie in the hallway. "What are you two turtle doves cooing about, as if I didn't know?"

"We've just narrowly escaped eating lunch with the terrible twos," Chad says.

"Well, that's good news for you, but keep me in your prayers. I'm heading that way with Tums in my pocket," Paul shakes his head. "Oh, by the way, did Katy have a chance to talk with you, Angie?"

"She tried, but we didn't make much headway. I told her we'd talk tonight. See ya."

"What's that all about?" Chad asks as he helps Angie into his car.

"About our wedding," Chad nestles behind the wheel and heads for The Grille. "Katy's been after me to start planning the wedding. Her mom volunteered to help line things up, you know, since I don't have anyone."

"We haven't set the date yet, so I guess we need to get a move on, huh?" Chad adds.

"Only if you're sure you still want to hitch your wagon to a—what was it that man called me, a call girl?"

"Only if you're sure you want to be married to a cradle robber."

They discuss some possible wedding dates as they nibble at leftovers on their plates. Angie gulps down the last of her sweet tea, clunks the glass down and exclaims, "I've got it, Chad! Before we set a date, there's a special place I want you to take me."

"Where?"

"It'll be a surprise, my prince. Pick me up tomorrow morning at the boarding house and I'll take it from there."

"Will I need my overnight bag?"

"Save it for the honeymoon, Mr. Overanxious."

"All right, but don't keep Katy on the phone too long tonight, I need her at choir practice."

"I'll try but she's the big talker, not me," Angie laughs.

Preparing for a big rehearsal, Chad has no time to think about Angie's surprise trip. His oboe/English horn player has cancelled and he spends the entire afternoon locating this most endangered specie of woodwind players hoping one is available on short notice.

From her dormer window the next morning, Angie watches the red Mustang approach and Chad jump out to ring the doorbell. She waits for her "arsenic and old lace" landlady to call up the stairway, "Miss Shook, you have a gentleman caller in the parlor." The archaic formality must be tolerated if Angie is to avoid another scathing lecture like the one that embarrassed her the first time Chad had arrived to pick her up, honking the horn as she bounced out to meet him.

"Morning *lover*," Angie shouts as she floats down the ornate staircase with exaggerated grace, kisses Chad on the lips and waves a hand over her shoulder. "Bye, Mrs. Kirkendall, y'all be good now, you hear."

"You shouldn't tease your landlady that way. She'll think you're a little hussy," Chad opens the car door.

"I know, but she needs to get a life. Anyway, I'm moving out of that creepy old house soon."

"Where to?" Chad arches his brow. She cuts her eyes at him and responds with only a pixie grin.

Chad drives several blocks from the boarding house before realizing he has no idea which direction to take.

"Just go west, young man, go west," Angie says when he questions their destination. "I'm your personal navigator." They skirt the northern edge of downtown through the pipe shop village. Angie holds her nose as the odor from the acrid smoke from the plant's mammoth chimney seeps into the car. "How'd you like to live in this stinky place?"

"Oh, one gets used to it. The smell was even stronger when I taught school here."

"I didn't know you taught near the pipe shop. Where is it?" Chad points to the right. "How far? Can we drive by and see it?"

"Sure, it's just a couple of blocks. I'd like to see what the years have done to the old girl." At first Angie had wanted to drive by the school. Now she insists on stopping.

"I wanna go inside," she bubbles. Chad is anxious to see his old music room and maybe talk to some of his former colleagues, but Fairway has changed. Heavy scrutiny by the media when the first black students were enrolled under armed guards has made the Georgian entrance an icon for school integration. They cross the street and pass through the gate of the new chain link fence to reach the front door. The oily pine floor creaks as they proceed to the office.

Angie tilts her head back and inhales the scent. "Smells just like my old school in Mimosa."

"All schools smell the same, I think they soak these floors in used motor oil," Chad jokes. When they enter the office Chad sees only one familiar face—the huge wall clock with its Victorian hands pointing to a circle of Roman numerals. Two women behind the counter exchange furtive glances before referring Chad's request for a visitor's pass to their boss. Responding to a buzzer, the principal emerges from his office shaped like a butter churn, sporting a size-too-small shirt with tightly stretched, short sleeves that cut into his ballooning biceps. *Another losing football coach*, Chad quickly surmises before he asks to see his former music room.

The muscle-bound principal shifts a toothpick to the other side of his mouth. "Won't do you any good, mister, we don't have music anymore, that's where we do special ed."

Forcing a smile, Chad thanks the principal and makes a hasty exit. "Now you see why I quit teaching," Chad starts the engine. "It's so depressing. When trouble knocks at the schoolhouse door, the music teacher is the first to get the axe. It's not fair that the kids have to muscle their way through the most vulnerable periods of their lives without legitimate music."

"Yeah, I couldn't have survived school without…wait, wait, we need to be going west," Angie shouts. Chad turns right along Ferndale Avenue.

"This will take us by the college."

"Yes, I know." Angie's eyes begin to sparkle.

They stop at a traffic signal near the Methodist College entrance. "Now I know this may sound silly to you, but I want you to take me to Coal City from here, and go the way you went when you were a student," Angie says.

"All right, but don't you want to see the campus again."

"Oh no, I ain't lost a damn thing here 'cept half a year of my life. Let's move on." Chad's innocent suggestion has churned up the anger she buried here over two years ago, has touched the raw nerve connecting the life stolen from her to that other far-removed coarse, black, coal-town life of her roots. Chad drives on in silence, baffled by Angie's vehement reaction, puzzled by this curious trip back in time.

Turning off the main thoroughfare onto Coal City highway, his nostalgia kicks in. "If this were in my old car, I could just turn the steering wheel loose right here and it would take me right to the church. Look, this hump is where the old trolley track ran down the middle of the road, and when we round this curve..." he hesitates "...there...I'll bet you won't see that anywhere else." He points to the asphalt covered trolley track line that angles through two blocks of the business section appearing to split the old brick buildings in half.

Angie studies the spectacle briefly and turns to gaze at a beaming Chad. When he realizes the tour guide is drawing more attention than the tour, he pulls over and stops the car. "I thought you wanted to see Coal City. What is it? Did I not wash behind my ears?"

Angie laughs and squeezes his arm with both hands. "No, silly, I want to see *you* in Coal City. That's all you and Katy ever talk about when we're together...Coal City this and Coal City that. I just wanted to get you over here and see if some of that magic might rub off on me. Where's the church that launched your career as a choir director?"

"A couple of blocks from that corner, let's go." Chad avoids driving over the track line strewn with empty bottles that peek through the weeds. "Boy, this place has changed," he says, pointing out the boarded up store fronts. "At least the church is still here," he tries to sift the ghostly images of former storeowners through his mind. As he nears the old brick building with the neon sign attached to its corner, Chad's glow of reminiscence fades. He parks in front of the empty building.

"What's wrong, Chad?" Angie watches him become mesmerized by the scene before him.

"Look at that, the church is closed down, abandoned." Shards of neon tubing litter the sidewalk. Gone is the blue glow that once beckoned worshippers to church. Boards nailed across the majestic oak doors bear a grim resemblance to the empty cross of Calvary. Compelled to get out, Chad stands beside the car and glances next door to the parsonage where he first met the Peterson family. Wind has ripped the rotted screen wire on the porch until it hangs like widows' veils, hardly hiding the grief behind the parsonage doors. Angie joins Chad on the sidewalk and clasps his hand, embracing his gloom.

"I'm sorry, Chad, I had no idea."

"It's O. K., it's O. K., I should've come back more often and the changes might not have been such a shock."

"So this is where my handsome young choir director got his start and swept all the girls off their feet." Angie tries to cheer him up.

"Who told you that fairy tale, Miss Nosy?"

"Didn't you know that Katy was in love with you until you broke her heart when you went to the army?" she twists her finger in his ribs.

"Oh, that. She was only a freckled teenager. You know how girls that age get loopy over any older guy whose pants don't come up to his armpits."

Angie looks around and heaves a sigh, "O. K., let's go, I've seen enough to convince me that Coal City is not really the Camelot that you and Katy thought it was."

"Wait a sec," Chad walks to the boarded up entrance. "Let's see what's on the door." A metal sign spells out the condemnation procedures and warns trespassers of the consequences for breaking the seal on the entrance. Chad runs his finger around the edge of the sign as if to bid farewell to the site of his basic training as choir director. His finger touches something barely poking out from under the edge of the sign. He wiggles it out, a piece of paper folded several times, fragile from the insults of weather.

"What is it?" Chad comes down the steps holding the paper gently between his thumb and forefinger.

"It's a note of some kind. Maybe you'd better help open it, I might tear it."

Angie unfolds the notepaper and delicately peels the two ends apart. "It looks like a kid's handwriting, manuscript. It's kind of blurred. Here turn it around."

"O. K., it says:

> *Deer God, Our hole church is moved over to Stoneburg. I hope you can find us. They have anuther Methodist church there too.*
>
> *Love,*
> *Bobby Parks.*

"O my God, he must be Rosemary Parks' boy. I sang at her wedding, must've been twelve years ago. I wonder why the church's been abandoned."

"Just look around," Angie nods her head towards some black children playing on the porch of the house across the street.

"Yeah, I see. Half my bass section lived in that house."

"Half?"

"Only had two basses," Chad heaves a sigh of melancholy as he opens the car door and presses the note between pages of a hymnbook in the back seat. He turns to Angie, "Where to now, Miss Navigator? I guess we're ready to roll."

"Not yet, there's one more thing. Remember a tiny little blond haired tot that sang a solo at this church years ago?"

"Vaguely," Chad replies. "She was related to the church treasurer, I think. Why? Do you know her? Her mother called her Lil Angel…wait a minute!"

Angie emits a mischievous giggle before lapsing into her childhood voice:
> *This little light of mine, I'm gonna let it shine..."*

"It can't be!" Chad exclaims.
> *This little light of mine, I'm gonna let it shine..."*

"I'm not believing this, you were that little girl?"

"Still am, but not so little anymore."

"O my gosh, do you remember I was the choir director back then?" Chad asks, still in awe.

"Not really. You see, I had blocked out that memory and many others, except one—a cold Christmas Eve when I sang *Jingle Bells* in a tiny church. I was afraid Santa Claus would skip my house that night because I was out so late. I didn't remember singing here at Coal City until Paul mentioned it a few days ago. Katy didn't even remember."

"So that's why you brought me out here today, to reminisce."

"Wrong again, my prince. This may sound silly, but I thought you'd show me around this church and I'd start talking about our wedding and...well, this is the silly part...and you'd start remembering all the good times you and the Petersons had here...and you'd say, 'Angie, why don't we get married right here' that's all."

"What brought this on, all of a sudden?"

"It's not all of a sudden. Do you remember when we went to your visit your mother? I just adored those little village churches staring across the road at each other, but you said you didn't want to get married there. When I told Katy my plans she agreed with you. It wouldn't be fair to ask your friends to drive that far. Well, she didn't hesitate to ask me to drive from New Orleans for her wedding, but I didn't bring that up. That's when I got the idea of checking out the other churches where you knew people. See what a ninny I'm being." Chad raises his eyebrows, scrunching his shoulders as Angie goes on. "Every day Katy tells me something else that I need to do before the wedding. First, it was deciding on bridesmaids and dresses. Then she said, 'Angie, you need to book a photographer, a cake baker, a florist…' on and on and on. When she got to the part about invitations and guest lists, I wanted to throw up my hands and scream. So I just told her right then and there, 'I'm not getting married at Hope Methodist Church. It's too much trouble'."

"Hold on a sec, didn't Lorna volunteer to help take care of all the details?"

"But the money…!"

"Now don't worry we'll work that out. I'll talk to your daddy and…"

"You will not!" she screams, "He is definitely out of the picture. He took all the fun out of singing at different churches, fussing and cussing at Momma. All she wanted was for me to be somebody."

Tears glisten in Angie's eyes. Uncertain how to respond, Chad starts the motor and meanders through several blocks of once majestic houses, fences and yards now marked by years of neglect. "I wonder where all the white people went," Chad attempts to change the subject.

But it doesn't work. Angie picks up where she left off, "And Daddy's not the only one," she sniffs. Chad's confusion intensifies as he continues to drive and point out former houses of choir members. "Katy said her daddy would invite the big Methodist muckity-mucks to your wedding."

"*Our* wedding."

"I know, but because of your position…you know…" She stops for a breath and decides to come to the point. "There are certain people I won't have at my wedding."

"*Our* wedding," Chad corrects, thinking she's referring to certain choir members. "All right, I agree with you. I am not going to fight over anything to do with our wedding. We can't start our honeymoon with a free-for-all. I know just the solution. There's a small chapel at the last church I served. We won't be able to crowd more than twenty or twenty-five people in there including the bride and groom."

"Where?" Angie recovers her excitement. "I didn't know there was another one. How far is it?"

"Not far. I don't talk about it much. It may have been the best and worst year of my life as a choir director, but I'm sure we can use their chapel."

"What was so bad about it, Chad? I didn't know you had any dark past."

"About four years ago, I left Fairway School when Paul Peterson offered me a full time job at his church."

"At Hope?"

"No, at his former church, St. Francis." Angie's heart sinks, she gasps for air. "Are you all right, Angel?" When she doesn't respond, he quickly slows the car and pulls over on the shoulder. "Now take a deep breath and relax," he massages her shoulders and back.

She momentarily recovers from the shock. "I knew Paul was the pastor at St. Francis when I first met Katy, but he was gone in a wink. She's never mentioned that church again."

"Paul doesn't talk about it either. He crossed horns with a church boss over integration and was transferred in the middle of his first year. We had that church on the upswing 'til that happened. Then, along came a red-headed Caesar in a fancy robe driving a baby blue chariot and I didn't last more than four months." Chad slaps his hand on the steering wheel so hard it sounds the horn. "Wow, listen to me. You can see why I've never mentioned St. Francis either."

Angie looks at Chad with new eyes. Thoughts flicker through her mind like lightening bugs in August. *Now I know where I've seen his face before. He's the one who showed me the office that day I went to see Ollie Barron for the last time. And I ran into him again on the way out. My God, he was there! What if he begins to remember, and realizes it was me behind the dark glasses and scarf. What if he figures out about me and Ollie? I have to think of something fast.*

"Chad, we can't put Paul through the pain of going back to that church, or you for that matter. So, I'm asking you to let me decide where we'll be married and please be on my side, no matter what anybody says. O. K.?" Chad looks at her pleading eyes, smiles and assents. "And we'll live happily ever after," she adds with delight.

~~~

A gray van parks near the playground fence just before seven a.m. the day after Easter Sunday. The man who emerges pulls an oil-smudged baseball cap down tight just above his eyes and scans the nearly empty parking lot. He zips his navy blue coveralls up to his neck and slips on a pair of tight fitting work gloves, takes a heavy toolbox from the side door of the van, looks around once more and then follows the path from the playground to the back door of the educational building. Once inside, he goes straight to the boys' bathroom, gently taps on the door and calls out, "maintenance." Repeating the same routine, the husky man inspects each bathroom on the first floor, turns the faucets on and off, flushes the toilets and then he heads for the stairs. The day-care workers are too busy helping the early arriving children with their coats to notice the man, but the janitor encounters him in the stairwell.

"Is something wrong?"

"Got a call to check out the plumbing, that's all," the man answers casually, keeping his head down as he continues up the stairs.

"Who called you?" the janitor shouts after him.

"No idea, I just picked up a work order. It says first thing this morning."

"O. K., holler if you need anything," the janitor watches him disappear to the second floor.

Hurrying down the empty hallway to the office suite, the husky stranger passes two more bathrooms on the way. Marge's office is locked, but he proceeds unperturbed to the adjacent Sunday school classroom and enters the unlocked door. He sets the toolbox against the wall he knows adjoins Paul's office. Working swiftly and silently, the stranger opens the metal box, takes off one glove and extracts an alarm clock. He pushes back his cap to see better in the semi-dark room and meticulously attaches some wires to the clock. After replacing his glove, he shoves an oak table over the open toolbox and leans a folded metal chair against the table to hide his work. He closes the door as he leaves the room and casually retraces his steps back to his truck.

An hour later, Katy drops Pauline off at the nursery and goes upstairs to see her dad. Marge unlocks the office door trying to balance a sloshing carafe full of water. "Good Morning, Marge, don't you just love Easter?" Katy greets the church secretary.

Marge nods her head, "But not the morning after, the sanctuary's a mess and the janitor says we have a plumbing problem."

"Looks like Dad's not here yet. He must've caught the post-Easter blahs from you," Katy laughs and winks.

"Oh, he'll be along shortly. Why don't you get comfortable and I'll have this coffee ready in a jiffy," Marge offers.

"No, thanks, I have to meet Angie for breakfast at Looney's before she leaves for class. I'll catch him when I pick up Pauline at noon."

Chad meets the two women at the restaurant hoping for closure on the dangling wedding date including the site. Just as they order bagels and juice, a loud thud stifles the chatter in the dining room. Then a cacophony of questions descends upon the silence. Speculations among the diners range from a sonic boom to a blast at the nearby quarry. When conversations return to normal, Chad re-opens the discussion pushing for an answer from Angie. "So what did you decide?"

"About what?" she asks with a coy expression.

"You know 'about what', Angel, our wedding date, or whatever."

Still playing the naïve role, she turns to Katy, "What do you think, madam consultant?" Katy doesn't answer. Her head is cocked listening to distant sounds that most city folks have tuned out of consciousness—sirens.

"Katy!" Angie insists as the sirens cease.

"Wait a minute," Katy becomes increasingly apprehensive. "They stopped pretty close by."

"Who, what are you talking about?"

"The fire trucks, ambulances...whatever just stopped." She jumps up and runs outside. Smoke rises from the direction of the church a few blocks away. "Oh, no!" she cries, "my baby!"

Her car is halted one block from Hope Methodist, the police have already cordoned off the area. Katy jumps out, breaks through the gathering crowd and rushes to a group of children huddled across the street from the church. Each nursery worker holds two babies, one in each arm. After a frenetic search under several blankets, Katy locates Pauline. "Oh, thank God you're all right," she retrieves her daughter and presses the baby close to her chest. As Katy's panic subsides, she notices the grim expressions of the nursery worker. "Did all the kids get out all right?" Katy asks, turning her face away from the encroaching smoke.

"All the kids are fine, but, look!" The woman points to a charred opening in the wall of her dad's office and the adjacent Sunday school classroom. Smoke pours from the gaping hole where mute isolated embers begin to supplant the diminishing flames.

"Dad!"

20

> *May 23, 1966*
>
> *Dear Bishop Grand,*
>   *First, I want to express my appreciation for your thoughtful notes during my recovery. I regret having taken so long to respond to all the kindnesses and prayers on my behalf. I should soon be back to normal.*
>   *Secondly, I do appreciate your appointing me to serve the congregation at Hope Methodist Church for another year; however, at the end of that year, I would like to be granted at-large status in the Conference. In that capacity I may work to unite people of faith in a common cause. I have neither a plan nor support for such an undertaking; however, I trust God will provide both in good time. Thank you for considering this humble request, I remain,*
>
> *A faithful servant of our Lord,*
>
> *Paul Peterson, Senior Pastor*

"Paul, it's Lorna, wake up, Honey, wake up." She anxiously hovers over him. His head wrapped tightly in bandages, Paul struggles to clear his mind through the fog of residual anesthesia.

Where am I? Can't move my head...feels like it's in a harness...is my body in some kind of strait jacket? Oh, my arms, my legs...wait...I feel some pain, they're O.K...still intact. Or...is that just phantom pains from missing limbs? I hear Lorna's voice but I can't see her.

"Paul, Honey, can you hear me?"

The right side of his head throbs as he strains to focus his uncovered left eye on the fuzzy image of his wife. He moistens his taut, dry lips with the tip of his tongue and labors to answer her, but there's no sound. He's determined to assure Lorna he hears her and manages to utter a few raspy words, "My eye...can't see...what..?"

Lorna carefully presses two fingers to his lips, "You're in the hospital, Paul. Your office exploded this morning, but you're going to be all right." She begins explaining what has transpired in the last eight hours, but the I. V. sedative kicks in and Paul drifts back into the healing sleep his assaulted body is demanding.

Katy, Chad and Paul's Associate, Edgar meet Lorna at the door of the waiting room, anxious to hear the doctor's report. Lorna takes a moment to wipe away tears of acrimony and relief. "His whole right side is bandaged, but there are no broken bones. We won't know about his right eye until they remove the bandage." She breaks down again. "He could lose it!"

Katy eases her mother over to a chair. "Edgar, would you call Marge and get the phone tree started? Call Leland and make sure Pauline's all right. I can run home for a while if he needs me." She hands him a list of people who have come by during the day and left their numbers. "Then call the Bishop."

List in hand, the Associate Pastor takes the elevator to the emergency room lobby and heads toward the bank of pay phones. A stranger wearing a London Fog topcoat loosely about his shoulders hails him, "Excuse me, Reverend, do you have just a second? I'm with the *New York Times,*" he flashes his identification card. "Can you tell me about Reverend Peterson's condition?"

Edgar suddenly swells with importance as he jumps at this chance to be the purveyor of the story. He gives the reporter a detailed account of the aftermath of the explosion near Paul's office, concluding with, "Yes, he was the only one injured. His secretary was only shaken up a bit...the firemen said it was probably a gas leak, an unfortunate accident."

"I see," mutters the reporter, biting his lip. "And what do you think happened?" Edgar flutters his eyelashes as though he doesn't understand the question. "I mean, did Reverend Peterson have any enemies?"

Edgar glances at the reporter in disbelief; then without hesitation, assures him, "Everybody respects Paul Peterson, even those who disagree with him."

"And who would that be?"

"Sir, I'm telling you he has absolutely no enemies that I know of," Edgar senses the pushy reporter is fishing for a story that has no grounds. "Excuse me, I need to make some phone calls."

The reporter stuffs the notebook back into his coat pocket as he watches Edgar walk away. His editor will never accept a story about a natural gas explosion, and he has no desire to write one. If this had happened anywhere else but Birmingham, he would leave the report to local newshounds. But ripples from the city's recent rash of church explosions urge him on, even though this is the first white church to be involved. He decides to at least personally view the damage, so he leaves the hospital and drives to the site of the explosion.

Wisps of white smoke that rise from the rubble cast an eerie specter in the glow of the mercury vapor light. Curious commuters stop in front of the church to behold the gaping hole where Paul Peterson's office had been, but others have already headed home, anxious to enthrall their families with their firsthand accounts of the scene. Volunteers in rubber boots, busy siphoning water from the ground floor of the educational building are sweeping and mopping while they try to keep the stubborn pump working. Several women mill about the sanctuary entrance handing out coffee and sweet rolls to help the men weather the cool spring air that settled in after sundown.

"Coffee?" one of them offers the reporter who wanders near their table.

"No thanks, what on earth happened here?" the reporter pretends he has just stumbled on the scene.

They all clamor to answer at once, but he manages to get the gist of the story. *Gas must have leaked into the pastor's office overnight and he accidently set it off somehow when he came to work this morning.* Once again, the reporter can find no evidence surrounding this incident that will support his gnawing curiosity. He makes a mental picture of the smoldering ruins of Paul Peterson's corner office and leaves the scene.

The next day, Paul is relocated to one of the private rooms at Methodist Hospital. Ollie Barron waits at the nurses' station for a signal to go in and visit his fellow pastor. As the attendants leave the room, Ollie strolls forward and taps on the door. "Knock, knock, anybody home?"

Lorna comes to the door. "Ollie, what a surprise. Paul isn't feeling so…"

Ollie brushes past her, ignoring the words of caution. "Everybody's been terribly worried about you, my friend," Ollie strolls over to Paul's bed. "I bring greetings and best wishes from Bishop Grand, who's tied up in meetings this morning."

"Thank you," Paul answers in a soft voice, still raspy from lingering effects of the surgical breathing tube. The brazen Dr. Barron arrogantly ignores Lorna's signals beckoning him towards the door.

"Excuse me," she relents, "I'm going to check on Paul's medication." Lorna leaves to seek someone at the nurses' station who will force Ollie to cut his visit short. She meets Chad and Angie leaving the elevator. "Hey folks, you're just in time. Paul has a visitor he doesn't need or want. What can we do to make him leave?"

"Who is it?" Chad asks, "Bull Connor?"

"Not that bad, but close. It's Ollie Barron," Lorna exclaims through clenched teeth. Angie startles them with a strangling noise, clutching her throat and gasping for breath. "My word Angie, are you all right?"

Chad pats Angie on the back until she catches her breath. "I'm all right," she tries to conceal the panic that seizes her. "My goodness, my stomach is turning flip flops. I think I'll go down to the cafeteria and get some juice."

"That's a good idea, I could use some breakfast myself," Lorna says. "We'll let Chad get rid of Ollie."

"O. K. girls, I'll rescue our leader from the notorious Red Barron."

Chad's entrance hardly makes a dent in Ollie Barron's ongoing monologue. His "Hi, Chad, how are you?" is imbedded in his continuing story about the Bishop having his sights on Ollie for the next opening in his cabinet a year from now. "Homer Dyer's term will be up in June of '67 and he's put the word out that he wants to move to his home at Lake Junaluska before he gets too old to fish. Since I don't necessarily want his district, I'm working on the Bishop to shift some people around so that I..." Paul closes his good eye hoping to block out Ollie's political speculations. A long interval passes before Ollie focuses on Paul's face, realizing that he has fallen asleep. "What do you think of that?" Ollie bends over Paul's bed. "Trying to bring him up-to-date and he goes to sleep on me. And he didn't even tell me how he's doing. Tell me Chad," he says still staring at Paul's face. "Can the eye be saved?"

"We're optimistic, but nobody's certain just yet. The doctor told Lorna..."

"Well, we'll all pray for his recovery. You tell him to let me know if there's anything I can do while he's laid up." Ollie gives Chad a condescending pat on the arm and leaves, his steely voice still vibrating off the walls.

Chad closes the door and switches off the light so Paul can rest. He goes to the window and adjusts the blinds.

"Is he gone?"

"I thought you were asleep...oh, I get it..." Chad chuckles, "You faked off the Red Barron. Now that was downright impolite of you."

"But effective, eh?"

Downstairs in the cafeteria, Angie fidgets with her nearly empty glass as Lorna crunches on dry toast. *There's no way, now way I can leave without going in to see Paul. But how can I avoid that red-haired demon from my past?*

"He's a fine man," Lorna offers when she observes Angie's worried look.

"He...he is?" Angie stumbles over her words, her thoughts still fixed on Ollie.

When Lorna explains, "Yes indeed, despite the pain, Paul's spirit remains high," Angie realizes she is not talking about Ollie.

"Oh, good," she replies softly.

Lorna tries to catch her attention, but Angie's eyes are darting back and forth from the windows to the hallway. "Angie? You've turned that glass every way but over. Is something wrong?"

Angie forces a jittery smile, "No, not really."

"Well, we'd better be getting back upstairs before Dr. Barron sends Paul's blood pressure through the roof."

Angie's anxiety kicks into high gear in again, not sure how she'll react to seeing Ollie again, or what he'll do. "You go on, Lorna. I'll just sit here and finish my juice and make a stop at the restroom before I come up."

As soon as Lorna leaves, Angie leans sideways to watch her disappear into the elevator bay. Then she positions herself for a view of the elevator from behind an artificial plant. It seems an eternity before the familiar figure emerges from the elevator. Angie presses the crystal angel necklace to her breast, hoping Ollie is not headed to the cafeteria. Her heart pounds furiously as she watches him draw his trench coat belt tight, cover his flaming red hair with a sportsman's cap, and stride across the lobby to the door. As she presses the "up" elevator button, Angie envisions Ollie driving off in his baby blue convertible.

Panic has erased Paul's room number from Angie's memory. After stopping once at the wrong floor, she gets lucky on her second try. Chad is standing there as the door slides open. "I was just coming to get you. Come say 'hi' to Paul. Then we need to go and let him get some rest."

Angie enters the darkened hospital room. Her knees wobble as the medicinal odors awaken memories of her brief stay in the Catholic hospital many months ago. She clutches Chad's arm for balance. "Look who's here, Paul, it's Angie," Lorna pretends not to notice Angie's queasiness returning.

Angie and Chad walk to the foot of the bed. The door, like a bolt of lightening, flies open flooding the room with light from the hall. Ollie Barron charges forward waving an envelope over his head. "I completely forgot to leave you this card," he bellows. "Betty wouldn't let me in the house if I came back with it still in my pocket."

Aghast at the specter from her past, Angie stands immobile, trapped, then edges behind Chad to fade into the shadows. "Oh good, you're finally awake," Ollie lays the card on Paul's hand urging him to open it. "Betty and Olive made it especially for you. Olive even signed it. Of course she can't write yet, but she made her mark." As Ollie prattles on about his remarkable daughter, Paul hands the card to Lorna.

"Oh how sweet," Lorna holds the construction paper message up for Paul to see in the dim light. Ollie points out the markings intending to interpret them, but pauses when he catches a glimpse of Angie almost hidden behind Chad. Noticing his curiosity, Lorna responds promptly, "I don't believe you've met Chad's fiancée. Reverend Barron this is Angie Shook." Chad moves over revealing Angie's distraught expression.

As if the wind is knocked from him with a violent blow, Ollie stutters a weak "h-h-how-do-you-do." The room falls coldly silent. Angie nods a response and stares intently at the wheels of the hospital bed.

Lorna eases the tension. "I promised the doctor I'd make Paul get his rest, so…"

"I really must go," Ollie checks his watch. "The Bishop is anxious to hear a report on Paul's condition." Ollie practically leaps through the doorway without closing the door.

Paul crooks his index finger beckoning everyone to come closer. As they bend over his bed, Paul whispers, "The Red Barron didn't ask about my condition," and smiles.

Lorna accompanies Chad and Angie to the door. "Did you know Ollie Barron when he served Mimosa First Methodist?" Chad asks Angie.

"Sorta."

"He acted like he didn't recognize you."

"I was just a kid," Angie responds, "and we didn't go to his church all that often."

Lorna intervenes to explain Ollie to Angie. "That man comes on like a swarm of hornets, enough to intimidate anybody. He used to be difficult to deal with, but since Angela Olive came along, he's become impossible. Good day, you two. I'll stand guard over Paul in case the Bishop's squire forgets something else."

~~~

The congregation stands and applauds as Edgar assists Paul Peterson up the steps to the pulpit dais. Paul props his cane against the oversized chair and braces himself, facing his parishioners. He stretches tall as his healing body will tolerate and grips the sides of the pulpit. "Don't let this patch over my eye fool you. Your pastor has not become a pirate." The worshippers flutter with nervous laughter. "I am very happy to see all of you again. I regret that I missed the last two Sundays, but the Lord had other plans for me. Thank you for your kind letters, flowers and get-well cards. I especially enjoyed this card from the Pastor-Relations Committee." He picks up a folded card and reads aloud: *The Committee met in your absence and passed a resolution in favor of your speedy recovery and return to the pulpit very soon. P.S. The vote was five to four."* As soon as the punch line sinks in, howls of laughter break forth.

In the choir loft, Evelyn whispers to Katy, "At least, he didn't lose his sense of humor."

"That's odd, Dad never makes jokes from the pulpit," Katy responds, "It must be the medication."

Paul makes no allusions to his own misfortune, but proceeds to deliver a brief sermon based on Thomas' hesitation to believe the risen Christ who stood before him. Throughout the sermon Paul keeps a small index card before him to which is taped the scrap of wood from Sixteenth Street Baptist Church, the memento from Jesse Shuman. Scenes of the gaping hole left in the building by that senseless blast continually flash through his mind as he speaks.

After the service, Evelyn comments as she hangs her choir robe in the closet. "I thought Brother Paul would at least mention how God had spared his life."

Katy overhears and springs to her dad's defense. "That's because he doesn't believe it!"

The rowdy choir room is instantly hushed as everyone pauses to listen. "Ohhhh?" Evelyn slides her vocal reaction up the musical scale without missing a note.

"Dad doesn't think that God goes around picking and choosing who lives and who dies," Katy continues. "God gives us life, God does not take away life."

Marge ventures into the timorous silence, "Well, God saved me that day. I would not be standing here if I'd been in your daddy's office instead of mine."

Uh oh, I mustn't press this issue of Dad's theology any further. In the end, I will only alienate my choir friends, the people I love. She hugs Marge, averting a no-win theological debate. "And we're all glad you're safe." The singers exchange smug glances, dismissing Katy's remarks as naïve utterances of a preacher's kid.

Monday morning Lorna drives Paul to his temporary office on the ground floor of the educational building. "Still smells like smoke," he observes, hobbling past the nursery. "I'm thankful that none of the children were injured." The janitor holds the door open as Lorna and Paul enter the classroom. "Which class did you bump to get this room, Jude?" Paul asks the janitor.

"Martha Henderson," he smiles, "but, don't worry, they're meetin' with the Wesley class 'til we get yo' office fixed up. First time those two classes got together since they split years ago. Reckon they forgot what all the fuss was about."

"Now, now, Jude, that's no way to talk about the pillars of this church. By the way, were you able to salvage any of my books?"

"Most of 'em, Brother Paul. Got 'em laid out to dry in the basement. The fire didn't touch your office, just the Sunday school room next door."

"That's strange...hm...very strange," Paul eases painfully into an upholstered chair behind a table.

Lorna makes sure he's comfortable before leaving. "I'm going to do a few errands. I'll be back in a while and bring you some lunch."

Jude starts out the door, but Paul stops him. "Sit down Jude. I understand you pulled me out and saved my life that terrible day. I really appreciate your fine act of courage."

"I got lucky 'cause I was on my way to see you when the bomb went off. I was just walkin' down the hall..."

"Just a minute," Paul interrupts. "Did I hear you right, a bomb?"

"Yep, that's all it could be, a bomb."

"What makes you think that? I understood a gas leak caused the explosion."

"Yep, that's what folks say, but it don't add up. In the first place, the gas lines a-comin' to that end o' the buildin' are closed off. They did that when the new furnace was put in."

"What about those overhead heaters by the front door?"

"Electric."

Paul nods his head. "Now that you mention it, I don't remember smelling any gas that morning. I was in the office maybe fifteen minutes before it happened."

"And in the second place, when I went in to get you, I smelled dynamite, just like when my church got bombed."

"Your church, bombed?"

"Yep, I helped dig those little girls' bodies outta the mess. I was s'posed to usher that day."

"Sixteenth Street Baptist was your church?"

"Still is. It ain't gone nowhere."

"I can't believe anyone would bomb our church. Did you tell this to the police?"

Jude grins and shakes his gray head. "The police? Huh, all they did was d'rect traffic. The firemen said it was gas. The gas company came out and shut off the gas for a day, but Miss Marilyn made 'em turn it back on so the kids could have some heat. Anyhow, who'd believe a black man goin' 'round sayin' that somebody done bombed a big white church like this'n? Nawsir, I ain't said nothin' to nobody 'cept you."

"But, who would do such a thing? I can't imagine…"

"It ain't for me to say, 'specially the way things goin' with white and black folks these days, seems somebody wanted you to get hurt, preacher, maybe even wants you dead."

"If that's true…I wonder how a bomb made its way into my office."

"It didn't go off in yo' office, it blew up in that Sunday school room. If it hadn't been for that bookcase 'gainst the wall you wouldn't be here talkin' to me now."

"Did you see anybody in the building that morning?"

"Just some of the day-care teachers and that plumber lookin' for a leakin' toilet."

"Plumber? What time was that?"

"He came right after I unlocked the building for the day-care people. Said he had a work order to check the toilets, but he wan't here more'n twenty, thirty minutes."

Paul pauses to consider if the janitor's tale has any credibility. *After all, he does have every reason to distrust the white police officers and firemen who responded to the explosion. It's unbelievable, his own church was bombed and not a thing has been done to bring the culprits to justice. I wonder how much of his version might be shaped by a subliminal quest for retribution.* "Thank you, again, Jude for saving my life. You've given me plenty of food for thought."

Marge passes Jude on her way into Paul's office. "Good morning, Brother Paul, would you like some coffee?"

"That'd be great, Marge. Are you back in your office?"

"No, it's still a mess. I'm just glad I wasn't in your office, glad I was at my desk when all heck broke loose. So I'm camping out with Marilyn. The telephone people will be here today to run a line to this room so we can talk without me running back and forth all day to check on you. I'll be right there with your coffee."

"Wait a minute, Marge. What time did you come to work the morning of the explosion?"

"I don't remember exactly, but it must have been early, maybe eight-ten, eight-fifteen. Wait a minute...I remember, I went to the sanctuary first, to see how many Easter lilies were left. Then I detoured to the kitchen to get some packets of coffee. Katy was just dropping off your granddaughter when I unlocked the office, must have been around eight-thirty. Why?"

"Oh, just trying to put my own memory back in place. Did you see anyone else besides Katy, the kitchen help, and day-care workers?"

"Now you've got me wondering about my own memory. Let's see...Jude and I had a friendly little argument that morning, nothing serious. He jumped on me about calling a plumber to check the bathrooms, because he said that was his job. I explained that I didn't call any plumber and I didn't know about any leaks in the building. He got over it pretty quickly."

"So you didn't see a plumber that morning."

"No. I never call anybody like that, except when Mr. Hawthorn authorizes repair work. Now, how about that coffee?"

Lorna returns to Paul's office, lugging a laundry basket full of mail. "I saw how much mail you have, so I put off my errands to open it for you. Looks like mostly get well cards. I know you don't have a one-handed letter opener."

Paul laughs. "You're so funny, Lorna, that's why I keep you around."

"Speaking of being funny, where on earth did you get that comedy routine you pulled in church yesterday? You were funnier than Bob Newhart." She hands him an opened card.

"Oh, I don't know, somewhere between being blown to kingdom come and being released from the hospital." He lays the card on the table. "I remember drifting in and out of consciousness, not sure whether something was really happening or I was dreaming. Sometimes I'd just burst out laughing. It hurt, but it felt good, too."

"Yes, I remember those bouts of hysteria. I'd ask you what's so funny and you'd just look at me like I was the one acting crazy."

"Oh, you weren't crazy and I wasn't hysterical. You see, it wasn't the dreams I had that made me laugh, it was the real stuff."

"Like what?"

"Like the day Ollie Barron came. He really hit my funny bone. I lay there hurting from head to toe, unable to focus with my one good eye, trying to piece together in my mind what you and Edgar had told me about the explosion. I wanted to be able to answer the obvious question about what happened. But Ollie never asked. Instead, he paced the floor, talking a blue streak like he was creating a roadmap for the remaining years of his ministry, a Triptik from here to retirement. Suddenly, a scene from an old Laurel and Hardy movie flickered in my mind—the one where Oliver gives Stan some elaborate directions for running an errand while Stan's attention is diverted by a butterfly on Oliver's hair. I looked at Ollie's wavy red hair and all I could see was that butterfly."

"And you thought that was hilarious? I guess I'd have to have been there," Lorna quips. "Here, you'll never get these cards read."

"Well, you're the one that asked about my sense of humor." .

"You two are in a jovial mood for a Monday morning," Marge enters and sets a steaming mug before her preacher.

"Forget it, Marge. You don't even want to go there," Lorna dismisses her comment with a wave of her hand.

"There's a man here to see you, Brother Paul, looks like a detective or something."

"Send him in. Ask him if he wants some coffee."

"I'll take some of this mail and go with you, Marge. Sounds like it's no place for a comedian's wife," Lorna says.

Wearing a tan trench coat, hat in hand, the man walks over and clutches Paul's good hand. "My name is Brian Peck. I'm with the *New York Times*. I know you're probably busy on this, your first day back in the office, but could you spare me a few moments?" After inquiring about Paul's recovery, the reporter adds, "Are you aware that there has been no formal investigation of the explosion?" Paul shakes his head. "Are you aware that local newspaper reporters have orders not to interview anyone connected with Hope Methodist Church? Again, Paul shakes his head, but this time with increasing concern. "Are you aware that the explosion is attributed to a gas leak in your office?"

"Yes, I've been told that."

"Are you aware that there are no gas lines anywhere near your former office?"

Paul straightens up, "Have you been talking to our janitor?"

"No, should I?"

Paul eases back in his chair. "Mr. Peck, I'm very curious as to how you got this information and if you can attest to its accuracy."

"A newspaper man has his sources, Reverend Peterson, and I can assure you that everything I just told you is true. The only other thing I need to verify is a rumor that I received from a reasonably questionable source."

"And what is that, Mr. Peck?"

"Are you aware that the Klan has a hit list of people in Birmingham whom they intend to annihilate?"

"No, I thought we had passed beyond that violent phase of our history."

"Like I said, just a rumor, Reverend Peterson, My source says he saw the alleged list and it contains an item that might be of interest to you."

"And that would be…?"

"Your name, sir."

21

> *May 29, 1966*
> *Dear Mrs. Ray,*
>   *Thank you for inviting me to Claude Ray Appreciation Day. I can't come because the celebration is the same day I plan to be married. It is hard to imagine it's been seventeen years since Mr. Ray came to Mimosa. I am sorry to hear he is giving up teaching to open a music store. I will always remember how he made me work hard to improve my voice. I hope he will continue to direct the choir at Mimosa Methodist. He was responsible for giving me my first solo gig. Please give Mr. Ray my best wishes.*
>
> *Sincerely,*
>
> *Angie (Angeline) Shook, soon to be Willis*
>
> *p.s. Reverend Paul Peterson sends his regards. He also told me about presiding at your wedding ceremony.*

"I'm not complaining, Angel Eyes, but I'm concerned about how strange you're acting lately. Tell me it's PMS, or test anxiety, or the explosion in Paul's office and I'll hush and ride it out," Chad tells Angie as she sits across the table with her anthropology book opened and tears flooding her eyes.

Angie just shakes her head and pulls another tissue from the box. She blows her nose and slams the book shut. "It's none of the above!" She rambles through her purse on the floor and finds a date book. "It's this damn wedding!"

"Our wedding? I didn't realize it was such a problem."

"I don't mean it the way it sounds. Katy and her mother are driving me crazy with details—dresses, shoes, caterer, photographer, invitations on and on and on. Why can't we just keep it simple?" Tossing the tiny book on the table, Angie screams, "We can't even agree on a damn date!"

"Hey! Back up a notch. That's our decision, not theirs." Chad takes the date book and opens it to August. "Here, pick a weekend."

Angie dabs her eyes with a clean tissue. "What about the week after finals?"

"Are you serious? That's only a month away." Angie widens her eyes and screws up her face. "O. K., O. K., don't go ballistic on me again. Let's see, that'll be June sixth. I always wanted to get married on D-Day." Chad marks an "X" on the first Saturday in June. "You break the news to Katy and Lorna and I'll check with Paul to see if he is available on the sixth."

Katy is unable to hide her disappointment when Angie phones her about the change in plans. "I thought you were aiming for an August wedding. There's no way we can pull this off so soon. Have you told Momma?"

"No, not yet."

"Then, we'd better do that right away—together. You'll need me—to stand by with the smelling salts."

Lorna receives the message with more grace than either of them expected. "Now you two have a seat while my granddaughter and I put a pot of water on the stove," Lorna says matter-of-factly, "Then, we'll discuss the matter calmly over tea." Katy hands Pauline over to Lorna and watches them disappear into the kitchen.

"That was too easy, Angie. Momma's up to something, maybe a ploy to change your mind."

"I've got to have you on my side, Katy, will you promise?"

During tea, Angie parries Lorna's questions about the sudden change of wedding plans with evasive and sometimes incoherent reasons. The conversation goes nowhere until Lorna mentions a bridal shower. "Betty Barron is planning to give you a shower before the wedding. What...?"

Crash! Angie drops her teacup. "No! Hell no, a thousand times no!" Lorna and Katy exchange looks of amazement at Angie's violent flare-up. Pauline, frightened by the shattered cup and Angie's outburst, begins to cry.

"There, there, baby," Katy lifts her out of the crib. "Everything's all right. Aunt Angie's not angry with you."

Katy sits in a rocker with seven-month old Pauline as Lorna and Angie clean up the broken china. "I'm so sorry, really, really I am," Angie apologizes, her hands still shaking.

"Don't worry, it's a cheap set—belongs to the church. I keep my good china there," Lorna points to a mahogany cabinet. She dumps the shards in a waste can, "Now where were we? Oh, yes." Lorna strokes her brow and drifts into deep thought. After a few moments, waiting for Pauline's whimpering to subside, Lorna announces, "There has to be a way out of this maze, if I could only get inside your head. If Paul were here he would stick a paper clip in his mouth, tape blank newsprint to the walls and make a flow chart. Pretty soon the solution would jump out at us."

Katy laughs, "You've got Dad down to a 'T'. Shall I get some paper and tape?"

"Not on these walls," Lorna rises from her chair and sweeps the air with her hands. "But maybe it would help to lay the pieces of the puzzle out in front of us." Lorna spreads her fingers and folds them one-by-one into her palm as she enumerates the obstacles Angie has mentioned. "Angie, you have a problem selecting a reasonable date for the wedding. You have no bridesmaids except your friend in New Orleans who isn't certain she can come. Chad has no best man or groomsmen. The two of you can't agree on where to have the ceremony. You made it quite clear you do not want a bridal shower." With one hand balled into a fist, Lorna starts counting on the other. "There's no caterer, no photographer and you don't want your father to give you away. Also, certain people are not welcome." Lorna extends a single pinky finger toward Angie. "Aside from the bride and groom, this is all we have left—a minister."

Angie forces a grin on her lips but retains a frown on her brow. "What else do we need?"

"Me!" Katy says, "You haven't asked me yet, I would like to be invited."

Angie lightens up, "Of course, I want…"

"Wait a minute; I think I know a way around your dilemma." Lorna taps the lone pinky against her temple.

"What?" Angie and Katy sing out in unison.

"It's all quite simple. Move your date forward one day and get married on Sunday. Following the sermon at the eleven o'clock service, Paul will invite you and Chad to the altar for a special closing ceremony, the same way he beckons parents to come forward to baptize a baby. You two will exchange vows and *voila*, it's done!" Lorna smiles, clasps her hands together and grins at the two astounded young women.

Angie cocks her head. "That might work, it just might work." She thanks Lorna for the suggestion and the tea. "I'll talk it over with Chad and see what he thinks. I can be pretty persuasive," she giggles.

"Wait a minute, I'll walk out with you," Katy says. Pauline has fallen asleep in her arms, so she gently passes the baby to Lorna. "You can hold her or put her down, Momma, I'll be right back."

Angie practically skips across the lawn as if she has been released from heavy shackles. "Your mother is a wonder," Angie fills her lungs with the sweet warm spring air. "The only problem I see is Chad's family."

"Not to burst your balloon, but there's another problem you have to face, either now or later."

"Is it bigger than a breadbox?" Angie asks, still exhilarated beyond worry.

"He certainly is…I'm talking about Ollie Barron."

Caught off guard, Angie staggers to a halt and fumbles her words, blurting out a telling question, "How, how...how do you know?"

"I figured he must have been the one who gave you money for an abortion, but I wasn't completely sure until Momma told me how you folded up inside yourself when you met him at the hospital. Then, when you went ape over Betty Barron's offer of a bridal shower, the whole jigsaw puzzle came into focus—even though a few pieces are still missing."

"Oh God, does your momma know?"

"No, I don't think so. She just said Ollie overwhelmed you, tied you up in a knot with his aggressive manner. But I knew better."

"Please, Katy, I don't want anyone else to ever know about this," Angie pleads.

"Then, you need to get over him in a flash. Ollie is omnipresent, he's everywhere. After you marry Chad, you'll run into that flaming parson at every Methodist event from now on. He has his eye on a position in the Bishop's cabinet."

"What...what will I do?"

"I'm not sure, but I know one thing you cannot do, and that is turn into an ostrich every time you two are in the same room. He's the one with the problem, not you."

"I...I don't understand."

"Whenever he sees you, he'll wonder if you will reveal his indiscretion or if you already have. Since the day he saw you at the hospital, Ollie has probably been obsessed with saving his reputation, he's undoubtedly on guard to stonewall any accusations you might make."

"He has nothing to be afraid of. He thinks I took care of his problem with an abortion, but there's a child running around somewhere sporting his conniving genes."

"As well as yours, my dear. Look at it this way, he thinks he paid for an illegal abortion. Therefore, in his mind, he's committed a crime on top of adultery. If that man's not suffering, he's more psychotic than I imagined."

"I find that hard to believe."

"I don't mean to sound so omniscient, but I've had a little experience with pastors carrying bags of smelly garbage under their lily white vestments."

"Oh?"

"It's mostly those preachers who, from the pulpit paint themselves as protagonists of justice and good will, yet suddenly become spectators when Dad puts shoes on his faith and invites them to hit the streets with him in the name of human rights. My point is that one day those candlestick jumpers will have to stand in their pulpits and preach sermons to mixed race congregations. Between now and then they had better find ways to address their moral failures, just like those priests that supported Bloody Mary and Hitler."

"You're losing me now with that history stuff."

"I guess I got carried away. The point is that many preachers live in fear that one day their sins against humanity will be emblazoned across the church marquees instead of their clever sermon titles. Ollie Barron's situation is more pressing. You're a stand-up-walking-around reminder of his moral failures he thought he'd never have to face, at least here on earth."

"That makes sense, Katy, but I don't know how to maintain control over my feelings about that bastard."

"It may take some time. Remember you've spent three years working up a poisonous concoction of hate, guilt and vengeance that won't be easy to neutralize. Think about what I'm saying, it's not *your* problem, it's Ollie Barron's problem. I'm afraid I've reached the end of my clinical rope...should've gone to graduate school," Katy muses. "One thing's for sure, if you and Chad follow Momma's suggestion, the Barrons will not be at your wedding. That face-off will come some other time."

"Thanks loads." Angie smiles and hugs Katy. "I'll call you after I talk with Chad."

At first, Chad cringes at the idea of a Sunday wedding, but is elated when his mother and sister agree to show up and bring his grandmother. Paul Peterson makes one final attempt to talk Angie into inviting Tucker. "Edgar has offered to pick up your father from the V. A. Hospital if you will only…"

"Thank you, but no," Angie cuts him off.

"Don't you even want your father to know the date of your wedding?"

"If it'll make you feel better, go ahead and tell him. Just make darn sure he doesn't show up to spoil everything."

~~~

Saturday before the wedding, Paul goes to the hospital to deliver Angie's disappointing refusal in person. As he enters the small ward, Paul notices Tucker's bed is vacant. Before he can ask, Ralph speaks with stark naked frankness, "He ain't here, preacher. They took ol' Tucker downstairs to die."

"My heavens," Paul exclaims, "where?" His three ward companions shake their heads and resume watching cartoons on television. Paul rushes to the nurses' station and learns that Tucker has spent the past two days in the first floor intensive care unit. To save time Paul takes the stairway rather than the elevator. He locates the hallway marked "I.C.U." and presses the button that opens the double doors. Inside the hall, a nurse intercepts him. He finally convinces her that he's Tucker Shook's pastor. She leads him to the patient who is tented and tethered to a green cylinder.

Raising one corner of the clear cover, the nurse calls as if he is across the room, "Mr. Shook, your pastor is here." Paul fights the urge to escape from the mixture of oxygen and body odors that assaults his senses. He draws closer. Tucker opens his eyes and smiles weakly.

"Hidee Preacher," Tucker rasps, his voice hardly more than a whisper. "Don't light up." He points to the *No Smoking* sign posted on the tent.

"If I had only known, Tucker, I would have come sooner."

Tucker rolls his head back and forth to signal "no problem." He lifts his hand. "Gimme my bag, Preacher."

The nurse says, "I'll get it." She pulls the canvas bag from under the foot of the bed and hands it to Paul.

"Take out the papers." Paul pulls out the Gideon Bible and a couple scraps of paper, but Tucker shakes his head. "No, the envelopes." Paul probes under a shirt and pair of pants before locating two worn envelopes. "Take 'em to Angeline, my weddin' gifts." His breathing becomes more labored as he struggles to talk, so Paul asks no questions. Instead he slips the envelopes into his coat pocket and reaches under the oxygen tent to lay his hand on Tucker's chest. Paul closes his eyes and prays softly. Tucker closes his eyes as Paul pleads with God to send healing balm to His suffering servant. Paul ends his prayer by reciting Psalm Twenty-three, "The Lord is my Shepherd, I shall not want..." concluding with "and I shall dwell in the house of the Lord forever. Amen."

Paul opens his eyes. Tucker's eyes remain closed. Paul becomes aware there's no movement beneath his hand on Tucker's chest. He panics, "Somebody do something!"

The nurse places her forefinger on Tucker's wrist. Feeling no pulse, she declares, "No resuscitation, Reverend. He requested we let him go."

Death is no stranger to Paul. He has held the hands of dying patients on many occasions. But this time is different. No friends and family surround the deathbed to seek pastoral comfort in their grief, only an indifferent uniformed observer for whom death has become an opiate.

After assuring the hospital administrator that he will notify Tucker's next of kin, Paul drives to the parsonage to meet with the betrothed couple. *Should I tell Angie about her father's death now? I hate to cast a pall over their plans. Maybe I should wait until after the ceremony to break the news?* Paul's dedication to truth and honesty make the decision easier, but the task will still be difficult.

Lorna meets Paul at the door, chastising him for being late. "What took you so long? Everybody's waiting on the back porch."

"I'll explain later." Paul goes directly to the back porch and greets Angie, Chad, Katy and Leland. "Where's Pauline?"

Katy laughs, "Didn't you see her asleep in the crib?"

"I guess I was too concerned with being so late," Paul looks directly at Angie. "I've just returned from Veterans Hospital with great sorrow in my heart." He walks over and kneels before her. "I'm sorry to have to bring you the news that your father died this morning."

The others gasp and utter words of disbelief, but Angie merely swallows hard and replies, "So?"

Paul takes her hands in his, a gesture of comfort, "If there is anything I can do for you, Angie, please let me know." But she remains stoic.

"I thought we came to practice the wedding," Angie says with no note of remorse.

"Of course," Paul rises to his feet. "I'll get my book."

The wedding rehearsal proceeds like a dispassionate recitation of a weather report on a clear day. The participants keep close watch on Angie, poised for signs of a delayed expression of grief. But her stoicism is unrelenting. Paul reads through the vows and exchange of rings as Katy stands in for Angie to ward off bad luck. Just as the walk-through concludes, the baby cries out, breaking a pall that had settled over the group. "What timing!" Lorna darts out. "I'll get her while you finish up here."

Paul pulls two envelopes from his pocket and offers them to Angie. "Your father asked me to give these to you before he passed on. He said they are wedding gifts."

Angie shies away, glaring at the worn envelopes. "What's in them?" she asks, clasping her hands together as if to forbid them from touching the gifts.

"I don't know. He never told me."

Chad asks Angie, "Do you want me to open them for you?" He takes the envelopes from Paul.

"Yes," Angie mumbles under her breath, "but not 'til we're married. I don't want to deal with anything now except plans for tomorrow." Chad folds and stuffs the envelopes into his pocket. "Thanks," she whispers.

The next day, Paul preaches a brief sermon and concludes with his surprise announcement. "As we sing our closing hymn, I invite Angie Shook, Chad Willis and his family to join mine at the altar for a special conclusion to our service today." Ladies in the congregation, who are normally waking their husbands and straightening their girdles at this point, preparing for a quick exit to the local restaurants, do not budge. They watch Chad, Katy and Lorna shed their choir robes and meet Angie and Chad's family at the altar.

Following the exchange of vows, Paul leads the recessional to the front door of the church where the newlyweds receive good wishes from the departing parishioners. Some choir members gently chide Chad for depriving them of the opportunity to bring wedding gifts.

After the crowd disperses, Lorna invites the wedding party to lunch in the fellowship hall. She had sworn Marge and Evelyn to secrecy when she asked them to prepare a light meal. The tensions of the day fade as they eat and gaiety overtakes the celebration. Marge whispers to Paul. "Someone's outside looking for the bride. What shall I tell her?"

Before Paul can answer, a tiny figure appears in the doorway carrying a grocery sack. She places the sack on the floor and removes the black hat that almost covers her eyes.

"Vicki!" screams Angie. She darts across the room to hug her New Orleans roommate. "You came!"

"Yep, I made it, finally. If that frigging taxi driver had not gotten lost, I wouldn't have missed the goddamn wedding." Everybody winces at the crude expression, except Angie. She dances around holding her friend's hands, squealing with delight.

Angie settles down enough to pull Vicki forward to meet Chad. "This is my Prince Charming. Chad, this is Vicki, my friend from New Orleans who...who," Angie weighs her words carefully. "...who put up with me...and we worked together."

Chad takes Vicki's hand and introduces her to his parents and Katy's husband and family. "A preacher? Omigod, sorry about the language," she drops her chin to her chest. Then she turns to retrieve the grocery sack. "Here, Crystal...I mean, Angie. I brought you a wedding present."

"Oh, my first and only wedding gift."

"Your second," Chad pats his coat pocket where he keeps the envelopes from Tucker.

"Oh," Angie rolls her eyes. "But it'll be the first one I'll open." Vicki hands her a box wrapped in silver paper, tied with a fancy gold bow. Angie slides off the bow and meticulously removes the tape holding the paper.

"I hope it didn't break getting bounced around on the bus," Vickie says. Everyone watches as Angie pulls away folds of white tissue paper, to unveil the treasure nestled inside. She extracts a smaller box and removes the lid to reveal a crystal bell. She lifts the bell and jingles it. "It's to ring up your husband when you need his attention," Vicki laughs.

Angie displays Vicki's gift in the palm of her hand. The silver handle is the figure of an angel's upper body. The angel's robe flares out below to form the cup, made of fine glass and etched with musical notes all around. "It's so beautiful!" Angie exclaims, now realizing it's more than just a fancy bell. Vicki's gift is a reminder of Crystal Angel's hard-bitten survival of New Orleans nightlife.

After the luncheon, Angie insists that Vicki spend a few days with her and Chad before returning to New Orleans. "Omigod, no! Three's a crowd on a honeymoon. I'm catching the first bus outta here. I didn't even bring a change of underwear."

"Don't be so dense, Vicki. We've already had our honeymoon—twice over," Angie whispers, blushing. "I moved in with him a month ago, but we didn't tell anybody."

"Nothing like getting a head start, I always say," Vicki nudges her in the side. "Looks like I'd have to rush to catch the New Orleans bus anyway, so I suppose I could hang around for one night."

Back at the apartment, Chad urges Angie to open the envelopes from her dad. "You go ahead and open them. Vicki and I have a lot of catching up to do and so little time." The two women plant themselves at the kitchen table sipping the champagne Chad opened. He takes his fluted glass to the couch.

Chad opens the small envelope addressed to Tucker. He unfolds three sheets of paper and presses them flat on the coffee table. "Angie, you won't believe this," he says after reading the papers.

"If it's bad news, I don't want to hear it. If it's good news, then it'll keep 'til we're through talking," Angie's head bubbles from the champagne.

"It's both."

Angie barely hears him as she pours Vicki another glass. Chad opens the longer and more tattered envelope. It also contains three pages; the letter from United Mutual Insurance Co., a claim form and a list of names with dates and telephone numbers. "Wow!" Chad shouts, this is fantastic, but I guess you're too busy talking to hear fantastic news."

"O.K., O.K., say it and get it over with so we can talk," Angie relents.

"Your mother left you twenty-thousand dollars and your daddy left you his house and five acres of land. That's the fantastic news," Chad waves the papers in the air.

"Twenty-thou....I'm not believing this. She couldn't have saved that much money." Angie walks over to inspect the papers on the coffee table. Chad points out the insurance claim form and a hand-written will leaving her the property. "I'll be damned," she says as she discovers the letter she had written to her mother before hearing of her death. "Shit! This is why I hated the son-of-a-bitch!"

"Here, before you get worked up all over again, read this," Chad shows her another sheet with hand-printed letters:

> *DEAR ANGELINE, MARIE PASSED AWAY WHEN SHE COULD NOT FIND YOU IN NEW ORLEANS. I WANTED TO COME FIND YOU BUT I GOT SICK. I DON'T KNOW WHERE TO MAIL THIS...*

Angie reads the note over and over, tears forming in her eyes. She eases down on the couch beside Chad. "Goodness and mercy, I didn't know Momma searched for me in New Orleans, did you, Vicki? Her friend shakes her head. Angie picks up the tattered envelope. "Damn my hide! I shouldn't have mentioned being in New Orleans when I wrote to Mama. I never dreamed she'd leave Mimosa and come looking for me in a big city."

Chad shows Angie the paper trail of Tucker's efforts to locate her. "Your dad called a lot of people searching for you before he went in the hospital." One name jumps out at Angie: Reverend Oliver Barron. Tucker had scratched a note beside Ollie's name, *lying bastard.* Chad continues talking about the contents of the papers, but Angie's mind is preoccupied with the encounter between Tucker and Ollie Barron. *What did they say to each other? How did Ollie upset Daddy? Did they talk about me?*

"Angie, Angie, are you listening?" Chad finally breaks through but then decides to drop the discussion. "Never mind, we can deal with this later. You and Vicki have a lot to talk about, so why don't I run out and get a pizza." The women give Chad thumbs up and he makes a hasty exit, leaving them alone.

Vicki tops off their glasses with more champagne. "Now, come clean, Angel. Something's in your craw."

Angie's mouth falls open as if she had been caught in a lie. "You know me too well, Vicki, could never hide anything from you." Angie sips her champagne and thrusts the list of names and numbers in front of Vicki. "Looks like my dad had it out with the father of my baby." She places a finger on Ollie Barron's name.

"So? You mean that's the preacher who knocked you up? Son-of-a..."

"That's not the worst of it. Now the bastard has come back into my life, uninvited! It turns out his wife is chummy with the Petersons and, get this, he was Chad's college roommate. I don't think any of them like him, but he pokes his red head into their business pretty often. Help me, Vickie. I can't face him without coming apart."

"But, who's going to know? Can't you fake it for a while 'til you get used to being around him?"

"Katy already knows. She figured it out from the way I acted when I met Ollie for the first time since...well, you know, since I hauled ass to New Orleans."

"This may be too simple to work, but why not go ahead and expose the sorry son-of-a-bitch, get it off your chest."

"And let people think Chad's married a slut? Some of those bitches in the choir would love that, no thank you." Angie gulps down the last shot of champagne. "I even thought about phoning Ollie to let him know that I did not get an abortion. I'm dying to tell him there's a kid running around somewhere with his red hair and green eyes and...one day the kid will walk down the aisle of the church and...and call him daddy and...and they'll kick Ollie Barron out on his holy ass and...and his wife will leave him and...and...and..." Angie paused and giggles. "Gosh, this champagne's made my tongue as slick as boiled okra."

"Sounds like a good idea to tell him off," Vicki chuckles, "but don't do it while you're smashed, you'll slur all those juicy words."

Chad pushes the door open and marches to the table with the large flat box. "Let's eat while it's hot, well at least lukewarm."

"Just in time, sir," Vicki announces with a flourish, "your bride's craving anchovies and pepperoni."

"God, I hope she's not pregnant," Chad laughs. Angie lobs the empty champagne bottle toward him. He catches it in mid-air. "Just kidding, Angel, just kidding."

22

> *October 20, 1966*
>
> *Dear Mrs. Willis,*
>
> *Angela Olive wishes to thank you for the birthday gift. I'm sure she will enjoy it when she is old enough to wear it.*
> *Regards to you and Chad,*
>
> *Betty Barron*

Chad Willis breaks his own tradition by giving the choir a two-week summer break from practice. He offers to help Angie arrange Tucker's funeral service and burial in Mimosa. But it is beyond his powers to exorcise the anxieties that rage within her troubled breast. Despite her father's skepticism of religion and her own experience with the church, Angie wants a proper funeral for him with chimes tolling, his body nestled in a silk-lined casket and Paul Peterson eulogizing eloquently from the pulpit of the First Methodist Church—in Mimosa, the town she pledged never to return. The grandiose funeral plans belie not only the simple, coal-miner, down-to-earth life that Tucker Shook had lived, but also the vow she had made to herself, serving only to compound the conflicts that already claw at Angie's insides.

"I just had a conversation with Claude Ray. He agreed to meet with the pastor at Mimosa First Methodist to make the necessary arrangements for Tucker's funeral, possibly for Thursday. Would that be suitable?" In spite of hearing Paul

Peterson's compassionate voice flowing from the receiver, the prospect of making the decision is still paralyzing for her. "Angie, are you there?" Paul persists.

Chad takes the phone from her limp hand. "I'm sorry, Paul, Angie is still overcome with grief. Allow me, please." Paul explains the situation again. Chad thanks his friend and hangs up. Wrapping his despairing bride in his arms, Chad longs to alleviate her pain, "I know what a strain you're under, my angel. You just take it easy and put these troubling details out of your mind. Paul and I will handle everything."

Angie sniffs and snuggles closer to Chad's chest. "Except the worst part...they want me to come to the hospital to claim Daddy's bo..." she releases a guttural moan, "Aaugh, I can't say the word."

"No you don't have to do that, Paul told me he took care of that chore this morning. He signed the release and requested the Mimosa Funeral Home to come and pick up the bo..." Chad stops as Angie gasps, "...your daddy."

There is much to do during the next two days before the Thursday afternoon funeral. Paul and Chad make most of the decisions and, to make the burial proper and legal, they present all the papers for Angie's signature. Chad sleeps well Wednesday night, but Angie wrestles until dawn with the prospect of returning to her hometown.

Early next morning, the phone rings. Chad answers and discovers that Tucker Shook's daughter has one last decision to make. The mortician from Mimosa asks to speak to Angie.

"Miss Shook, would you like to come by the funeral home before noon today to approve the arrangements?" When Angie declines, the velvet-voice confirms, "Well then, Miss Shook, I must know if you prefer an opened or closed casket—that would be during the service."

"Why?"

"Some loved ones prefer to say their final goodbyes in private and others during the service." His mellifluous voice however, does not assuage her turmoil.

"O my gosh, I hadn't thought of that!" She turns to Chad. "He wants to know if they should close the casket or leave it opened. I just don't know…"

"Tell him you need time to think about it, that we'll be by the funeral home later this morning to let him know what you have decided." Angie relays the message and hangs up the phone.

~~~

"I've never been to Mimosa, what's it like?" Chad asks Angie as the car speeds along Highway 78, the bright morning sun at their backs promising another warm June day.

"Just a town," Angie intends to divert Chad's attention with the terse reply. *This may not be such a hot idea, going back to where my troubles began. It makes me feel sick to think about it.*

"I'm anxious to see your church. You should be glad it's not all boarded up like my old church at Coal City."

"Just a church." *How can I explain to him the church means nothing to me? Daddy never went and Momma thought of it as a theatre where I could become a star. Then there was Ollie Barron, the slick talking preacher that came along and used me—in more ways than one. I hope the service won't last very long.*

A few moments of silence later, Chad slows the car to a halt at a stop sign. Angie glances out the window and recognizes the motel at Sargent's Crossroads. She covers her eyes and slides down in her seat. "What's wrong, my angel, do I need to pull over?"

"No, no, I'm all right, just a little dizzy. Keep on going." *I tried to forget about this place where that red-headed bastard sent me down a path to hell. He never gave a damn about me.*

As they pass the stop sign and speed up, Chad asks, "So what do you plan to tell the undertaker?"

Angie heaves a sigh and attempts to chatter away the despair of her dilemma. "I don't know what to do. I haven't seen Daddy in over three years. I don't even remember the last words I spoke to him. I didn't even tell him goodbye when I went off to college. He'd gone fishing that day. And the next thing I knew about him was when you told me he looked like walking death, and that was six months ago. I want to remember Daddy like he used to be, but somehow it doesn't seem fair."

"Fair? How so?"

"Because I owe Daddy an apology. It will be terribly difficult, but I need to tell him—to his face—what a total asshole I've been. All this time I thought it was because I had run away that he didn't tell me Momma died. But I didn't give him a bat's chance in daylight to say so. Like a typical coal miner, Daddy wasn't handy with words, so he took up Momma's search and died the same way she did—looking for me." Angie pauses to blow her nose.

"Don't be too hard on yourself, Angel. You didn't give your daddy black lung disease or buy him any cigarettes. It seems to me there's enough blame for everybody to have a share."

"I have to face him, Chad, no matter how bad he looks, but I can't let anybody else see my daddy all withered away."

As they enter Mimosa's city limits, Angie directs Chad to the funeral home. He parks on the concrete apron in front of the converted two-story house laced with gingerbread across the eaves and front porch. Angie laments, "Let's get this over with."

A well-dressed gentleman meets them in the reception room that still bears the trappings of a Victorian parlor—floral wallpaper, ornate fireplace, dark trim molding and a fussy crystal chandelier. "May I be of service?" he asks. Before Angie can respond, he adds, "Oh, you must be Mr. Shook's family. We have him all ready and prepared for your visit. If you will just follow me…"

Angie doesn't budge. "Sir, could we have a moment?" Chad asks. The man stops in the archway that leads to what was once a formal dining room. The edge of a gray casket is barely visible against the back wall. "My wife has not yet decided if she wants to view her father's bo..., her father."

Angie bites her lip. "Yes, I have. I do." The man turns sideways and extends his hand toward the open casket. Angie grips Chad's hand as she steps gingerly beneath the arch. She stops before entering the room. "Please let me be alone for a minute."

The attendant wrinkles his brow and glances at Chad for affirmation. "Are you sure?" Chad asks Angie. She nods and the two men remain behind as she approaches the casket but then stops halfway.

God, I didn't expect it would be this hard, but I've got to talk to my daddy. I just wish he could hear me. Why was I too hard-headed to do it sooner?

For the longest moments of her life, Angie stares in silence at Tucker's pale profile nestled among the white silken tufts. Then she speaks softly, "Daddy, I know you can't hear me, but I have to talk to you anyway. Maybe whatever spirits or angels are hovering over you will deliver my message." Angie sniffs and pulls a tissue from her purse. "I'm trying to do this without bawling like a baby. Momma always told me not to cry in front of you because you'd leave the house." She steps forward and breathes deeply. "I came by to talk to you about mistakes, one you made and a big one I made. We were both wrong but that's no excuse for what we did. You said singing was a waste of time. Well, Daddy, I proved I could make a living as a singer. What's more, it was my voice that led me to the most wonderful husband in the world." Angie moves to where she can peer down at Tucker's drawn face. She musters enough fortitude to whisper, "Just once, you could've said, 'Angeline, I love to hear you sing.' But I didn't hold that against you. What I really wanted was for you to love me. I know, I know you always told Momma it was enough that you built us a house, kept us from starving and drove me places to sing. I never knew how to tell you there was more you needed to do. Fact is, you had more coal dust under your fingernails than love in your heart. I wish you could've held me on your lap like a baby doll, just once. But you always pushed me away, afraid I'd get dirty. Couldn't you understand? I didn't mind when you were all black and sweaty, you were my daddy."

Angie realizes her voice has risen above a whisper. "Excuse me, Daddy, that's not really what I came to say. I made a huge mistake by not talking to you after Momma died. I should have realized you didn't want to tell me about Momma over the phone. How stupid I was!" Her voice gets louder. "I'm so sorry, Daddy, really, really sorry." She regains control and gently touches his hands that are folded across his chest, then bends forward with a whisper. "There's one other thing you ought to know. I overheard you accusing Momma of shacking up with the preacher. When you meet her in heaven, she'll straighten you out. But I'm here to tell you, Momma wasn't the one messing around with the preacher." Angie stares at Tucker's waxen face, incredulous that she has just admitted this to his deaf ears. Then she gently pats her daddy's cold hands and backs away from the casket. "You have some mighty pretty flowers. In case nobody's told you, they're from the union," she says in a composed gesture of closure. She calls Chad to come view Tucker's body before instructing the undertaker to seal the casket.

"And please leave it closed for good," she adds, walking away and drying her remaining tears.

After the funeral service at the church, the National Guard provides a military ceremony at the cemetery. Lieutenant Sawyer presents Angie with a folded triangle of white stars on a blue background, salutes her and dismisses the uniformed honor guard. The large contingency of union members files by Angie and Chad offering condolences. After all the other cars have driven away, as Katy, Leland and the Petersons say their goodbyes, Angie hands the folded flag to Chad and wraps both her arms around Paul. "I appreciate your kind words about Daddy and I can't thank you enough for all you did for him. I just wish I hadn't been so hardheaded. I left too many things unsaid, so did Daddy."

"Don't be so hard on yourself, Angie, death often comes before any of us can get around to saying proper farewells. It may be of consolation to you to know that Tucker kept a Bible with him in the hospital."

"He did? That's strange. We never owned one."

"It belonged to the hospital," Paul says, not wishing to pursue the conversation further.

Angie takes one last look at the casket before heading for the car. "Chad, can we go by my old house before we head back to Birmingham? I need to see if there's anything I want to keep before turning it over to the real estate agent."

~~~

Brian Peck's story appears in the *Times* in mid July, about the time Paul and Lorna Peterson prepare to leave for a vacation. With the car laden with luggage, Paul stuffs his briefcase just as full with unread journals, articles, and letters. The phone rings. "Ignore it," Lorna shouts from the front porch, "everybody knows we're headed out of town." But Paul's premonition of an unexpected crisis compels him to respond to the phone's persistent summons.

"Hello, Paul Peterson speaking…Oh, hello Ollie, I'm sorry, but I was just going out the door to spend a week…no, I haven't seen today's *News*."

"I'm not speaking of *The Birmingham News*," Ollie's voice blusters in the receiver, "It's in the *Times,* the New York paper!"

"I do not subscribe to a New York newspaper, Ollie, so I am not aware of the 'it' you are referring to."

"Your name…your picture…all over the page…says the Klan bombed your office...You never told me somebody tried to kill you, Paul...What on earth is going on?" Ollie continues ranting nonstop, ignoring Paul's attempts to respond. "Who fed the reporter all that nonsense? I'd hate to be around when the Bishop reads the paper; he's going to have a…"

"Wait a minute, Ollie," Paul interrupts loudly, seeking clarification. "Read me the part about the explosion," Paul finally breaks in seeking clarification.

"I can't, I don't have the paper."

"Then how do you know what's in it?"

"I just talked to H. R. Wood. He reads the *Times* regularly."

Paul releases an impatient sigh, "I know you will excuse me, Ollie," he interrupts the incessant blather, "this is my vacation week and I don't want to waste another minute of it, goodbye." As soon as Paul hangs up, the phone rings again. As his hand reaches for the receiver, he freezes, pivots to face the door and heads to the car, refusing to surrender to the rising anxiety. Lorna and Paul take off for a relaxing week in a cottage at Lake Junaluska.

Katy and Marge call the Petersons the next day to report the flood of requests they've fielded from various news media for "just a minute of Reverend Peterson's time."

"Please hold them at bay until we get back. Paul desperately needs this vacation and I'm going to see that he gets it," Lorna asserts.

The Petersons return to the parsonage late Saturday night in time for Paul to deliver his sermon the next day. Katy had stacked their accumulated mail on the kitchen table along with a copy of Monday's *Times,* with pages folded to reveal his picture. Paul takes time to read the article before unpacking. "Look Lorna, this reporter says he gave the Birmingham Police all the evidence, including a name, that they need in order to arrest the bomber, but nothing was ever done."

"Like I said before, I'm still not convinced someone was out to get you. It was obviously a case of mistaken identity." Then she looks over Paul's shoulder and changes the subject. "Your picture looks like Moshe Dyan with hair," she snickers, referring to the patch over his damaged eye. "And that caption, now I understand why Ollie Barron got so excited—Reverend Paul Peterson, Bombingham's Newest Prophet."

"A prophet, I'm not," Paul mutters. "Would you please open the mail for me while I go in the study to polish up tomorrow's sermon?"

The next morning as Paul finishes adjusting his necktie before going to the church, the doorbell rings. "Good morning, Brother Mack is something wrong?"

"Don't know Brother Paul, but Channel 6 is setting up a television camera in the sanctuary balcony and I thought you should know." Paul grabs his coat and hurries to the church.

"Good morning, Reverend Peterson, I'm Hank Davis from Six News. We're here to…"

Paul cuts him off, ignoring his extended hand. "I'm sorry, but I made it clear to your station manager last night that no cameras will be allowed during the service. This is a place of worship."

"I'm sorry, we didn't get the word. You may not realize it, Reverend, but you are big news. Perhaps we can just shoot a little footage of you in the pulpit, very quietly…" the man insists.

"No sir, I'm afraid that would not be possible," Paul glances at his watch. "It is almost time for the service to begin."

"But, I understand a delegation of black pastors will be here today to pay tribute…"

Paul raises his hand to curb the television reporter's appeal. "Then your news story will occur outside the sanctuary." He motions to some members who are milling around. "Perhaps you fellows will help Mr. Davis remove his equipment from the balcony before the processional."

The morning service commences with a standing-room-only crowd, a rare sight for summer. The overflow wedged in the vestibule blocks the entrance, so Chad cancels the processional and leads the choir to enter the choir loft through the back doors. The alternate route has diminished the chance of theatrics as Paul makes his appearance from the side door. After placing his Bible on the pulpit, he looks up to witness an unbelievable scene on the second row pew. There, in his puffed up splendor, is Bishop

Grand seated next to a slender black man in a clerical collar. This solitary face of color is a striking contrast to the packed sanctuary of whites.

The service proceeds at the usual pace until Paul stands for the pastoral prayer. One look at Bishop Grand's expectant glow prompts him to call on his superior to do the honors. The Bishop relishes the opportunity to gain the spotlight. His prayer uniquely offers more information than supplication.

"Our most gracious and holy Heavenly Father, we most humbly beg forgiveness for our sins..." the Bishop begins his prayer. A few moments later he concludes with praise for Reverend Peterson, "...We thank Thee for our Brother Paul's leadership in promoting brotherhood within our church and community. Thou hast imbued your servant with sufficient integrity and courage to offer his own life on the altar of racial equality. As Thou plucked Isaac from the throes of death, Thou saw fit to save our brother from the inferno of bigotry. And now as we remember the high ideals of the Methodist Church, we ask Thy blessings in the name of our Savior, Jesus of Nazareth. Amen."

The Bishop's effort to hitch his chariot to Paul Peterson's star draws a sprinkle of "amen's" from men in the congregation that barely muffles the sound of Paul choking.

After the service, reporters are drawn to the Bishop like nails to a magnet. Meanwhile, Paul stands by the door as usual and speaks to each worshipper leaving the sanctuary. As he shakes hands with the last one in line, an usher tugs at Paul's robe. "The Bishop would like to for you to join him up front."

Reverend Peterson moves down the aisle toward a small crowd surrounding the Bishop and his guest. "A wonderful service, Brother Paul," exclaims the Bishop. "I would like for you to meet Reverend Arthur Towns, pastor of Mt. Signal Methodist." Paul shakes the hand of the black preacher as a newspaper photographer's camera flashes several times. Reporters levy a barrage of questions at Paul, but Bishop Grand raises his hands and takes charge of the interview.

"Please, gentlemen, I want to make a special announcement that may be of considerable interest. As you may have read in the newspaper, Brother Paul has asked to be relieved of his charge at this church in order to more effectively serve the ministry of the Methodist Church. Therefore, I am pleased to announce, after consultation with Reverend Towns, that my office will create a new and innovative charge to serve the disenfranchised residents of Birmingham's inner city." A clamor for more information follows his announcement, but the Bishop again raises his hands. "Furthermore, it shall be my distinct pleasure to appoint Reverend Paul Peterson as Pastor of what we shall call 'Aldersgate Ministry' in honor of the site of John Wesley's life-altering experience."

Paul is stunned, caught completely unaware by the Bishop's announcement. *What a turn-around. I expected no support from the Bishop in my new venture. But here he stands in the church designated as my exile, making a stand for racial equality. He's a bit late, but a welcome transformation. Thanks be to God.* Still in awe, Paul observes the converted Bishop intercepting each reporter's question followed by an extended response.

~~~

"Hon, are you going to accept the new assignment?" Lorna asks watching the Channel Six evening news.

"Not until I've read thoroughly between the lines of Bishop Grand's offer."

"Good, like where we will live, how much you'll be paid and who'll be your boss," Lorna says, "I shudder to think where we'll set up housekeeping next. I wonder if we could use some of the donations you've received to buy a modest home here in the Hope neighborhood."

"I couldn't possibly touch that money for our personal needs, Lorna. It's earmarked for my new charge. It's hard to believe that one newspaper story would initiate so much generosity from people we don't even know," Paul smiles as he strokes his chin.

"You know, this is the first time there's ever been enough money at my disposal to dictate the direction of my ministry, to actually be in charge of my own destiny!" He pauses and adds "...with God's help."

"That's wonderful my brave heart. But promise me you won't become another Ollie Barron, or J. B. Colley, or H. R. Wood, or..."

"Hold it, you made your point," Paul exclaims, squeezing his wife. "That will never happen—with you and Katy watching my every move."

~~~

Leaves on the parsonage sycamore tree have begun their transition to a golden glow by the time Lorna remembers to give some attention to Betty Barron's unrelenting obsession—a shower for Angie. Lorna suggests a linen shower is an appropriate substitute for the aborted bridal fete. But Angie curtails that suggestion, fearing another confrontation with Ollie Barron. However, Angie gives in when Katy assures her that no man would be caught dead in a parsonage full of giddy women showering a new bride with bed sheets, towels and pillow cases.

Angie starts fall classes at the university and resumes her job singing at a dinner club in the evenings. Chad remains disappointed that he is unable to lure her back to the Hope choir. "Not yet, my prince, I'm not quite ready to sing again with those gossiping bitches that tried to break us up, maybe later when the goblins in my mind settle down." She relies on this excuse, not yet prepared to chance an inevitable encounter with a redheaded preacher.

"Not making any progress, huh?" Katy sits at Angie's kitchen table addressing invitations to the shower.

"Oh, I've finished half the stack you gave me."

"I wasn't referring to the envelopes, Mrs. Willis. By the look of those lines etched across your forehead, you haven't figured out what to do about the Red Barron, have you?"

"Does it show? That must be why Chad's been asking about my health. Every night before I go to work at the club, he asks, 'Angel, are you coming down with something?'" Katy laughs at Angie's treble imitation of Chad's bass voice. "But I have to confess, the thought of that bastard Ollie haunts me constantly. I'm so afraid I'll bump into him at the grocery store, or the Spinning Wheel, or just walking down the street. He might even come to the club for dinner and then my only choice would be to sing with a paper sack over my head."

"Have you thought any further about meeting him somewhere, just to talk?"

"I wouldn't know what to say, except to call him every bad name I picked up from Vicki. Anyway, I'd freeze up if he actually spoke to me."

"I know this is going to sound like a preacher's kid talking, but you could forgive him."

"Forgive him, hell! After all he did to me? I don't think so. You don't realize how hard it was to forgive my own daddy. And he'd done nothing intentional to hurt me. Wiping Ollie's slate clean would take seventy times seven more guts than I have. Besides, he ought to suffer for his sins."

"Don't look now, my friend, but Ollie's not doing much suffering. All I'm saying is, no matter how hard it is to forgive him, the very act of forgiveness will go a long way toward resolving your own anxiety."

"There, I've finished these. How many do you have left?" Angie changes the subject by returning to the task at hand.

"Just a couple, and then I have to pick up Pauline at day care," Katy replies. "But think about what I said."

"I will, I really will, but don't get your hopes up. If only I could figure a way to hand him all my emotional baggage, let him drag it around. Do psychologists have a formula for transferring misery to another person?"

"Sorry, I don't know of any therapy that would make that possible," Katy retrieves her sweater from the couch.

Angie walks her to the door. "I wasn't thinking about therapy, Mrs. Freud, I was thinking about medieval torture, like the iron maiden or the rack."

Katy shakes her head and gives Angie a quick hug. "And I thought you hated history."

~~~

The day before the linen shower, Angie lapses into a rare state of giddiness. Katy notices, "I'm pleased to see you in a party mood."

"It's Saturday, no classes today and tomorrow I'll finally replace those old jungle bed sheets Chad's had since college." They laugh and joke together as they help Lorna decorate the parsonage with frilly yellow and white ribbon.

"Wouldn't want your guests to think they're coming to a baby shower," Lorna jokes as she tapes a large yellow bow to the dining room chandelier. Katy scrunches her shoulders, extending her upturned palms, a signal to Angie that Lorna's remark is strictly out of the blue. Angie grins and lets it roll off.

"I'll get it," Katy responds to the door chimes. She opens the door to a curious sight—Betty Barron holding a beautifully wrapped gift in one hand and little Angela Olive's hand in the other. "Mrs. Barron, what a surprise. The shower's not 'til tomorrow."

"I know, darling, but I'm afraid I made a big *faux pas*. Tomorrow's Angela Olive's birthday and…"

"Well, come on in, Betty," shouts Lorna perched on the stepladder. Katy steps aside. Angie stands face to face with Betty Barron and a little toddler with hair the color of rust and sparkling green eyes. She gulps for air and feels herself shrinking into a ball.

Mrs. Barron eyes Angie carefully. "Oh, you must be Chad's wife…Angie, is it? I haven't seen you since you served pizza in Mimosa. How long has it been?"

"I sang in the choir, too," sputters Angie, miffed at Betty's condescending remark.

"So you have a birthday coming up?" Lorna kneels and takes Angela's hands.

"Yes, she does, Lorna, and I feel like such a dunce. Oliver and I failed to coordinate our calendars. Tomorrow is Angela Olive's birthday and he invited the Bishop and his wife over for cake and ice cream after church. I planned a little party for later in the afternoon, after the shower, but now...I suppose it's the curse of being married to a preacher. One never knows when one must be about the Lord's business. Anyway, I brought our gift over so you would have it in time for the unveiling." She extends the package toward Angie, lifting her eyebrows.

Angie catches herself staring at Angela, almost missing Betty's comment. "Oh...thanks."

Katy comes to the rescue, taking the package from the petrified Angie. "That's very considerate, Mrs. Barron, but I could have picked up your gift if you had just called," Katy says.

"Well, we owe it to Chad. He was always special to Oliver; you know they were roommates in college."

Angie bites her tongue. *Damn, another put-down, the second one today. I could work up a craw full of resentment—except I know that her majesty treated all the folks in Mimosa this way. I'm not the only one to be put down by this queen of faint praise.*

"I thought Angela's birthday was last May," Katy says. "I remember it was the same day as our anniversary."

"True, my dear, Oliver and I could never agree on when to celebrate Angela's birthday, the day she was born or the day we adopted her. To tell the truth, Oliver didn't like the Catholic connection associated with her date of birth, so he declared the date on the adoption papers as the official date for celebration purposes."

"Catholic connection, I don't understand."

"Oh, it's nothing really...all in Oliver's mind. He thinks because she was born in a Catholic hospital on Columbus Day and cared for by nuns for seven months that she's been imprinted with the curse of Catholicism. Ridiculous, isn't it?"

Angie's knees weaken. She backs up against the wall, unnoticed by Lorna and Katy as they continue chatting with their visitor. Angie finds it difficult to restrain herself from questioning Betty Barron further. She fiddles with the crystal angel pendant underneath her blouse, all the while staring at the beaming three-year-old. As if reading Angie's mind, Lorna comments, "I understand you went out of state to adopt Angela."

"That's true, but I'm afraid I've said too much already. Oliver and I agreed not to discuss the details of the adoption until Angela is twenty-one. He's so paranoid about it. He thinks the anonymous birth mother might show up on our doorstep one day to claim the child she gave away. He nearly came apart after we lost our little Amy. Not many people know this, but Oliver almost gave up the pulpit after the accident. If the Bishop hadn't moved him from Mimosa, I'm afraid to think what he would be doing now, probably selling real estate."

Angie's mind spirals faster trying to follow the path of the adoption maze Betty has drawn, while she rambles on about her *gift from God*. From the corner of her eye, Katy catches a glimpse of Angie and moves over beside her. "What's wrong?" she whispers. "You're digging a hole in your blouse."

"Nothing," Angie licks her dry lips and heads toward to the kitchen. "Excuse me, I need a drink of water."

Angela Olive toddles behind Angie to the kitchen babbling "wa-wa, wa-wa."

"Would you mind?" Betty calls to Angie, without relaxing the pace of her conversation.

Angie fills a glass half full and kneels before the dimpled child, gripping the glass with both hands to subdue her nervous trembling. Placing the empty glass on the counter, Angie cannot take her eyes off the three-year-old redhead looking up at her with crystal green eyes.

"Wuv me?" Little Angela asks in fractured baby talk. Angie reaches out to hug the smiling toddler, but simply holds her by the shoulders, compelled to study this face.

"Yes, I love you." Tears swell in her eyes as she senses a strong attachment to this child who mirrors Angie's persistent gaze. Angie's quandary flashes through her mind: *Could God be trying to mend the bond that was broken in that lonely hospital delivery room three years ago? Maybe it's just my imagination fanning the flames of hope?*

She rises and touches the crystal angel resting next to her heart, then lifts the silver chain from around her neck. "So you have a birthday tomorrow?" Angela nods and holds up three fingers. "Well, Miss Angela Olive, three-year-old, I have a birthday present for you." Angie loops a knot in the chain to shorten it and places it over the child's head. Then she holds the disc flat against her palm for Angela to see. "My precious, this is your special angel, a friend you can tell all your secrets to and she will always listen."

Angela trots back to the living room, dangling the angel in her hand. Her mother finally looks down at Angela Olive tugging at her dress. The afternoon sun from the window strikes the crystal, causing it to sparkle as it rotates on the silver chain. "My, my, how lovely, Angela. Now give back Miss Angie's trinket so we can go."

"No, no, Mrs. Barron. It's a gift...for her birthday," Angie exclaims.

Betty examines the pendant more closely, "But it looks expensive, are you sure?"

"Absolutely, someone gave it to me many years ago for luck. And now, since I've had more than my share of good luck, I'm passing the charm on to Angela. I call it my crystal angel, but Angela may want to give her another name."

Angie lifts her chin and enjoys a breath of new-found freedom as Lorna accompanies Betty and Angela to the car. Katy studies Angie's profile in the doorway momentarily. Angie turns to see Katy's quizzical gaze, "What?"

"That was very nice of you, Miss Crystal Angel, to give away your namesake. I know how much that little angel means to you...but why?"

Angie leaps into the room, spins around several times and collapses on the sofa. "I suppose there are some things you will never know, Miss Psychologist," Angie laughs, wiggling her fingers wildly in the air.

"That's true, but there is one thing I do know."

"What?"

"Those worry lines on your face, they have completely vanished. Where did they go?"

"Again, my dearest friend, some things will remain a mystery...but, I will say this: that therapy you said was not in the books, it just got invented. I have discovered a special angel, an angel who will deliver all my pain and fears to the mighty Reverend Oliver Barron. Now I can lie down at night, close my eyes as he twists and turns in the wind, wondering when his sins will be exposed, sending him crashing down in flames. My guess is that the Red Barron will pray that he never encounters another angel."

23

September 4, 1969

Dear Mrs. Black,

Today I enrolled my daughter, Angela Olive, in your first grade class. Her teacher, Miss Sullivan, informs me that Charter Christian Academy does not employ a music teacher. If it is agreeable with you, I would like to volunteer to teach music in the first grade three days a week. Angela Olive has a wonderful voice already and sings in the Muffins Choir at the church where my husband, Dr. Oliver Barron, is pastor. I consider music to be very important in the development of a young child's mind as well as providing the groundwork for serving the church in the future as a choir member or soloist.

Please let me know your decision on this important matter soon. I am prepared to begin this volunteer effort next Monday.

Sincerely,

Betty Barron

The end

www.ingramcontent.com/pod-product-compliance
Lightning Source LLC
Chambersburg PA
CBHW022001160426
43197CB00007B/223